# Pollution Control and Environmental Management

# Pollution Control and Environmental Management

Nikhil Mukerjee

**2008**

**CYBER TECH PUBLICATIONS**
4264/3, Ansari Road, Daryaganj, New Delhi-110002 (India)
Ph.: 011-23244078. Fax: 011-23280028
E-Mail: cyberpublicationsdelhi@yahoo.com

*Pollution Control and Environmental Management*



First Edition 2008

Published by G.S. Rawat
**For Cyber Tech Publications**
4264/3, Ansari Road, Daryaganj, New Delhi - 110 002
E-mail : cyberpublicationsdelhi@yahoo.com
Phone : 011-23244078,
Fax : 011-23280028



Printed at
**Amit Enterprises, Moujpur, Delhi. Ph. - 9810878184**

# PREFACE

This book Pollution Control and Environmental Management has been prepared by deeply concerned about environmental issues. It aims at creating a society of motivated citizens committed to conservation, preservation and protection of the environment and striving towards a life in perfect harmony with nature. Learners have to be made aware through proper guidance, about the nature of environment problems. They have to be imparted knowledge about why environment problems arise and why they should be tackled immediately. This knowledge will help learners to develop necessary skills and attitudes and motivate them to work together and individually for a better man-nature relationship.

Environmental Protection Act of protecting the environment by regulating the discharge of waste, the emission of pollutions, and other human activities.

Last but not the least. my publishers who appreciated this book and brought this work out in a record time.

*—Editors*

# CONTENTS

# 1

# OBJECTIVES OF ENVIRONMNTAL IMPACT ASSESSMENT

The main objective of Environmental Impact Assessment by industrial establishments involves evaluation of environmental implications of their units and to achieve sustainable development with minimum degradation of environment by incorporation of necessary safeguards and suitable mitigative measures against such activities which may have bearing on disturbing the environmental quality. According to Singh et al. (2001): "EIA can be considered as a mechanism which maximizes the efficient use of natural and human resources. It can also reduce cost and time taken to reach a decision by ensuring that subjectivity and duplication of efforts are minimized., as well as identifying and attempting to evaluate the primary and secondary consequences which might require the introduction of expensive pollution control equipment or compensation and other costs at a later date."

Commenting on Environmental Impact Assessment in Indian context he writes: "Environmental clearance on the basis of Environmental Impact Assessment is mandatory for various development projects in most parts of the world today. In India, this was introduced as an administrative measures in 1978-79, initially for river valley projects and extended later to industrial projects. There are about 29 categories of projects for which Environmental Clearance, was made mandatory by the Environmental Impact Assessment (EIA) Notification issued in January 1994 under the Environment Protection Act, 1986. Certain activities permissible under the Coastal Regulation Zone Notification 1991also require clearance. Environmental Clearance is granted by the Impact Assessment in the Ministry of Environment and Forest. This power has been delegated to the State governments in the case of co-generation power plants of any capacity, gas/naptha based and coal based power plants with fluidized bed technology of up to 500 MW capacity and conventional coal based power plants of up to 250 MW capacity when located within 25 km. Of the boundary of reserved forests, biosphere reserves and critically polluted areas or within 50 km. Of inter-state boundary. In 1985, the Government had published a set of guidelines, recommended by a working group, for setting up various development projects including industries, power plants and mining. In addition, Government offices notifies, from time to time, certain areas in the country as ecologically sensitive and development activities to be taken up in these areas are regulated through the provisions of these notifications. Such areas include Coastal Regulation Zone (CRZ), DOON valley, Murud-Janjira, Dahanu Taluka, Numaligarh, Taj Trapezium and Aravalli ranges in Gurgaon (Haryana) and Alwar (Rajasthan) districts. Activities to be taken up in forest areas are to be governed by Forest (Conservation) Act and Wild Life Protection Act, 1972. An amendment to the EIA notification introduced in April 1997 has made public hearing mandatory for all cases where environment clearance is required."

Having already amended the EIA rules half a dozen times during the last about a decade (1992-2002), the Union Minitry of Environment and Forests is once again planning to "simplify" regulations on the mandatory Environmental Impact Assessment of developmental and industrial projects as well as the procedure for clearance to chop forests (Times of India, 8.1.2003, p. 11).

The large scale expansion of industrial base in India during the last about 50 years has resulted considerable increase in high risk pollution of our ecosystem. It is an accepted fact globally that to achieve any sustainable development it is essential that a balance is maintained between industry and environment. This can be achieved by adopting latest scientific practices of environmental management and making pollution control programmes cost-effective and feasible so that investment for protection of environment by industrial managements are not considered as a liability on them. Standards play an important role in sustaining development technology and measures so that our environment does not get destroyed beyond a limit. In fact, standards are meant to strike a balance between economic progress and protection of environment.

World Standard Day is celebrated every year on 14th October to mark the birth of International Organisation for Standardisation (ISO). Bureau of Indian Standards (BIS) has launched Environment Management Systems (EMS) Certification. It is the sole national agency authorised to operate EMS Certification in India under Act of Parliament as per International Standards ISO 14000 Series. Industry should voluntary adopt prescribed standards and take advantage of BIS's certification scheme of management systems to combat the menace of pollution. Statistical data collected by BIS is reported to have shown that industrial wastes are the major cause of air, water and land pollution. Nearly 500 Indian standards are presently available in the field of environment protection. These include standards for sampling, testing and analysis of air, water and air and multitude of physical products pertaining to electrical, electronic and telecommunication spheres. BIS also provide standards and information to industries on environmental aspects like materials, industrial processes, recycling and waste disposal. Commenting on standardisation for environment, V.K.Kapoor writes (Tribune, 14.X.2001, p. 2):

"Standardisation is a natural phenomenon and as a human action it is a continuous effort with a purpose to make sense in its interaction with the surroundings to help us handle repeatable situations. It is the standardisation, which formed the basis for evaluation and further development of society, its value system and its numerous dimensions leading to present day civilisation. An indepth analysis of development since the dawn of civilisation reveals that standardisation is a pervasive feature in the Nature, the sunrise and sunset takes place in well-defined directions, orderly pattern of seasonal changes exists and bring definite changes in flora and fauna.

Till date, nearly 500 standards are available on environmental issues. In addition standards are also available on a number of allied aspects, including estimation of the volume of water flowing in water courses, requirements of water supply and sanitation and detection of pesticidal residues and handling of cases of pesticidal poisoning. The government has promulgated comprehensive Environment Protection Act – 1986. Under this Act, the Ministry of Environment and Forest (MEF) had been assigned the responsibility of developing and enforcing the needed standards in regard to liquid and gasesous emissions. MEF interacted closely with the Bureau to ensure proper co-ordination and harmonisation of eggorts persued by the two bodies for sustaining the purity of environment. BIS responsibility includes development and supply of standards. In this perspective, particular significance attached to the nation wide programmes initiated by the Central Pollution Control Board for containing the menace of water and air pollution arising from specific categories of industries. The Board has established national and zonal task forces in respect of industries like cement, thermal power plants, fertilisers, oil refineries and pulp and paper industries. Assistance for implementation of the programmes of pollution control is also being provided by bodies like industry departments in the Central and state governments, financial institutions, municipal corporations, statutory bodies, association of manufacturers, chambers of industry and trade etc. It would be imperative to strengthen their efforts still further. It may be mentioned that pollution aspects and the need for compliance to prescribed standards should be taken into account right at the stage of planning of an industry.

With a view to providing organisations world over with the structure for managing environmental impacts of their activities, products and services and to have a uniform International Environmental Management Systems (EMS) for use as environmental management tool, for achieving sustainable development, the International Organisations for Standardisation (ISO) 14000 series of standards. Together, these standards provide the necessary guidance for implementing an effective environmental management system. While ISO 14001, the environmental management systems specifications, is a standard which can be audited against and is voluntary in nature, other standards provide guidelines that support implementation of a management system. These standards have become an integral part of the business to make them competitive in the world markey. They have already been popularised in industry and service organisation for handling their environmental issues either by implementing on their own or through third party certification. With the growing concern for environmental-friendly industrial activity, BIS launched Environmental Management System (EMS) Certification. BIS is the sole national agency authorised to operate Environmental Management System (EMS). Certification in India under an Act of Parliament as per International Standard ISO 14000 series. BIS has so far granted 48 licenses. In these types of certification, the companies are not only required to comply the national regulations related to environment protection but also its commitment to environment management in toatality. It will be appropriate to all concerns to adopt this certification, timely and efficient service.

The Bureau with its proactive and professional approach is fully committed to advise the Indian industry on core environmental issues and foster its confidence in new business paradigm of making business 'green', through standards on environment which in turn will pave the way to achieve business sustainability in their respective spheres of activities."

More and more industrial establishments in the advanced countries like USA, EU, Germany, Japan, France have resorted to getting their industrial units environmentaly audited in view of the valuable environmental impact such an audit has on their companies overall performance. It is reported that 10,000 companies in 72 countries are already having ISO-14001 certification for environmental management systems. Of these, 320 companies are located in India. The number of companies falling under this category is highest in Japan followed by Germany and United Kingdom. It is expected that in the near future, Asian countries may have the same growth and popularity of environmental management system by adopting ISO standard as has been the case in industrially developed advanced countries like USA and

European Union. The ISO management standards which have, so far, been published and have acquired considerable presence in the market include the following:

- ISO 14001: Environmental Management System – Specifications with guidelines for use.
- ISO 14004: Environmental Management Systems – General guidelines on Environmental Management Principles, Systems ans Supporting Techniques.
- ISO 14010: Guidelines for Environmental Auditing – General Principles.
- ISO 14011: Guidelines for Environmental Auditing – Audit Procedures – Part-1: Auditing of Environmental Management Systems.
- ISO 14012: Guidelines for Environmental Auditing – Qualification Criteria for Environmental Auditors.

In addition to the above, the work on the following standards is in progress:

- ISO 14020: Environmental Labelling.
- ISO 14030: Environmental Performance Evaluation.
- ISO 14040: Life Cycle Assessment.
- ISO 14050: Terms and Conditions.
- ISO 14060: Environmental Products Standards.

According to Bhargava and Welford (1996):

"More and more companies are finding it valuable to undertake and audit their environmental impacts. This commonly leads to the identification of risks as well as pinpointing cost saving opportunities. However, owing to the undue emphasis being laid on complying with current legislation, too many companies are using environmental audits only in order to evaluate and verify compliance. This is very narrow approach and misses the many more positive reasons for undertaking the audit. Moreover, in the spirit of the environmental management systems standards environmental audits are an important tool for any company taking a proactive stance towards environmental issues. While a passive or reactive stance towards the environment focuses on doing the minimum that is required by law, a proactive stance aims at moving beyond compliance. Environmental auditing is not a particularly new discipline; however its popularity as a means to assessing environmental performance has recently increased substantially. Indeed, the first environmental audits can be traced back to the US, where corporations adopted this methodology during the 1970s in response to their domestic liability laws. During the 1980s these audits were extended beyond simply adhering to legislation and regulations. In general, environmental auditing is a series of activities initiated by management, to evaluate environmental performance, to check compliance with environmental legislation and to assess whether the systems in place to manage environmental improvement are effective. Audits are undertaken at regular intervals to assess the environmental performance of the company in relation to the company's stated objectives and environmental policy. The environmental audit is therefore an integral part of the environmental management system."

The Government of India issued notification on March 13, 1992 making it mandatory for industries to submit an environmental auditing statement of the financial year ending on March 31 in prescribed form to the concerned Pollution Control Boards of the state concerned on or before September 30, each year beginning 1993 (financial year 1992-93). The Department of Company Affairs also accepted this proposal and agreed to include this requirement as part of the Director's Annual Report. To meet this mandatory requirement it became imperative for the industries to regularly develop, update and maintain complete record on the various aspects of environmental performance (including raw materials used, process followed and products generated) of their industrial units.

Prior to the notification issued by the Government of India, making it mandatory for the industries to get environmental auditing conducted of their industrial units, the practice of looking after the environmental health and safety was being conducted by some of the industrial concerns since early 1970s as part of their routine activities for reviewing and evaluating environmental problems associated with their operations. The environmental auditing for the industrial establishments has been intrduced with the objectives that such concerns comply with the established environmental standards and good industrial practices. The definition of the term "Environmental Auditing" (EA) as adopted by the International Chamber of Commerce (ICC) is as follows:

"A management tool comprising a systematic, documented, periodic and objective evaluation of how well environmental organisation, management systems and equipment are performing with the aim of (i) facilitating management control of environmental practices, and (ii) compliance with company policies, including meeting regulatory requirements. It may be noted that the process of auditing as seen here is an internal process that should become a necessary and routine part of most, if not all industrial management, irrespective of the size of the company".

The Confideration of British Industry defines environment audit as:

"The systematic examination of the interactions between any business operation and its surroundings. This includes all emissions to air, land and water; legal constraints; the effects on the neighbouring community, landscape and ecology; and the public's perception of the operating company in the local area......Environmental auditing does not stop at compliance with legislation. Nor is it a 'green-washing' public relations exercise. Rather, it is a total strategic approach to the organization's activities."

The definition as given within the eco-management and adult scheme based on the ICC definition, is:

"A management tool comprising a systematic, documented, periodic and objective evaluation of the performance of the organization, management system and processes designed to protect the environment with the aim of: (i) facilitating management control of practices which may have impact on the environment; (ii) assessing compliance with company environmental policies."

The Central Pollution Control Board, Delhi has brought out the following two publications as part of their "Programme Objective Series" (PROBES/ 50 and 51/ 1993-94) to provide necessary guidelines pertaining to "Environmental Auditing":

Guidelines for Environmental Audit – 1993

Environmental Auditing in Polluting Industries – 1994

The following are some of the details pertaining to "Environmental Auditing in Polluting Industries" as published by the Central Pollution Control Board, Delhi (PROBES/ 51/ 1993-94):

## Need for Environmental Information

The need for environmental information could be two main types namely, (i) internal, and (ii) external, as far as the industry's perspective is concerned. The internal needs are to ensure that the industry has accurate, up-to-date information at hand on environmental performance of its construction contractors, plants, technologies, waste contractors, products, raw materials and all related activities. Such a need has in fact made environmental auditing in atleast some of the developed countries, a part of the industry's overall drive for quality assurance.

The growing concern for the protection of human resources is making this area, increasingly useful and interesting even to the external agencies (i.e. other than the industry).

Among these, who are seen demanding or requesting such information are: National and international regulatory agencies and research institutions; Environmental crime investigation, environmental courts etc.; Insurer and risk managers, particularly those involved in environmental impairment liability insurance field; Employees and trade unions; - share holders;

Local, communities and environmental officers/planners; Environmentalists; and Ethical investment funds wanting priority investment in companies with ecofriendly products.

The environmental audit studies serve atleat the following three basic purposes:

Compilation of the complete information on the operation of the industrial facility and its potential sources of pollution through technical inspection. This inspection, which is conducted at a facility allows the activities that are programmed and entrusted to the operational branches to be carried out in order to correct the different problems detected at their source or to foresee conservation and maintenance measures need to prevent major pollution problems.

Evaluation of the conditions surrounding the industrial facility in order to estimate possible impacts which may be caused and the suggested recovery measures for such situations. Preparation and implementation of action plans for better control of the environment, and the environmentally related industrial activities, including further development activities of the areas.

The primary and obvious advantage of environmental auditing is to help safeguard the environment and to substantiate compliance with local, regional and national laws and regulations, and with the company policy and standards. There can be several other benefits, the importance of which may vary from situation to situation. These benefits include:

Reduced exposure to litigation and regulatory risk (e.g. prosecutions, penalties, etc.); - facilitating comparison and interchange of information between operations or plants; Increasing employer awareness of environmental policies and responsibilities; Identifying potential cost-savings including those resulting from waste minimisation; Evaluating training programmes and providing data to assist in training personnel; Providing an information base for use in emergencies and evaluating the effectiveness of emergency response arrangements; Assuring an adequate, up-to-date environmental data base for internal management awareness and decision making in relation to plant modification, new plants etc; Enabling management to give credit for good environmental performance; Helping to assist relations with authorities by convincing them that complete and effective audits are being undertaken; Facilitating the obtention of insurance coverage for environmental impairment liability.

The general approach followed for environmental audit studies cover three main phases, namely collection of information, evaluation of information collected, and formulation of conclusions, including identification of aspects needing improvement. These phases cover, pre-audit preparation, a site visit normally involving interviews with personnel and inspection of facilities and post-visit activities. A team of experts and assisting officials, generally completes the site assignments which involves gathering all the required data/ information, analysing these, drawing conclusions regarding the status of the industrial facility audited with respect to specific criteria/objectives, and reporting the conclusions.

These activities are conducted within a formal structure in a sequence that is repeated in each location audited to provide a level of uniformity of coverage and reliability of findings.

This covers a number of activities including, selection and review of site and audit team, development of an audit plan which defines the technical, geographic and time scope, arranging for the expected sample collection, preservation, transport and analysis, and obtaining background information on the plant, as well as the criteria to be used for evaluating the programme. Questionnaires are preferably prepared to cover maximum data collection and wide coverage of the industrial activity as well as its surroundings and the industrial area. Depending upon the need arrangements for assistance from the local environmental authority/laboratories may have to be also made before the team leaves for the audit studies.

The site activities include, identification and assessment of the management control systems, data collection and their evaluation, and reporting audit findings. The various arrangements existing for environmental management and related aspects are identified and understood. This is followed by evaluation of the arrangements with respect to the requirements in the sense of meeting the standards regulations. The data collection include almost every aspect of the facility which may be related directly or indirectly to the emissions/discharges, as well as the details regarding the location's surroundings i.e. other industries in the vicinity, weather, soil and rain – data, ground water quality in immediate vicinity and little away. Wastewater, sludges, air quality samples, are taken depending upon the type of industrial activity and possible impacts. The data collected are collated, compiled and evaluated, and findings are finalised on the basis of the evidence collected, some of the findings may require transportation, for analysis of the samples collected in a laboratory, before the same are finalised.

The activities that follows after visit to the site is completed, mainly include (i) preparation of the final report, and (ii) development and follow-ups for implementation of a corrective action programme.

Problems which the audit team may face are likely to vary from facility to facility. However, what could be generally expected and needs attention, are as follows:

The prior history of the site.

The age of the relevant equipment.

Lack of records related to the relevant equipment.

The attitude of the concerned personnel on site towards such audit studies.

Problems as well as responses of the concerned management for implementation of the corrective measures.

The concept of environmental auditing in industrial facilities in India, appears to have first got into meaningful discussions in the beginning of nineties. Efforts were initiated to see the practicability of this programme before it could be made mandatory. This area gained further movement with the Govt. of India's action plan for pollution control in the critical areas including heavy polluting industries. The Central Pollution Control Board accordingly initiated a programme of such audit studies in 18 major polluting industries (Aluminium Smelter, Basic Drugs and Pharmaceuticals, Caustic Soda, Cement, Copper Smelter, Distillery, Dyes and Dye Intermediate, Fertiliser, Iron and Steel, Leather Processing Industries, Oil Refinery, Pesticides, Petrochemicals, Pulp and Paper, Sugar, Sulphuric Acid. Thermal Power Plant, Zinc Smelter), in 1991-92. Meanwhile a discussion paper on "Outline of Environmental Auditing" was prepared by the Ministry of Environment & Forests (MOEF) and circulated for comment. This process finally resulted into issuing of a gazette notification on March 13, 1992 through which submission of the environmental audit reports has been made mandatory. The term 'Audit Report' has also been changed to 'Statement' through a revised notification of April 22, 1993. The industries are now supposed to submit their auditing reports to the concerned State Boards on or before 30th day of September every year beginning 1993. All environmental audits involve gathering information, analysing that information, making objective judgements based on evidence and knowledge of the industry and of relevant environmental legislation and standards. There is also need to report the results of the audit to senior management with recommendations and possible strategies for the implementation of the findings. This all needs considerable preparatory work as well as follow-up time in order that the findings are accurate and comprehensive. Ideally, therefore, there needs to be three clear stages of an audit. The first stage, the pre-audit activities, will aim to minimize the time spent at the site and to maximize the audit team's productivity, and will involve the following:

Planning the nature and scope of the audit and providing a framework for setting goals and objectives, developing strategies for their achievement and specifying accountability for accomplishing the work and scheduling the audit process. Information must be gathered from secondary sources like previous audit reviews and other corporate reports. Sites and facilities must be prioritized according to risk involved with regard to hazardous wastes, air pollution, water pollution, soil contamination, inventory, non-compliance with legislation and worker health and safety. Then a framework for an environmental audit programme with clearly defined procedures must be developed.

. Selecting members of the audit team and allocating resources to the strategies and policies determined in (I). The audit team will consist of people chosen for their expertise not only in environmental matters but also having knowledge of the industry in which a company operates. An assignment of audit responsibilities should be made according to the competencies and experience of the team.

Getting to know the industry and company to be audited. A useful strategy here is to use pre-survey questionnaires submitted to management in order for the audit team to familiarize themselves with the type of instalment, the site and location. It will also focus the minds of management on what will be required of them during the audit. In addition, the geographic area, as well as the areas within the field of health, safety and environment, that have to be covered by the audit should also be clearly defined, as also should the total time allocated for conducting the audit.

Questionnaires may also be sent to a representative sample of the workforce (to be filled out in confidence) asking about key issues such as communications, planning, health and safety and working conditions.

The second stage is the on-site audit itself. This will include:

An inspection of records kept by the company, certificate of compliance, discharge consents, waste licenses etc.

The examination of inspection and maintenance programmes and the company's own policy on what to do in the event of spills and other accidents. Auditors will have to assess the soundness of the facility's internal controls. Such controls will include management procedures and the equipment and engineering controls that affect environmental performance.

Examining lines of management and responsibility, competence of personnel and systems of authorization. There needs to be a working understanding of the facility" internal management system and of its effectiveness.

A confidential interview of selected staff at all levels of operation with a view to collecting information, particularly in the area of the effectiveness of systems and waste management.

A physical inspection of the plant, working practices, office management systems and surrounding areas including a check on safety equipment, verifying the company's own sampling and monitoring procedures, investigating energy management systems and where necessary taking samples of waste, liquids, soil, air and noise.

The final stage of the audit will involve:

Confirming that there is sufficient evidence on which to base and justify a set of findings and evaluating the audit information and observations. Such evaluation will involve the audit team meeting to discuss all facets of the environmental audit.

Reporting the audit findings in written form and in discussion with the management of the audited company. This entails a formal review of the audit findings to avoid misinterpretation and discussion about how to improve the environmental performance of the firm based on the audit report. Management is thus provided with information about compliance status and recommendations regarding action which should be taken.

This will often result in the development of an action plan to address deficiencies. This will include assigning responsibilities for corrective action, determining potential solutions and establishing timetables. Recommendations for the next audit may also be made. Much stress needs to be placed on the idea that audits should be seen by management as a positive help rather than a threatening or hostile exercise. Management must feel that they own the audit and even though some external expertise may be used it is an activity which is promoted and driven internally rather than externally. In the early 1990s when we experienced a rapid growth in environmental awareness in industry, it was the environmental audit which was seen as the first step towards improving environmental performance and many companies boasted about the fact that they had an environmental audit.Because of the developments such as the introduction of BS7750 and ISO 14000, businesses are coming to realize that it is the environmental management system which should be at the centre of the organization and that environmental auditing is an integral part of that system, which checks not only compliance and measures environmental improvements, but also checks the effectiveness of the system itself. What we mean by an environmental audit and how it is implemented is also becoming clearer and the key difference between a review and an audit needs to be clearly recognized. However, there are still many firms who, having undertaken a single environmental audit, subsequently claim to be an environmentally conscious firm. Conscious they might be but effective they are not. As with so much of environmental management, the audit has to be an ongoing process which never ends. The key role of the audit must be to check and assess all the other activities of the firm in relation to environmental improvement. EU moves to standardize the auditing process and an encouragement to publish audit reports to be welcomed. But auditing is a technique which is still in its infancy and there is much scope for experimentation.

# 2

# APPROACH TO SUSTAINABLE DEVELOPMENT BEYOND ENVIRONMENTAL PROTECTION

Countries and regions where the economy is driven by the tourism industry have become increasingly concerned with the environmental, as well as the socio-cultural problems associated with unsustainable tourism. As a result, there is now increasing agreement on the need to promote sustainable tourism development to minimise its environmental impact and to maximise socio-economic overall benefits at tourist destinations. The concept of sustainable tourism, as developed by the World Tourism Organisation (WTO) in the context of the United Nations sustainable development process, refers to tourist activities "leading to management of all resources in such a way that economic, social and aesthetic needs can be fulfilled while maintaining cultural integrity, essential ecological processes, biological diversity and life support systems"

Although domestic tourism currently accounts for approximately 80% of all tourist activity (UN, 1999a), many countries tend to give priority to international tourism because, while the former basically involves a regional redistribution of national income, the latter has now become the world's largest source of foreign exchange receipts. According to the latest figures compiled by the World Tourism Organisation (WTO), foreign exchange earnings from international tourism reached as peak of US$ 476 billion in 2000, which was larger than the export value of petroleum products, motor vehicles, telecommunications equipment or any other single category of product or service (WTO, 2001a).

International tourist arrivals grew at an annual average rate of 4.3% during the1990s, despite major international political and economic crises, such as the Gulf War and the Asian financial crisis. According to the latest WTO figures, the turn of the millennium recorded one of the most impressive annual growth rates in international tourism. As table 1 shows, all regions of the world recorded significant growth in international tourism in 2000, during which the number of international arrivals grew at an extraordinary rate of nearly 7% to reach almost 700 million arrivals.

The September 2001 terrorist attacks in the United States, however, appear to have had a more serious impact on the tourist sector than any other major international crisis in recent decades. The attacks had a particularly severe impact on air transport, business travel and long-haul travel. Worldwide travel reservations were estimated to have dropped by 15% at the end of October 2001, although not every destination nor every part of the tourism sector was badly affected. For example, while air transport and luxury hotels have suffered from considerable fall in demand, travel within the same country or region, as well as travel by rail and road, appear to have weathered the worst effects of the crisis, or even benefited from it.

Nevertheless, initial forecasts of 3-4% rise in international tourist arrivals for 2001, made before the September 2001 attacks, were subsequently revised downwards to around a 1% increase over the 2000 figures (WTO, 2001c). The latest WTO (2002) data show that there was an actual decline of 0.6% in international arrivals, to a total of 693 million, in 2001. Given that the northern hemisphere summer holiday season was coming to end by the time the attacks took place, this significant drop confirms that the short-term impacts of the attacks were devastating to international tourism as a whole. The last four months of 2001, in fact, recorded a drop of almost 9% in arrivals worldwide and substantial decreases in all regions of the world.

It is worth noting, however, that this considerable fall in international arrivals was caused not only by a widespread fear of travelling generated by the attacks—particularly in airplanes and to certain destinations—but also by a downturn in the world economy. The economic downturn that began in the United States during the first half of 2001 had already been affecting the tourism sector before the terrorist attacks were carried out. The attacks aggravated the economic slowdown already under way. The expected recovery in world tourism in the near future will thus depend on the evolution of the world economy, amongst other factors, including the possibility of further terrorist acts or regional conflicts. Some destinations will in any case experience a prolonged decline in tourism revenues—regardless of any world economic improvements—for various reasons, including proximity to areas of regional conflict.

In the medium and long term, however, international tourism is expected to resume its rapid growth, in view of rising living standards and discretionary incomes, falling real costs of travel, expansion and improvement of various transport modes, increasing amounts of free time and other factors. This helps to explain why WTO (2001c) has reiterated its long-term forecasts, made before the September 2001 attacks, of an average annual growth rate in international arrivals of over 4% in the period upto 2020. The number of international arrivals is thus expected to reach the striking mark of 1 billion by 2010 and 1.6 billion by 2020. Tourism comprises an extensive range of economic activities and can be considered the largest industry in the world.[5] International tourism is one of the fastest growing sectors of the global economy. During the 1990s, when the globalisation of tourism reached unprecedented proportions, international tourism receipts had a much higher average annual growth rate (7.3%) than that of gross world product. By 1999, international tourism receipts accounted for more than 8% of the worldwide export value of goods and services, overtaking the export value of other leading world industries such as automotive products, chemicals, and computer and office equipment.

A significant proportion of world tourism expenditure takes place within industrialised countries: Europe alone accounts for around half of annual international tourism receipts. Tourism, however, is the only major service sector in which developing countries have consistently recorded trade surpluses relative to the rest of the world. Between 1980 and 1996, for instance, their travel account surplus increased from $4.6 billion to $65.9 billon, due primarily to the impressive growth of inbound tourism to countries in Africa, the Caribbean, and the Asia and Pacific regions (UN, 1999a). The 1990s also experienced a significant growth of international tourism receipts in the 49 least developed countries: total tourism receipts in these countries more than doubled from US$ 1 billion in 1992 to over US$ 2.2 billion in 1998. Tourism is now the second largest source of foreign exchange earnings in the least developed countries (LDCs) as a whole.

Tourism has also become the main source of income for an increasing number of Small Island Developing States (SIDS). Foreign exchange earnings can, however, vary significantly among these tourism-driven economies because of 'leakages' arising from imports of equipment for construction and consumer goods required by tourists, repatriation of profits earned by foreign investors and amortisation of foreign debt incurred in tourist development.

Besides export earnings, international tourism also generates an increasingly significant share of government (national and local) tax revenues throughout the world. In addition, the development of tourism as a whole is usually accompanied by considerable investments in infrastructure, such as airports, roads, water and sewerage facilities, telecommunications and other public utilities. Such infrastructural improvements not only generate benefits to tourists but can also contribute to improving the living conditions of local populations. This increase in social overhead capital can also help attract other industries to a disadvantaged area and thus be a stimulus to regional economic development. The tourism sector is an increasingly important source of employment—including in tourism-related sectors, such as construction and agriculture—

primarily for unskilled labour, migrants from poor rural areas, people who prefer to work part-time, and notably women. Because the sector is relatively labour-intensive, investments in tourism tend to generate a larger and more rapid increase in employment than equal investment in other economic activities. Furthermore, given that the sector provides a considerable amount of jobs for women and unskilled workers, tourism can significantly contribute to empowering women and alleviating poverty.

At the same time, available data suggest that most workers in the tourism sector, notably in hotels and catering, tend to earn less than workers in socially comparable occupations in both developed and developing countries (ILO, 2001). In addition, the differential tends to be larger in less developed countries and regions, particularly those with high rates of unemployment amongst unskilled labour. Informal employment relations in small and medium-sized enterprises, which employ about half of the labour force in the hotel and catering sub-sectors worldwide, also contribute to a relatively high proportion of child labour and non-remunerated employment and other unacceptable forms of social exploitation in many countries.

The increasing reliance of less diversified economies on tourism also increases their vulnerability to seasonal aspects of tourism and to shocks, such as, natural disasters, regional wars and other unexpected events. The recent crisis generated by fear of international terrorism is and regional conflict, for example, caused devastating immediate effects on tourism dependent economies.[12] In addition, sudden changes in consumer tastes and sharp economic downturns pose significant risks to such economies, given that demand for mass tourism-tends to be relatively income-estatic and can produce drastic negative responses to economic recession in source markets.

Nonetheless, it is now generally recognised that tourism can make a vital contribution to employment, export receipts and national income in most countries and regions, Furthermore, tourism is often identified as the most promising driving force for the economic development of less developed countries and regions endowed with areas of natural beauty—including Small Island Developing States—because it offers them a valuable opportunity for economic diversification.

## Interaction Between Tourism and the Environment

While tourism provides considerable economic benefits for many countries, regions and communities, its rapid expansion can also be responsible for adverse environmental, as well as socio-cultural, impact.[13] Natural resource depletion and environmental degradation associated with tourism activities pose severe problems to many tourism-rich regions. The fact that most tourists chose to maintain their relatively high patterns of consumption (and waste generation) when they reach their destinations can be a particularly serious problem for developing countries and regions without the appropriate means for protecting their natural resources and local ecosystems from the pressures of mass tourism.

The two main areas of environmental impact of tourism are: pressure on natural resources and damage to ecosystems. Furthermore, it is now widely recognised not only that uncontrolled tourism expansion is likely to lead to environmental degradation, but also that environmental degradation, in turn, poses a serious threat to tourism activities.

## Pressure on Natural Resources

In addition to pressure on the availability and prices of resources consumed by local residents—such as energy, food and basic raw materials—the main natural resources at risk from tourism development are land, freshwater and marine resources. Without careful land-use planning, for instance, rapid tourism development can intensify competition for land resources with other uses and lead to rising land prices and increased pressure to build on agricultural land. Moreover, intensive tourism development can threaten natural landscapes, notably through deforestation, loss of wetlands and soil erosion. Tourism development in coastal areas—including hotel, airport and road construction—is often a matter for increasing concern worldwide as it can lead to sand mining, beach erosion and other forms of land degradation.

Freshwater availability for competing agricultural, industrial, household and other uses is rapidly becoming one of the most critical natural resource issues in many countries and regions. Rapid expansion of the tourism industry, which tends to be extremely water-intensive, can exacerbate this problem by placing considerable pressure on scarce water supply in many destinations. Water scarcity can pose a serious limitation to future tourism development in many low-lying coastal areas and small islands that have limited supplies of surface water, and whose groundwater may be contaminated by saltwater intrusion. Over-consumption by many tourism facilities—notably large hotel resorts and golf courses—can limit current supplies available to farmers and local populations in water-scarce regions and thus lead to serious shortages and price rises. In addition, pollution of available freshwater sources, some of which may be associated with tourism-related activities, can exacerbate local shortages.

Rapid expansion of coastal and ocean tourism activities, such as snorkelling, scuba diving and sport fishing, can threaten fisheries and other marine resources. Disturbance to marine aquatic life can also be caused by the intensive use of thrill craft, such as jet skis, frequent boat tours and boat anchors. Anchor damage is now regarded as one of the most serious threats to coral reefs in the Caribbean Sea, in view of the growing number of both small boats and large cruise ships sailing in the region (see Michael Hall, 2001). Severe damage to coral reefs and other marine resources may, in turn, not only discourage further tourism and threaten the future of local tourist industries, but also damage local fisheries.

## Damage to Ecosystems

Besides the consumption of large amounts of natural resources, the tourism industry also generates considerable waste and pollution. Disposal of liquid and solid waste generated by the tourism industry has become a particular problem for many developing countries and regions that lack the capacity to treat these waste materials. Disposal of such untreated waste has, in turn, contributed to reducing the availability of natural resources, such as freshwater.

Apart from the contamination of freshwater from pollution by untreated sewage, tourist activities can also lead to land contamination from solid waste and the contamination of marine waters and coastal areas from pollution generated by hotels and marinas, as well as cruise ships. It is estimated that cruise ships in the Caribbean Sea alone produced more than 70,000 tonnes of liquid and solid waste a year during the mid-1990s (UN, 1999a). The fast growth of the cruise sector in this and other regions around the world has exacerbated this problem in recent years. In fact, it is sometimes argued that the rapid expansion of cruise tourism calls for "the enforcement of an environmental protection 'level playing field' across the world's oceans and between the world's maritime tourism destinations" (Johnson, 2002).

In addition, relatively high levels of energy consumption in hotels—including energy for air-conditioning, heating and cooking—as well as fuel used by tourism-related transportation can also contribute significantly to local air pollution in many host countries and regions. Local air and noise pollution, as well as urban congestion linked to intensive tourism development, can sometimes even discourage tourists from visiting some destinations.

Uncontrolled tourism activities can also cause severe disruption of wildlife habitats and increased pressure on endangered species. Disruption of wildlife behaviour is often caused, for example, by tourist vehicles in Africa's national parks that approach wild cats and thus distract them from hunting and breeding; tour boat operators in the Caribbean Sea that feed sharks to ensure that they remain in tourist areas; and whale-watching boat crews around the world that pursue whales and dolphins and even encourage petting, which tends to alter the animals' feeding and behaviour (see Mastny, 2001).

Similarly, tourism can lead to the indiscriminate clearance of native vegetation for the development of new facilities, increased demand for fuelwood and even forest fires. Ecologically fragile areas, such as rain forests, wetlands and mangroves, are also threatened by intensive or irresponsible tourist activity. Moreover, as will be discussed below, it is increasingly recognized that, the rapid expansion of nature tourism (or 'eco-tourism') may also pose a threat to ecologically fragile areas, including many natural world heritage sites, if not properly managed and monitored.

The delicate ecosystems of most small islands, together with their increasing reliance on tourism as a main tool of socio-economic development, means that this environmental impact can be particularly damaging since the success of the tourism sector in these islands often depends on the quality of their natural environment (UN, 1999b). In addition, pollution of coastal waters—in particular by sewage, solid waste, sediments and untreated chemicals—often leads to the deterioration of coastal ecosystems, notably coral reefs, and thus harms their value for tourism.

The equally fragile ecosystems of mountain regions are also threatened by increasing popular tourist activities such as skiing, snowboarding and trekking. One of the most serious environmental problems in mountainous developing countries without appropriate energy supply is deforestation arising from increasing consumption of fuelwood by the tourism industry (see, for example, CDE/SDC, 1999). This often results not only in the destruction of local habitats and ecosystems, but also in accelerating processes of erosion and landslides. Other major problems arising from tourist activities in mountain regions include disruption of animal migration by road and tourist facilities, sewage pollution of rivers, excessive water withdrawals from streams to supply resorts and the accumulation of solid waste on trails.

## Environmental Threats to Tourism

In many mountain regions, small islands, coastal areas and other ecologically fragile places visited by tourists, there is an increasing concern that the negative impact of tourism on the natural environment can ultimately hurt the tourism industry itself. In other words, the negative impact of intensive tourism activities on the environmental quality of beaches, mountains, rivers, forests and other ecosystems also compromise the viability of the tourism industry in these places.

There is now plenty of evidence of the 'life-cycle' of a tourist destination, that is, the evolution from its discovery, to development and eventual decline because of over-exploitation and subsequent deterioration its key attractions. In many developing and developed countries alike, tourism destinations are becoming overdeveloped up to the point where the damage caused by environmental degradation—and the eventual loss of revenues arising from a collapse in tourism arrivals—becomes irreversible.

Examples of such exploitation of 'non-renewable tourism resources' range from a small fishing village in India's Kerala state—which saw its tourist sector collapse after two decades of fast growth, because inadequate disposal of solid waste—to several places in the industrialised world, such as Italy's Adriatic coast and Germany's Black Forest. It can also be argued that environmental pollution and urban sprawl tend to undermine further tourist development in major urban destinations in developing countries, such as Bangkok, Cairo and Mexico City.

In addition, tourism in many destinations could be particularly threatened by external environmental shocks, notably the potential threat of global warming and sea-level rise. Significant rises in sea level could cause serious problems to tourism activities, particularly in low-lying coastal areas and small islands. Global warming is also expected to increase climate variability and to provoke changes in the frequency and intensity of extreme climate events—such as tropical windstorms and associated storm surges and coastal flooding—that may threaten tourism activities at certain destinations.

Although tourism was not specifically addressed in Agenda 21—the international action plan on sustainable development agreed on at the 1992 Earth Summit in Rio de Janeiro (Brazil)—its growing economic importance, significant use of natural resources and environmental impact all contributed to its gradual introduction into the international sustainable development agenda over the past ten years. One of the first concrete sectoral action plans arising from the increasing cooperation between the tourism industry and inter-governmental agencies was 'Agenda 21 for the Travel and Tourism Industry' an action plan for sustainable tourism development launched by the WTO, in cooperation with two business associations in 1996.

In 1997, the United Nations General Assembly, at its special session to review the five-year implementation of Agenda 21, decided that there was a need to consider the importance of tourism in the context of Agenda 21 and to "develop an action-oriented international programme of work on sustainable tourism" (see UN, 1998). This request was followed up during the seventh annual session of the United Nations Commission on Sustainable Development (CSD), held in New York in 1999, which considered tourism as an economic sector, held a multi-stakeholder dialogue on the topic and adopted an international work programme on sustainable tourism development (UN, 1999c). One of the major follow-up activities to the CDS international work programme on sustainable tourism has been the ongoing development of international guidelines for sustainable tourism by the Convention on Biological Diversity. The draft international guideline stress that "to be sustainable, tourism should be managed within the carrying capacity and limits of each ecosystem and site" (UNEP, 2002a).

The seventh session of the CSD also invited the WTO to further develop its proposed global code of ethics that had been drafted in consultation with the tourism industry over the previous two years. The 'Global Code of Ethics for Tourism,' introduced by the WTO in late 1999, sets a frame of reference for the responsible and sustainable development of international tourism (WTO, 2001f, Appendix I). It includes nine articles outlining the basic rules for governments, tour operators, developers, travel agents, workers, as well as host communities and the tourists themselves. The tenth article includes a proposed mechanism for conciliation, through the creation of a World Committee on Tourism Ethics made up of representatives of each region of the world and representatives of each group of stakeholders in the tourism sector. Governments, the private sector, and labour and non-governmental organisations. The United Nations General Assembly adopted the Global Code of Ethics for Tourism in 2001.

The Plan of Implementation adopted at the World Summit on Sustainable Development (WSSD), held in Johannesburg (South Africa) from 26 August to 4 September 2002, identified further measures to promote sustainable tourism development, with a view to increasing "the benefits from tourism resources for the population in host communities while maintaining the cultural and environmental integrity of the host communities and enhancing the protection of ecologically sensitive areas and natural heritages" (UN, 2002b:ch. 1.2). As similar international actions plans show, the WSSD Plan of Implementation is likely to induce States to take more progressive steps towards better governance and sustainable development (see Haas, 2002). However, achieving the sustainable tourism goals contained in the WSSD Plan of Implementation will require systematic action and the availability of adequate resources at both national and international levels.

The WSSD Plan of Implementation makes particular reference to activities carried out in conjunction with the 2002 United Nations International Year of Ecotourism, amongst other international activities, in the implementation of its sustainable tourism goals. The International Year of Ecotourism offered an ideal opportunity not only to review ecotourism experiences around the world, but also to promote worldwide recognition of the important role of sustainable tourism in the broader international sustainable development agenda. There is however, a crucial distinction between ecotourism and sustainable tourism: while the former can be broadly defined as an alternative, nature-based type of tourism, sustainable tourism calls for adherence to the above mentioned sustainability principles in all types of tourism activities and by all segments of the tourism industry.

Ecotourism is still a relatively small segment of the overall tourism sector. At the same time, it is one of the fastest growing tourism segments and further rapid growth is expected in the future. There is, however, little agreement about its exact meaning because of the wide variety of so-called ecotourism activities provided by many different suppliers (both international and domestic) and enjoyed by an equally broad range of diverse tourists. Its main features include (a) all forms of nature tourism aimed at the appreciation of both the natural world and the traditional cultures existent in natural areas, (b) deliberate efforts to minimise the harmful human impact on the natural and socio-cultural environment and (c) support for the protection of natural and cultural assets and the well-being of host communities.

Consensus on some of these issues was reached during the World Ecotourism Summit—held in Quebec City (Canada) in May 2002-although many questions need to be explored further (see UNEP, 2002b). The Quebec declaration stresses that, if carried out responsibly, ecotourism can be a valuable means for promoting the socio-economic development of host communities while generating resources for the preservation of natural and cultural assets. In this was, ecologically fragile areas can be protected with the financial returns of ecotourism activities.

Ecotourism has been particularly successful in attracting private investments for the establishment of privately owned natural parks and nature reserves in an increasing number of developing countries, such as Costa Rica, Ecuadol, Malaysia and South Africa. Many such reserves are well managed, self-financed and environmentally responsible, even when profit remains the main motivation behind the operation of a private reserve (see, for example, Langholz *et al.*, 2000). In this way, the tourism industry can help to protect and even rehabilitate natural assets, and thus contribute to the preservation of biological diversity and ecological balance.

However, if not properly planned, managed and monitored, ecotourism can be distorted for purely commercial purposes and even for promoting ecologically-damaging activities by large numbers of tourists in natural areas. Given their inadequate physical infrastructure and limited capacity to absorb mass tourism, the fragile land and ocean ecosystems of many developing countries can be literally overwhelmed by large numbers of tourism. It is increasing recognized, therefore, that eco-tourism activities can also cause adverse ecological impact, particularly if they are not properly managed or if they involve tourist numbers beyond the local carrying capacity (Gossling, 1999).

Furthermore, even when ecotourism activities are carried out in a responsible manner, they tend to give priority to environmental protection, mainly by focusing on providing financial incentives for environmental conservation by local communities. Similarly, while broader sustainable tourism strategies contain economic and social objectives, these objectives tend to be complementary to a central focus on environmental sustainability Greater priority should thus be given to socio-economic objectives in general, and to poverty reduction in particular.

While responsible ecotourism and other sustainable tourism strategies may bring significant socio-economic benefits to host communities, they are not necessarily aimed at poverty alleviation. Given that the *United Nations Millennium Declaration*[19] has placed poverty at the centre of the international development agenda, it can be argued that sustainable tourism development should go beyond the promotion of broad socio-economic development and give greater priority to poverty reduction. This priority shift would also address a somewhat ignored recommendation of the seventh session of the Commission on Sustainable Development which, *inter alia*, urged Governments "to maximise the potential of tourism for eradicating poverty by developing appropriate strategies in cooperation with all major groups, and indigenous and local communities" (see UN, 1999c).

A pro-poor tourism (PPT) approach differs from ecotourism and other sustainable tourism strategies in that its overriding goal is to deliver net benefits to the poor.[20] While PPT and ecotourism may have some similar objectives, the key difference is that poverty reduction is the core focus of the PPT approach, rather than a secondary component of a mainly environmental sustainability strategy. In other words, although environmental protection remains an important PPT goal, the quality of the environment in which targeted poor groups live is only one part of a broader poverty reduction strategy.

There are several reasons why tourism development could

be a particularly effective tool of poverty reduction. First, as discussed earlier, tourism offers considerable employment opportunities for unskilled labour, rural to urban migrants and lower-income women. Second, there are considerable linkages with the informal sector, which could generate positive multiplier effects to poorer groups that rely on that sector for their livelihoods. Third, tourism tends to be heavily based upon the preservation of natural capital—such as, wildlife and scenery—and cultural heritage, which are often "assets that some of the poor have, even if they have no financial resources" (Ashley *et al.*, 2001:2).

It is increasing realised that promoting greater community participation in tourism development not only provides stronger incentives to conserve natural capital,[21] but can also lead to a more equitable sharing of benefits and thus greater opportunities for poverty alleviation. But while ecotourism and PPT both aim to increase community participation in general, PPT also goes beyond this goal in that it includes specific mechanisms to enhance the participation of and opportunities for the poorer segments of society. Three key components of the PPT approach are:

(a) *improved access to the economic benefits of tourism* by expanding employment and business opportunities for the poor and providing adequate training to enable them to maximise these opportunities;

(b) *measures to deal with the social and environmental impact of tourism development,* particularly the above-mentioned forms of social exploitation, as well as excessive pressure on natural resources pollution generation and damage to ecosystems; and

(c) *policy reform*, by enhancing participating of the poor in planning, development and management of tourism activities pertinent to them, removing some of thc barriers for greater participation by the poor, and encouraging partnerships between government agencies or the private sector and poor people in developing new tourism goods and services.

Some of these PPT concepts are beginning to be implemented

in several developing countries, such as Ecuador, Namibia, Nepal and Uganda. In Namibia, for example, the implementation of a PPT approach to the development and management of the country's community-based tourism segment appears to have made a significant contribution towards poverty reduction.

Several studies have shown that financial returns from community-based natural resource management and tourism ventures in Namibia usually exceed their investments and are thus a viable option for generating sustainable economic returns, while promoting environmental conservation and cultural traditions in rural areas (see, for example, Barnes et al., 2002). There is now evidence of a successful introduction of the PPT approach by the Namibia Community-based Tourism Association (Nacobta), a non-profit organisation that supports poor local communities—including small entrepreneurs with inadequate skills or access to financial resources—in their efforts to develop tourism enterprises in the country (see Nicanor, 2001).

Nacobta supports its members at both micro and macro levels, mainly through the provision of grants, loans, training, capacity building in the areas of institutional development and marketing training, as well as in negotiations with relevant government agencies and the mainstream tourist industry. Nacobta is explicitly pro-poor not only because it represents the poorest segment of the country's tourism industry, but also because most of its members live on communal land areas, where the majority of the inhabitants have an average per capita income of less that US$1 a day[22] and depend on subsistence agriculture. One of the main objectives of Nacobta is "to raise the income and employment levels of these areas through tourism, in order to improve the living standards of people in communal areas" (Nicanor, 2001:5).

The pro-poor tourism approach of Nacobta is thus different from conventional tourism because members of local communities both own and manage the tourism enterprises, who economic benefits flow directly into community funds or as formal sector wages, temporary remuneration to casual labourers and income to informal sector traders.

As stressed at the beginning of this paper, tourism is expected to resume its rapid growth in the near future. This growth can be harnessed not only for the enjoyment of tourists themselves but, more importantly, for maximising economic benefits and thus increasing the living standards of host communities and countries. At the same time, unless corrective measures are taken, it is bound to have negative environmental and socio-cultural impact on those communities.

Ecotourism and other sustainable tourism strategies have gone a long way towards minimising this negative impact and ensuring that the economic benefits of tourism can contribute to environmental protection and the sustainable use of natural resources. But while environmental sustainability must remain a key component of sustainable tourism strategies, another challenge for the international community is to devise ways and means to place poverty reduction at the centre of tourism planning, development and management. This will require, amongst other things, genuine community participation, greater technical and financial assistance, human resources development, and institutional capacity building in many developing countries.

# 3

# STUDY OF ENVIRONMENTAL MANAGEMENT

Until quite recently, when one spoke of the environment, one usually meant pollution. One meant that industry is inherently bad and that it had to be traded-off against clean air water, land and scenic areas. The criterion for making this trade-off between economic development and environmental quality lay in society's desire for further material prosperity. The lower the existing level of development, the greater was the perceived need to sacrifice the environment as a luxury in order to meet the more urgent priorities of generating employment and eradicating poverty.

This view of the environment is gradually being recognised as both narrow and counter-productive in the long run. It is still true that we have to exploit the environment and its various resources if we are to prosper. Indeed, there is practically no development project which does not have some detrimental impact on the environment. What we are realising, however, is that just as there are different measures of "prosperity", different types and degrees of environmental exploiration are possible. All of these choices are offered by the environment provided we can interpret the latter broadly enough. It is in this spirit that the 1972 Stockholm Conference on the Human Environment declared:

"Man is both creature and moulder of his environment, which

gives him physical sustenance and affords him the opportunity for intellectual, moral, social and spiritual growth. In the long and tortuous evolution of the human race on this planet, a stage has been reached when through the rapid acceleration of science and technology, man has required the power to transform his environment in countless ways and on an unprecedented scale. Both aspects of man's environment, the natural and man-made, are essential to his well-being and to the enjoyment of basic human rights—even the right to life itself."

The environment can, therefore, best be defined as the *totality of man's surroundings.* Such a definition is not too different from the one adopted by the Environment Pollution Panel of the U.S. President's Science Advisory Committee as far back as 1965 which referred to the environment as "the sum of all social, biological and physical or chemical factors which compose the surroundings of man". Each element of these surroundings constitutes a resource on which man draws in order to develop a better life. For purposes of analysis, these resources can be grouped under two broad categories:

— *Natural*: land, water, air, biota (including fauna and flora), energy and fuels, and raw materials (such as minerals),

— *Man-Made:* socio-economic Infrastructure, human population and cultural heritage.

Also, just as droughts, famines and pestilences are a negative feature in natural resources, a number of man-created components of the environment may in fact be inimical to his survival. Hence, while knowledge, attitudes, skills and various institutions assist in the use of the environment for promoting human welfare, overcrowding, ignorance, crime, poverty and social alienation make the task more difficult. As illustrated by a number of recent studies, we do have the means to satisfy minimum physical needs sustainably for an indefinite period while minimising the impact of the environmental problems alluded to in the previous section. Any failure in our attempt to muster the will and undertake the required institutional changes to do so will lie in our socio-political environment. Unlike all other forms of life, human beings are capable of exerting environmental effects that extend, both quantitatively and qualitatively, far beyond their influence as biological organisms. The way in which we organise and harness this potential depends to a great extent on the kind of society we create. This is one of the challenges of environmental management.

## What is Environmental Management

The fact that the environment covers just about every activity of man makes it extremely important for us to develop a practical yet comprehensive definition of the term environmental management. To start with, it is obviously beyond the capacities of any 'Environmental manager" to master the detailed functioning of each of the individual components of the environment. Nor is he required to do so. Pollution, depletion of resources and the socio-politico-cultural heritage constitute vast technical subjects of themselves and are best left to the specialist concerned with them in isolation. The environmental manager's job is merely to study and control the process by which these factors interact with one another and the manner in which they ultimately contribute to his particular objectives.

Since each action or decision in any of the individual areas will have multiple reactions and repercussions, the essential characteristic of environmental management is not that it jumps to an extreme conclusion about the need to protect nature or the need to stop growth, but rather that it leads to a careful weighing up of all the consequence of these decisions such that the final decision reflects a balanced view of the whole physical, biological and social environment. Furthermore, environmental management as a means of managing this very special decision making process is equally relevant to the public domain where the decisions are directly, and specifically, concerned with environmental protection, as it is to the private sector where decisions have a major but localised repercussion on the environment.

Like all other forms of management, environmental management needs a set of criteria for evaluating goals and for measuring performance. These criteria can be of two types, depending on the influence exercised by the manager in shaping his particular environment. For corporations, the criteria are essentially *internal* in nature and linked to the overall objectives of the firm such as profits, growth, conflict avoidance (social acceptability) or, simply, survival. The environmental management function is one among many corporate functions contributing to these objectives. In the public domain, the criteria are broader and *external* in the sense that they are addressed to society as a whole.

The distinction drawn between 'internal' and 'external' criteria is, of course, only superficial. Both of them call for a resort to some value system in weighing overlapping concerns about the natural environment, the industrial environment, and the socio-economic environment. These values can be either parochial, national or global. To be meaningful, they must further conform to societal desires as well as meet certain espoused standards of justice. It is becoming increasingly obvious that any corporation that adopts environmental criteria that run counter to the wishes of society is not likely to meet its other long-term objectives. This is specially true in areas where societal desires are rapidly expressed and where resources are mobilised to carry them out. With growing communication capabilities, the matching of internal criteria with those external to the firm is not only becoming more imperative, but the type of external criteria themselves are moving away from the parochial level to the national and even sometimes international level.

But it is not always easy to quess what societal desires really are. They change with time and may conflict with one another. The most common situation of such a conflict arises when one group wishes to preserve the environment in its pristine form while another wants all the economic benefits that would result from industrial exploitation of the environment. The operational meaning given to individual criteria in such cases depends to a large extent on the relative power of the two positions. Part of the job of the environmental manager is, in fact, to interpret and continually update his own reading of the expressed utility of society around him and to design compromise strategies long before such conflict situations arise. It is not always possible to do so, but that should not prevent us from trying.

There are, however, certain trends in societal thinking that have significance for the choice of environmental criteria in the immediate future. "Growth at any cost", for instance, has all but disappeared as a philosophy, even in the poorest of societies. It is being replaced by a variety of indicators measuring the "quality of life" instead of the narrower term GNP. What is more, the structure of economic activity itself is being questioned with greater frequency. "Bigness", "Technological Fix", "Rationalised Production" and "Automation" are losing some of their earlier magic and are now almost disparaging descriptions of the industrial society. When Stephen Bennet remarked a few years ago, "We don't know where we're going, but we're on our way", he probably meant it as a witticism. Today, it is a critique; tomorrow, perhaps, a response will be demanded.

Technology in general is becoming suspect. This is, of course, nothing new, as there have always been sceptics regarding the miracles of science. The trend is rather that technological fixes cannot solve every problem, particularly the man-nature interface. As the *Ecologist* points out:

"To suppose that we can ensure the functioning of the ecosphere ourselves with the sole aid of technological devices, thereby dispensing with the elaborate set of self-regulating mechanisms that has taken thousands of millions of years to evolve, is an absurd piece of anthropocentric presumption that belongs to the realm of pure fantasy. It may be possible to replace certain natural controls locally and for a short while without any serious cataclysm occuring, but if we push things too far, if for instance, the insecticides we use to replace the self-regulating controls that normally ensure the stability of insect populations were to destroy nitrogen-fixing bacteria or pollinating insects, all the money and all the technology in the world would not suffice to replace them and thereby to prevent life processes from grinding to a half."

Yet another trend, initiated recently in a number of international fora, is the New International Economic Order with its emphasis on Basic Human Needs. Contained in this trend are two important implications for world environmental policy-making. First, the emphasis is being shifted from pure intergenerational equity as a consideration in environmental conservation, towards current inter-societal equity. Partly out of altruism and partly out of fear of the consequences, commitment seems to be building within some nations to the goal of satisfying at least the basic human needs of all individuals before the end of this century. According to Lester Pearson:

"No planet can survive half slave, half free; half engulfed in misery, half careening along toward the supposed joys of almost unlimited consumption from unprecedented production with less work; and all in an atmosphere of greater ease and luxury than man has known since the declining days of Rome. Neither our ecology nor our morality could survive such contrasts. And we may have perhaps ten years to begin correcting this unbalance and to do so in time."

Second, the provision of basic human needs should be undertaken in such a fashion that it is sustainable over time. What this means in terms of *Cocoyoc Declaration* is the meeting of the "inner limits" of poverty, malnutrition, illiteracy and shelter without transgressing the "outer limits" of the planet's physical integrity through environmental degradation. Conscious strategies have to be adopted which minimise the "boom and bust" characteristic of most of today's development and to husband resource for the future so that human progress may continue.

All of these trends have far-reaching implications for environmental management. They are also interrelated. Behind all the international dialogue and rhetoric on individual issues lies a growing concern for the environment which bridges the old gap between development progress and environmental protection and reinterprets them as interlocking facets of the same problems—how to improve the present conditions and future prospects for human life on this planet. According to Rudolf Peterson, Administrator of the United Nations Development Programme, "development—properly defined—is much more than a process of stimulated economic growth, fuelled by the endless consumption of resources. On the contrary, development must also seek to conserve, replenish or improve both natural resources and human potentials. Otherwise, it is bund to be self-defeating, because it will eventually devour its own life substance."

The purpose of environmental management is to see that development does in fact take place sustainably. Whether we speak of a corporation, region or a nation, the type of products, the type of technology and the needs fulfilled must be in harmony with this concept. By managing the complex web of man's surroundings, one could hope for a world where the all remains fit to breathe and the water fit to drink, where sea and soil stay productive and resource supplies of all kinds are adequate to meet all needs. It could give us a world where a great majority of the people would be well fed, well housed and well schooled—enjoying full and healthy life-spans and the chance to earn decent livings. Environmental Management is, in essence, the process of allocating natural and man-made resources so as to make optimum use of the environment is satisfying basic human needs at the minimum and more, if possible, for an indefinite future.

Environmental management is not yet a full-fledged discipline taught at schools and universities. Some people believe that it never will become one since it is too vague, general or trivial. In developing countries, it is further viewed as being irrelevant and counter-productive. In advanced industrialised countries, on the other hand, it is often interpreted as a means of coping with the nuisance of environmental legislation and the problems created by over-zealous "environmentalists". This situation cannot last. Except for some remaining optimists, most people are today in agreement that the environment is in fact deteriorating. Whether it is industrial pollution, toxic chemicals, oil spills, resource depletion or the march of the desert, environmental "problems" are constantly in the news. What is more, the frequency with which these problems are occurring and being reported is rising every day. It is only natural, therefore, that a greater number of people want to learn about what is happening and perhaps to do some thing about it. After all, skepticism regarding the existence of a problem especially if it is based on ignorance, may very well force us into cynicism against our will. Like in many other reallife situations, the old Chinese proverb that "a calamity is a time of great opportunity" is perhaps also applicable. In order to realise the opportunity, however, we must first understand what the calamity is all about.

The root of the problem lies in too many people using too many resources wastefully. This is nothing new, of course. Malthus knew about it when he demonstrated the unfeasibility of supporting growing populations on limited agricultural land. So did every society in history that was occasionally ravaged by droughts, famines and pestilences. But, each time round, new resources or a technological breakthrough came to the rescue. In the case of the American cowboy, there was always another frontier to settle in once the old one had been rendered sterile by overgrazing, deforestation and excessive cultivation. In other instances, the use of fertilizers, new agricultural techniques and substitutes derived from technological innovations averted, or at least postponed, disaster. The panacea of science gave rise to a complacent feeling that no problem was beyond the grasp of human ingenuity.

This seems no longer true. Perhaps for the first time, even scientists are beginning to fear that we have indeed gone too far. As eloquently, though perhaps controversially, brought out by the Project on the Predicament of Mankind[6] sponsored by the Club of Rome in 1971, the natural environment is being depleted at too rapid a rate for man-made resources, especially technological and economic, to cope. The project report entitled *The Limits to Growth* has been widely read and commented upon. Since it needs very little description, it is enough to merely list the three broad conclusions that it arrived at:

"1. If the present growth trends (exponential) in world population, industrialisation, food production, and resource depletion continue unchanged, the limits to growth on this planet will be reached within the next one hundred years. The most probable result will be a rather sudden and uncontrollable decline in both population and industrial capacity.

2. It is possible to alter these growth trends and to establish a condition of ecological and economic stability that is sustainable for into the future. The state of global equilibrium could be designed so that the basic material needs of each person on earth are satisfied and each person has an equal opportunity to realise his individual potential.

3. If the world's people decide to strive for this second outcome rather than the first, the sooner they begin working to attain it, the greater will be there chances of success."

Environmental deterioration is in fact a multi-dimensional problem of which resource depletion is only a minor part. For instance, pollution in its various forms is increasingly becoming an obstacle to resource use. Air pollution generated to a great extent by automobiles, has reached intolerable levels in many localized areas since World War II. The disastrous smog of December 1952, which caused the death of about 4,000 people in the London area, may have been followed by similar incidences had it not been for active clean air measures taken throughout the world over the past two decades. But carbon monoxide, hydrocarbons, lead, carbon dioxide, sulphur oxides and particulate matter, especially beryllium, asbestos and mercury continue to be released into the atmosphere. The burning of fossil fuels now releases about $1.5 \times 10^{16}$ grams of carbon dioxide per year. This is an alarming amount because the amount actually consumed in photosynthesis is estimated to be about $1.1 \times 10^{17}$ grams. Not only is the artificially introduced amount large compared with natural processes, but it is 1,000 times greater than the return of carbon to the fossil reservoir. At the current rate of disposition in the atmosphere, the amount of man-made carbon dioxide doubles every 23 years and the total amount of carbon dioxide in the atmosphere has increased by about 8 per cent since 1900.

Water pollution, which used to be a local problem, has also begun to receive global attention. As a direct result of industrial activity, a number of heavy metals that are highly toxic have entered the natural water systems through sewage discharges, drainage from mines and agricultural irrigation. These include mercury, lead, arsenic, cadmium, chromium and nickel. Also a number of non-degradable wastes composed mainly of inorganic chemicals such as chlorides, synthetic organic chemicals, oil and inorganic suspended solids are being discharged into water in growing amounts. Judging from the state of Lake Erie or Lac Leman in Switzerland, the hazards are clear. On an oceanic plane, Captain Jacoues Cousteau has estimated, for example, that the damage done to the oceans in the past 20 years is somewhere between 30 percent and 50 percent of the which would be required for most life in the oceans of the world to die. Of all the resources available to man, water in a form suitable for drinking, sanitary use and for agriculture and industry might be the first to pose problems of scarcity.

Man-made chemicals, the products of the growth industry of the twentieth century, have never been more suspect than now. A growing number of them have been found to have debilitating effects on various components of the ecosystem as well as being toxic for man himself. The case of DDT and related organichlorine compounds (chlorinated hydrocarbons) like dieldrin, aldrin and heptachlor was the first to be brought to the public's attention through Rachel Carson's epoch-making book *S lent Spring*. Initially discovered as in insecticide, DDT found vital uses in controlling body lice that carry typhus and fleas that transmit bubonic plague. Its subsequent use in controlling crop-destroying insects was even considered a boon to agriculture. Research on the side-effects of DDT since 1966, however, has led to its being banned in some countries while those that depend heavily on its use in agriculture have begun actively searching for substitutes. The fact is that even though we have no clear evidence of DDT being a carcinogen (producing cancer) or mutagen (creating genetic changes) when ingested by man, it is known to present a significant hazard to fresh water fish, marine bacteria and certain predatory bird populations. It cripples the capacity of marine bacteria to find food and causes birds to either cease reproducing or lay eggs too thinly shelled for hatching, with serious consequences for the natural food chain.

Polychlorinated biphenyls (PCBs) which are used commercially in plasticizers, dielectrics and lubricants, is another recent example of the harmful side-effects of man-made chemicals. Like most chlorinated hydrocarbons, PCBs are extremely resistant to biological degradation and get stored in fatty tissues of organisms. When ingested by man in large quantities, as happened in Japan in 1968, they cause severe acne, eye discharge and darkened skin plus affect a variety of enzyme systems.

Worse still are the synergistic effects of chemical contaminants. For instance, in mixing the organic phosphorous (TOCP), the combined toxicity of the two is from 88 to 134 times greater than their effect administered singly. Given the existing research effort to achieve more effective pesticides by creating synergisms, and danger of accidental or unintended side-effects is always present. As D.N. Thompson puts it "the risk to be assessed is not that of a few thousand deaths, or obvious cases of genetic mutation, but that in the long run, we shall all be dead of synergistic poisoning."

Man-made chemicals that have potential carcinogenic, mutagenic or teratogenic (prenatal deviation) effects are only beginning to be identified. Even so, according to the World Health Organisation's International Agency for Research in Cancer (Lyon, France), "there is good circumstantial evidence that 80-90 per cent of all cancers are dependent, directly or indirectly, on environmental factors...and at least 90 per cent of these factors are chemical in nature." At present, seven groups of carcinogens have been identified: polycyclic aromatic hydrocarobons, aromatic amines, azo compounds, peroxy compounds, alkylating agents, metals and metalloids (especially beryllium, chrome, nickel, arsenic, selenium) and agents such as asbestos, certain polymers and pesticides. There are several hundred among these that are also muta-genically active with intensities that in some cases exceed that of ionising radiation.

Health hazards associated with pollution is perhaps the most compelling reason to study the environment. But there are other aspects of environmental deterioration which impact significantly on resource generation and use as well. Energy, for instance, is at the base of nearly all human endeavour. Because of the rapid increase in the consumption of energy world-wide during the past few decades, it has become scarce in the form we have conventionally used it in, *i.e.,* fossil fuels. The conjunctural events surrounding the precipitation of the "oil crisis" at the end of 1973 has very little to do with the problem as such. Fossil fuels, which today constitute 97 per cent of our primary energy supply, are nonrenewable except in geological time. According to current estimates, oil and natural gas will be exhausted in about 50 years while coal will last for another 150 years if it use increases after the oil is gone.

Future scarcities in fossil fuels are disturbing for two reasons. First, substitute energy sources such as nuclear energy tar sands and oil shales are likely to have a greater detrimental impact on the environment. Some of these sources are already being opposed by citizen groups in many parts of the world. Second, renewable sources of energy such as solar, wind, forests, tides, etc. will probably not be able to meet energy demands at today's levels as far as we can tell. Conservation is necessary but will be inadequate without a fundamental change in our economic and industrial structure. The fact is that the energy input in mining, food production, manufacturing as well as in the repairing of environmental damage rises each year.

A reduction in future food supplies on ecological grounds is yet another aspect of scarcity. World food demand is expanding more rapidly than ever before in history, partly because of population growth, but also because of an increased consumption of animal protein in the form of milk, eggs and protein among affluent societies. The pressure to increase food supplies has resulted in all the good land in the world being farmed and a steady encroachment into marginal lands. According to the FAO, even marginal lands will be exhausted by 1985. In many parts of the world, one already witnesses a number of ecologically unsound practices that have resulted in short-term production gains at the expense of a long-term sustainable food output. Over-grazing, slash-and-burn agriculture, deforestation and the expansion of agriculture to steep hillsides are only a handful of the many examples that can be cited.

Finally, while the will to alter growth trends and to establish a condition of ecological and economic stability that is sustainable far into the future may be present, the social dimensions of our environment may perhaps not be conducive to implementing it. Social inequities, both within and between nations, crime, alienation and various other forms of social blight are as big a hindrance to human progress as a lack of physical resources. A pre-requisitc for a clean and sustainably productive environment is, in fact, a healthy society where basic human needs are taken care of any where values and instructions reinforce the development efforts. Human beings are, after all, our main resource and constituency.

## A Suggested "Model" for Environmental Management

There is no unique "model" of environmental management. The best one can do is to make an inventory of the various environmental components that need to be considered and relate them through the corporate (or national) development process to the achievement of certain objectives. By doing so, one can highlight where environmental management fits in and what is expected of it. More importantly, since there is always the pragmatic criticism that if the environment is everything, then it is nothing, a scheme of this sort needs to emphasise the precise function of the environmental manager.

The main functions of the environmental manager are information gathering, evaluation and coordination. His job entails active involvement in the strategy formulation process as well as subsequent review of the performance of individual projects. Because of the general and broad-based nature of his task, his performance cannot be measured in conventional terms such as contribution to output, profits or cost reduction, but in terms of his overall contribution to the organisation's long-term success. In so far as this is true, it is logical that he report to top management in the case of a corporation, and to the planning authorities or equivalent in the case of a region or state.

With these general considerations in mind, Figure 4.1 outlines the type of process that environmental management is based upon. It is essentially a development process, but one that gives explicit recognition to environmental resources and the manner in which they are used. Since environmental management is concerned with taking decisions which promote environmental improvement, its first task is to assess the type of environment which is wanted by people whose lives will be affected by the decision in question. This stage derives from Box 6, which is a representation of some of the factors contributing to human well-being. These have been divided into three broad categories:

A. Satisfaction of basic human needs which are material and quantitative in nature, such as: health, food, water, education, housing, transportation and clothing.

B. Satisfaction of qualitative needs such as peace, equity, justice, a sense of belonging, freedom, recreation and entertainment, conditions of work and social security.

C. Satisfaction of some wants in excess of needs sustainably.

The actual level of material and non-material requirements which are necessary for adequate participation in the social and cultural life of the society will indeed vary from one region to another. This is specially true of the non-physiological needs which are culture-specific and value-specific. These can only be fully specified by continuous interaction between the environmental manager and the society to which he is immediately responsible.

The type of environment desired by society is, of course, seldom articulated by citizens in a continuous and coherent manner. As indicated in Box 1, The process of environmental management begins by receiving signals on the satisfaction of human well-being that are voluntarily forthcoming from society as well as the generation of this information by the environmental manager himself. The latter can be done in practice by means of surveys, polls, citizen group participation in project formulation and a variety of "open planning" techniques. Information generated in this manner will have the advantage of being structured to suit the environmental manager's objectives and at the same time, help develop consensus between corporate and social groups during the planning process. Judging from the billions of dollars that are being wasted today in post-project conflicts, the importance of this consensus building can hardly be over-emphasised.

Of the many demands that a corporation or national planner perceives, only a few can be fulfilled on economic, financial or technical grounds. The second major task of environmental management (IB) is to add certain environmental constraints to the selection procedure as well. The formulation of these additional constraints can take many forms in practice. Thus, when speaking of air pollution, the constraint can be interpreted as the absorptive capacity of the air surrounding the project (and particularly, the area where people live). The extent to which this resource constraint will be binding on project design will in turn depend upon the existing pollutants in the atmosphere, climate and wind conditions. No two places are, therefore, likely to have the same constraint in terms of magnitude. In generla, the criterion of sustainability, in terms of magnitude. In general, the criterion of sustainability, when applied to the various environmental resources, will provide a comprehensive guide to choosing which constraints are to be taken into account for a particular situation. The basic principle is that, while resources are there to be used, they should not be permanently impaired unless an adequate substitute is forthcoming.

Though not explicitly formulated as such, the environmental impact statement (EIS) is a means of establishing this resource constraint in practice. The EIS requirement was first introduced in the United States under the National Environmental Policy Act of 1969 and has since either been, or is in the process of being, introduced in all of the OECD countries. In needs to be pointed out, however, that the manner in which it is currently prepared makes it an inadequate instrument for environmental management as we interpret in this note. This is for two main reasons. First, while environmentalists are in general agreement that the EIS should identify, predict and evaluate the impact of a given project on all of the relevant physical, biological and economic and social factors, only a handful of these factors are considered in reality. Second, which is a more important criticism, the EIS is not designed to study alternatives in any comprehensive fashion, though it is required to include them formally. This problem arises partly because the statement is prepared after all the other project parameters have been considered and partly because of limits on choice imposed by a rigid economic structure. Whereas a corporation can only initiate improvements in the former regards, the responsibility of creating an economic system that can accommodate a wider range of environmental strategies lies in the public domain. In both cases, it is necessary to realise that a final environmental impact statement is no more than an instrument for communicating a project's effect on the environment and that actual strategy formulation should consist of an evaluation of the impact of a range of possible alternatives. Also, that public measures such as pollution taxes and natural resource use taxes can significantly affect the final choice made.

Some of the alternatives that can be considered in evaluating resource constraints are listed under item IC. These are: pollution control, non-waste technologies and resource augmentation. The first, pollution control, needs no elaboration as it is currently being induced by emission standard regulations in many parts of the world. The last two are relatively new concepts whose full exploitation will have to wait until government policy measures come round to making them profitable. Some types of non-waste technologies can, of course, be implemented even under existing market conditions. Thus, instead of discharging the by-products of industrial activity into the environment as pollutants, some of these can be recycled to produce saleable products. The example of the North British Distilleries in Edinburgh is a case in point. This company, which was dumping its waste into a nearby river, was threatened by law either to clean up or to close down. It decided to clear up by concentrating and drying its wastes and selling the resulting product as highly nutritious animal feed. The revenue generated by this activity (£1 million a year) was enough to pay for the additional expenditure within 6 months and now constitutes a net benefit to the corporation. Yet, another example of this "product-not-waste" approach was that adopted by a Tel-

Aviv instant coffee manufacturer. By installing an electrostatic precipitator to recover the coffee dust which was previously being discharged into the asmosphere, it was able to add sufficiently to its coffee sales to pay for the new expenses, again over a 6 months period.[10] The same principle of waste recovery has already been applied in the recycling of metals (at a lower energy cost), the recovery of valuable materials from urban solid wastes (worth as much as $250 per ton in the U.S.) and the utilisation of organic wastes as fertilizer (in most developing countries).

Resource augmentation is further possibility to be explored within the context of environmental management. Contrary to popular belief, the environment is not totally finite and when one thinks of "space-ship earth", one does not necessarily have to imagine a perpetually deteriorating one. This applies specially to the man-made component of the environment but has important implications for natural resources as well. Human resources, whether they consist of trained manpower, scientific knowledge or organised institutions, all have the potential for development. If properly mobilised, they can contribute to the effective management and regeneration of natural resources themselves. It is true that every natural resource is not capable of augmentation or renewal, but a large number of the essential ones are. Land and water, which together contribute to food production, are the best examples. If properly managed, they can yield a greater quantity and variety of food on land on a sustainable basis and multiply several-fold the current output of fish and other sources of food from the sea.

The essence of environmental management is thus not only to minimise the environmental impact of a particular project, but also to husband and add to existing resources for the future. In formulating strategies based on the resource constraints mentioned above, explicit account should be taken of actions that might serve to prolong the life of a non-renewable resource or add to the existing stock of those that have growth potential. Account should also be taken of the fact that the line of demarcation between renewable and non-renewable resources is really quite thin, despite all the rhetoric to the contrary. A positive approach to formulating environmentally sound strategies should consider a resource non-renewable only if its exhaustion will impair current and future human welfare and if no substitute yielding equivalent utility is likely to be found before the forecost date of exhaustion. It could further be considered non-renewable if an inordinate amount of economic resources will be needed to find substitutes for it. With such a definition in view, the scope for implementing alternative plans is vast and full of opportunities.

As listed under item ID., the actual implementation of a strategy could be in terms of a new product, new technology or a complementary project that benefits the environment. Since these are necessarily a part of the development process, the impact of each change should further be evaluated against conventional development criteria. The first stage in this evaluation is shown in Box 2, Where each project, technology or complementary project is assessed according to its contribution to human well-being. This contribution could be the satisfaction of a basic need (a first priority), the meeting of certain "wants" in excess of "needs", a by-product takes will depend on the activity in question and could be either beneficial (spin-off, derived demand, etc.) or detrimental (pollution, waste, etc.) to human welfare.

Boxes 3 through 5 represent the development process which results in products and services. This process consists of strategy formulation, allocation of man-made resources (capital, labour and technology) and the use of environmental resources in production. Alternative ways of describing the same set of activities exist, but the difference here is the explicit recognition given to environmental resources. Furthermore, these resources are treated as a means to an end (human well-being) rather than the ultimate constituency to which development efforts are to be accountable. This is done on purpose. Underlying the framework for environmental management presented here is an open systems concept where the feedback on the functioning of the system comes not from the state of the environment but from the state of human well-being. Environmental resources are a component of the overall system and have no utility except for the services they provide. In other words, environmental management which consists of "managing" the various interactions depicted in Figure 4.1 should be accountable to man and only indirectly to the environment which provides him sustenance.

## Quantification of Environment Relevant Activities of Industries

The course topic on tourism was introduced so that the participants have an understanding of the impact of a service sector (such as tourism) on the environment. The course topic was treated under five main headings and these were:

- The life cycle analysis of tourism products;
- Tourism development world-wide and the transport problem;
- The domain of tourism definitions;
- Approaches to measuring tourism on the environment; and;
- Building up an information system on "Tourism and Environment."

The life cycle analysis of an inclusive tour is a conceptual framework utilised to analyse the impact of the tourism sector on the environment. In the life cycle analysis several materials are utilised. There different stages of the life cycle have different implications on the environment.

The greatest impact of tourism on environment is high air emissions as a result of air transportation. To get an impression of the magnitude of the problem the participants were requested to calculate the amount of energy that has been utilised in soming to the Munich Centre from their respective countries.

1. visitors who spend at least one night in the country visited, but less than one year.
2. visitors who arrive and leave the same day for leisure, recreation and holiday; visiting friends and relative; business and professional; health treatment; religious pilgrimages and other tourism purposes, including transit day visitors en route to or from their destination countries.

3. Persons who arrive in a country aboard ship even when disembarking for one or more day visits.
4. Foreign air or ship crews docked or inlay over and who use the accommodation establishments of the country visited.
5. Crews who are not residents not the country visited and who stay in the country for the day.
6. As defined by the United Nations in the "Recommendations on the International Migration Statistics, 1980."
7. Who do not leave the transit areas of the airport or the port, including transfer between airports or ports.
8. As defined by the United Nations High Commissioner for Refugees, 1967.
9. When they travel from their country of origin to the duty station and vice-versa (including household servants and dependants accompanying or joining them.

**Carrying Capacity**

The concept of carrying capacity was outlined as follows:

> "How many tourists can I put there before I threaten the long term viability of the system?"

This concept of carrying capacity is founded on the experience of pastoral agriculture which is based on the principles that a pasture can support only a particular number of cattle in perpetuity. If this threshold is exceeded, the supporting system is damaged often to point where it can support no more grazing at all.

This concept only deals with one product (in this case cattle), the tourism product includes a variety of products and services. Tourism depends on many attributes of an environment – the aesthetics, wildlife, access to shoreline, ability to support active uses (*e.g.,* Sports); each attribute has its own response to different levels of use. Different types of uses have different impacts. Different cultures have different levels of sensitivity towards change. Human activity's impact can be gradual, affect different parts of the systems at different rates. Tourism environments are mostly multipurpose environments. Other uses have to be considered when determining the correct level of development.

Hence the concept of carrying capacity is not an ideal concept for evaluating impact of tourism on the environment. The simplistic concept of carrying capacity involving identification of a single threshold value is inadequate for tourism management. An approach should rather reflect the sensitivity of the different attributes of the environment to various types and levels of use. At each level of use certain trade-offs have to made.

The dimensions of carrying capacity for sustainable tourism are highlighted in Box 5.1 below:

---

**Dimensions of Carrying Capacity for Sustainable Tourism**

**Environmental carrying capacity:** The degree to which an ecosystem, habitat or landscape can accommodate the various impacts of tourism and its associated infrastructure without damage being caused or without losing its "sense of place."

**Cultural and social carrying capacity:** The level beyond which tourism development and visitors numbers adversely affect local communities and their ways of life.

**Psychological carrying capacity:** The leave beyond which the essential qualities that people seek in the protected area (such as peace and quiet, few other people, few signs of human development) would be damaged by tourism developments.

*Source:* Federation of National Parks in Europe, 1993.

---

Carrying capacity is a concept beyond ecological matters. A policy for sustainable tourism development avoids serious environmental problems such as congestion, pollution of air and water, noise or degradation, degradation or ecosystems overload of infrastructure. It also avoids loss of culture identity of the host society or serious social problems (e.g., Crime). It avoids serious economic distortions, while still bringing economic benefit. A sustainable policy for tourism development maintains tourists satisfaction levels so that the desired tourist markets continue visiting the area.

**Approach by World Tourism Organisation**

The aim of the approach proposed by World Tourism Organisation are

- To develop an international system of indicators for sustainable tourism;
- Measure sensitivity of environment rather than carrying capacity;
- To develop warning systems for areas of concern in order to improve decision making with regard to sustainable tourism development; and;
- Reduce number of crucial indicators.

The characteristics of indicators developed are grouped into two dimensions the core indicators for general application and destination specific indicators applicable to particular ecosystems or types of tourism. This disaggregation enables the understanding of tourism and environment as a two way relationship including socio-economic indicators. The areas of concern covered in this approach are environmental sensitivity, stress on the environment, results of tourist use and human, biological consequences of tourism use.

The IUCN Protected Area Categories are as listed below

I. Scientific reserve/strict nature reserve

II. National park

III. Natural monument

IV. Managed nature reserve or wildlife sanctuary

V. Protected landscape

VI. Resource reserve

VII. Natural biotic areas of anthropological reserve

VIII. Multiple use management areas/managed resource

IX. Biosphere reserve

X. World Heritage Site.

This approach of sustainable tourism has been developed in conjunction with the IFTO/EU and the DWIF. The aims of the approach are: to provide a model for analysing the basic objects and requirements for the long term maintenance of a tourist destination; to develop a reduced number of indicators, comparatively easy collection of relevant data, significance, quantification, if possible; determining points/threshold at which critical values or situations are reached in order to know that action is required (identifying standards/limiting factors/carrying capacities).

The characteristics of this approach is that it is management oriented. Tourism is understood as an equilibrium between three major objectives/aims which are protection of population's prosperity/ socio cultural identity; preservation of the destination's attractiveness for tourists and preservation of destination's ecological functions. This approach has been applied to destinations such as Malloca, Rhodas, Ibiza whereby stress on socio-economic indicators/welfare in these destinations measured. Figure 5.3 show the pyramid of sustainable tourism.

For each of the major aims special targets/variables can be attributed. For example the major aim of securing population's prosperity in the socio-cultural identity is represented by security of the population's prosperity, security of the economic efficiency and preservation of the population's socio-cultural identity.

**Approach by Eurostat**

The aim of the approach that has been developed by EUROSTAT is to build up a European community system of integrated environmental and economical indicators for monitoring. Tourism is one of the priority economic sectors identified for assessing impact of the economy on the environment. The approach also aims to integrate environmental aspects by calculating physical indicators/indices related to the pressure of human and economic activities on the environment.

This approach is on the UN framework for inter-relationship between tourism and environment. Social/economic activities describe human activities impact on the environment. Environmental impacts of tourism can be described as changes in the quality of the environment. Stock, inventories, background conditions are needed to described the qualities of environment which include tourism demand. Responses to environment impact as actions/measures taken for environmental and nature protection.

Hunting and fishing are environment topics which lead to increased tourism activity in certain areas. The major environmental problem caused loss of biodiversity. Increasing tourists leads to increased use of various means of transport and the consequence is the green house effect, destruction of the ozone layer, air pollution. With regard to water used for human consumption, with increasing number of tourists leads to increased consumption of water and in small islands this may lead to water scarcity. The construction of hotels and roads, ski lifts and other infrastructure leads to land use and environmental restructuring, this leads to loss of biological diversity and soil erosion. Increase in the number of persons in tourism areas implies an increase in the amounts of waste.

The TMAP and TMEG approach has been used to assess the state of the Wadden Sea a famous ecosystem in Northern Germany. The target was to monitor the development in space and time.

The characteristics of this approach is that it is applied to a specific ecosystem the Wadden sea of the Netherlands, Germany and Denmark. It only measures the impact of human activity on the ecosystem (one-way relationship between tourism and environment!) and is based on selection of issues of concern and corresponding hypothesis.

The approach is being utilised to test a particular hypothesis that recreational activities can affect the occurrence and abundance of species. This includes the population size, growth and reproduction of species. The main impact of recreational activities may be related to the presence of visitors inside the Wadden Sea and their activities. National fluctuations have to be taken into account.

In this approach the impacts of land based pollutant inputs, dumping, military use, fisheries, recreation, shipping/harbour, oil/

gas extraction and sand gravel grading, coastal change on the eco-system is studied.

## REFERENCES

Dasman, R.E., (1975), *The Conservation Alternative*, New York, John Wiley and Sons Inc.

Herrera, A.O., Scolnik, H.D. *et. al.* (1976), *Catastrophe or New Society? A Latin American World Model*, Ottowa, International Development Research Centre.

Lovins, A.B. (1975), *World Energy Strategies: Facts, Issues and Opinions*, New York, Friends of the Earth Inc.

Parson, L.D. (1970), *Partners in Development, Report of the Commission on International Development*, New York Frederick A. Praeger, Inc.

Peterson, R.A. (undated), "Solvable by definition", in *Beyond Conflict or Compromise*, brochure prepared by the United Nations Development Programme.

Roschin, A.V. (1974), "Protection of the Working Environment", *International Labour Review*, September, 1974, Vol. 110, No. 3.

Royston, M.G. (1976), *Eco-Productivity: A Positive Approach of Non-Waste Technology*, background paper prepared for the UNEP seminar on the Principles and Creation of Non-Waste Technology and Production, Paris, November 29—December 4, 1976.

Thompson, D.N. (1973), *The Economics of Environmental Protection*, Cambridge, Mass., Winthrop Publishers.

# 4

# EFFECTS OF TOURISM ON THE NATURAL ENVIRONMENT

The investigation identified a great range of effects, both environmental and non-environmental, as well as some which may be considered environmental in some contexts. Environmental effects may include social, economic, aesthetic and cultural aspects where those matters are related to effects on the physical environment. People and communities are part of the physical environment in the sense that they are parts of ecosystems.

All types of effects associated with tourism in New Zealand identified in this investigation are listed and briefly characterized in Table 6.1. However, those which are not environmental effects will not be discussed in any detail in the body of the report.

The grouping of effects in the table reflects the framework used by the consultant. The 'effects identified in the literature' column is summarised from the consultant's report (PCE 1997b). This report includes more complete references, including overseas work. Here, comments relating to research in the fourth column refer only to key New Zealand references. The amount of relevant New Zealand research is characterised as: none, little (one or two studies), some (several studies, but gaps), or significant (comprehensive work).

This approach is appropriate because the context and content of the interviews in which effects were identified different significantly, precluding a rigorous, quantitative approach to the analysis of the responses. Each effect is listed only once, regardless of how many times it was cited, and no attempt was made to restrict the scope of effects raised by people interviewed. However, the effects are characterised in the 'type' column using the values.

Features of the effects identified in discussed in the next section. An assessment of what are considered to be the principal environmental effects is given in the preceding section.

In order to evaluate the management of the environmental effects associated with the tourism sector, it is necessary first to determine what these effects are. In this chapter an attempt is made to identify these effects to provide both a focus and a context for the evaluation carried out in subsequent chapters. This chapter addresses the first term of reference for the investigation.

Two approaches were taken:

- a literature review was commissioned from a tourism research consultant, to summarise the environmental effects associated with tourism identified in research literature both in New Zealand and overseas'; and
- environmental effects associated with tourism identified in interviews during the investigation were collated and evaluated, together with those noted in written submissions.

In this report the term 'environmental effect' includes reference to both positive and negative environmental effects. The term 'impacts', used in some work to refer to negative effects (*e.g.*, DOC 1997) is not used. The phrase 'environmental effects *associated with* the tourism sector' is used throughout this report because a causal relationship between tourism and some of the effects identified by those consulted is not clear. For brevity, the term 'the tourism sector' is generally abbreviated to 'tourism', but this does not imply that all effects identified are associated with tourism activities *per se;* they may be associated with any part of the tourism sector as defined at the beginning of this report.

A number of inventories of different environmental effects associated with tourism have been undertaken in New Zealand recently (DOC 1997; Ward and Beanland 1996; TPG 1995a, 1996a; Devlin *et. al.* 1995). However, this investigation is thought to be the most comprehensive attempt to date to broadly identify all environmental effects associated with the tourism sector in New Zealand.

***Range of Effects***

The breadth of the effects identified goes beyond what are generally considered as 'environmental effects.' Tourism in New Zealand "is primarily a recreation activity which results in many positive outcomes for the participating individuals, the majority of whom are New Zealanders" (P Winter, NZTB, letter to PCE, August 1997). Most of those positive outcomes for tourists are experiential, in that the quality of the outcome or experience involves intangible and subjective factors. As part of the tourist experience, tourists interact with the host community and environment and have effects on them. As the table shows, many of these effects are also experiential or perceptual, such as crowding or social effects. Perceptions of effects are likely to be related to people's reaction to the changes brought about by tourism. It is difficult to distinguish between real and perceived effects because of lack of research and because and because of the subjectivity of many effects. However, because tourism relies so heavily on positive perceptions, and since perceptions affect the way people (both hosts and visitors) feel and behave, perceived effects cannot be discounted as unreal or unimportant.

In the interviews it was evident that different groups of people identified different effects. Many community groups focused on social effects as well as cost of living, infrastructure and lifestyle effects, whereas industry representatives tended to emphasise economic effects. It was frequently impossible to distinguish the effects of domestic from international tourists, or to distinguish effects associated with the tourism sector from those associated with everyday activities and with day trips. Similarly, there is not always a clear distinction between social and environmental effects.

### *Positive and Negative Effects*

Most people consulted identified positive economic effects from tourism, but some (particularly by those people in the districts where profiles were undertaken) identified more negative than positive effects in the other groupings. Other surveys have found broad acceptance of tourism among many communities (*e.g.*, NZTB 1992 NZTB 1997a; Rotorua District Council 1997), suggesting that identification of negative effects does not necessarily equate with rejection of tourism.

Strong positive effects in economic terms were identified throughout, indicating a general appreciation of the contribution that tourism makes to the economy. This dichotomy between negative and positive attitudes suggests that a key issue for tourism management generally is to reconcile the beneficial effects on the economy with any detrimental effects on the environment.

### *Environmental Effects*

It has been noted that in identifying and managing environmental effects associated with tourism, there are both temporal and spatial dimensions which need to be taken into account. Economic effects of tourism tend to be beneficial in the short term, while the natural, physical, and socio-cultural effects tend to become apparent in the longer term and may be both interactive and cumulative. Factors determining significance include:

- characteristic of the place where the effect occurs;
- carrying capacity or sensitivity of the place;
- mitigation measures in place;
- services required compared to services provided;
- visitor numbers and frequency of visits; and
- reversibility of the effect.

From the point of view of ecological sustainability, the most important characteristic is reversibility. Many of the effects identified are reversible, especially where they are minor in intensity or scale but reversibility is hard to predict and depends enormously on the environment and the way the effect is managed.

'Reversible' should not be confused with 'temporary'. The cumulative nature of many effects suggests that reversible effects may become irreversible if their cumulative impact reaches a threshold level. Likewise, temporary effects can have permanent implications if they occur in a sensitive environment or occur so frequently as to be quasi-permanent. The gradation from specific to general shown in Figure 6.1 does not imply a parallel gradation of reversibility, as effects in all types 1 to 4 can be either reversible or irreversible.

Some researchers have attempted to assess the reversibility of some of the effects identified (e.g. Cessford and Dingwall, 1996). Most of these assessments are for individual effects, so more work will be needed before that information can be used to rank the significance of a number of recognised and potential effects. Those consulted were more specific about effects, possibly as a result of personal experience. For example, people gave a number of specific examples of 'disturbance of wildlife from tourist interactions' including feeding keas, poking seals and sea lions, disturbing penguins by standing between them and their nests, and changing albatross nesting patterns by the building of lookouts.

People consulted also put a stronger emphasis on community and infrastructural effects than did the literature. In relation to the social environment, they noted the effects that tourism has on local people and the differences between local and tourist needs. Some consulted felt that more negative effects on local communities occurred from overseas tourists than from domestic tourists. In some other locations, however, domestic visitors are seen to have the greatest and most detrimental effect, notably on the Coromandel Peninsula. It seems that the density of various types of tourist relative to the host community affects the perception of their effect on that community. 'Crowding' was mentioned by many people as a negative effect, expressed as a social rather than a physical effect.

From both consultation and the literature, effects on infrastructure included both positive and negative aspects, depending on the circumstances of the community and the type and extent of tourism it hosts. The financial commitment required for the infrastructural needs of the tourism sector and the demands this places on local communities were widely noted, and are discussed in later chapters.

Concern was also shown by those consulted about the behaviour of some business operators and the effects their practice can have on the environment. Allegations of 'fly-by-night' operators using and sometimes damaging an area for a short time and then leaving show concern about the implications of the operations of some in the tourism sector.

Specific localised environmental effects associated with tourism constituted a significant proportion of the effects noted by those consulted, often reflecting very personal responses to change. The taking of shellfish from a local resource base, mention of specific developments such as a tourism-oriented tram in Christchurch, and people feeling 'displaced' from their usual haunts, all reflect the personal and local nature of many of the effects identified. The significance of these effects to individuals largely depends on how they perceive the effect changing the condition and character of the environment.

### *Cultural Effects*

People consulted noted several positive cultural effects of tourism, which were not identified in the literature, including the fostering of relationships with other cultures and communities, and the maintenance and revival of cultural activities. Many of these positive effects were identified by industry sources, while, in general, most of the social and cultural effects identified by those consulted were negative. The negative effects tended to be cited by environmental and community groups, but not exclusively.

Many cultural issues specific to Maori were identified. These generally confirm the more generic effects identified from the literature, including both positive and negative effects for tangata whenua.

Adverse environmental effects where there are also cultural and spiritual dimensions include the desecration of waahi tapu sites. Differences over the management of specific sites of significance to Maori, where tourism may be incompatible with Maori values, highlight the particular significance of some effects for tangata whenua.

### *Effects of Tourism on the Natural Environment*

Some people consulted identified positive effects of tourism on the natural environment. There is a relatively common perception that tourism revenue can contribute to natural environment or wildlife protection and that tourism can be a strong argument for protection. While this has been identified in overseas literature, it is not clearly documented in the existing New Zealand literature.

In practice, the relationship between tourism and nature conservation or preservation is not clear. Concessions revenue has been used to further environmental protection (*e.g.*, Kawerau Bridge, Waimangu Valley). However, where money has been spent on visitor services in natural areas, the expenditure appears, in most cases, to have been for developing the area or mitigating adverse effects rather than for conservation or preservation *per se.* Penguin Place on the Otago Peninsula is an unusual example. Here, a tourism opportunity arose from a private conservation project to protect yellow-eyed penguins. For Penguin Place, tourism has provided money for further conservation work, but it was the landowner's conservation initiative, rather than a tourism initiative, that created the tourism opportunity.

It appears that where the environment benefits from tourism, the benefits may be indirect. On the West Coast, tourism revenues have not directly paid for the network of national parks and conservation reserves, but the potential for tourism revenue has no doubt been a factor in its development. Tourism was also part of the argument for reserving more areas for parks and reserves in the West Coast and was a strong consideration in the recent proposals for Kauri National Park in Northland, and for major extensions to Whanganui National Park. Considerably more research is needed to understand the relationship between tourism and environmental protection in New Zealand.

There was limited comment from those interviewed about lack of data on the environmental effects associated with tourism. Some concern was expressed about specific developments being permitted with inadequate information about possible effects, resulting in unforeseen outcomes with no avoidance or mitigation measures in place, but this is a general resource management rather than a tourism issue. Concern about lack of data was much more significant in the written submissions. It is clear that there is a need for more tourism research, especially into its effects on the social aspect of the environment (including community structures and culture) where so many effects are based on perceptions and values.

Those consulted often noted that many environmental effects associated with the tourism sector are cumulative, whereby individually small and gradual changes can over time accumulate to erode a resource or undermine a valued aspect of the environment, sometimes irreversibly. Concerns about the lack of knowledge about cumulative effects both tin relation to the physical and social aspects of the environment were widely expressed. Many of those consulted were concerned about the inability to determine when the 'carrying capacity' of an area has been reached.

Tourism, being a diverse sector, has effects on the whole range of environments – urban, rural, natural, and marine – and it affects the social, economic and cultural aspects of life in New Zealand. Based on work undertaken for this investigation, the principal positive effect associated with tourism in New Zealand is identified as:

- revenue generation and contribution to diversified employment and economic development (locally, regionally and nationally).

The principal negative environmental effects include:

- loss of quality of some relatively unspoilt parts of New Zealand's natural environment (both physical and intrinsic values);
- loss of amenity values from incremental development (in both rural and urban environments);
- pressure on infrastructure, such as sewerage and roads (often seasonal), resulting in significant costs to small communities.

These effects are of particular concern to Maori. In some cases, Maori are more likely to be affected than non-Maori; for instance, where key tourism attractions are based in Maori communities (*e.g.,* Whakarewarewa), or in places of great significance (*e.g.* Tane Mahuta at Waipoua).

Although all of these principal effects are strongly associated with tourism, they can also result from 'everyday' activities of New Zealanders. Probably all of them have 'perceived' as well as 'real' elements. These factors make such effects extremely hard to measure and assess. However, all these negative effects have some documentation to support their significance and all were frequently cited by those interviewed during the investigation. Also, they are cumulative, and at least have the potential to cause irreversible change to the natural environment and/or human communities.

## Distinguishing between International and Domestic Tourism Effects

Many of the people consulted in this investigation focused on the effects and perceived effects of overseas visitors. Comments about bus-loads of tourists, foreign-language signs, and poor driving on New Zealand roads, illustrate a general perception that tourists are people who come from overseas. Such comments and perceptions are reinforced by many official New Zealand publications (eg NZTB reports, New Zealand yearbook statistics) which refer to 'tourism' without qualification when in fact they are referring only to international tourism.

However, it is apparent that in most instances the effects of one person are the same as the effects of another, regardless of their origin. This principle is more relevant when considering the physical effects (erosion, car use, crowding, etc) than the social effects, where cultural differences can result in conflicting behaviour in certain environments. New Zealanders tend not to regard themselves as tourists in their own country, but it most be acknowledged that domestic visitors are very similar to overseas visitors in placing demands on certain services and infrastructure.

New Zealanders have strong expectations about their rights as citizens to freely access recreational opportunities in natural areas, and tenacious beliefs in the clean green qualities and reputation of this country. These factors have a strong influence on their responses to tourism and its environmental effects. Conflicts between different groups of users of the natural environment, particularly traditional back-country recreational users who feel their experience is compromised or diminished by such encounters, are often based in these deep-rooted cultural values and assumptions.

Distinguishing tourism effects from general effects arise from tourism and which are part of wider trends and patterns in everyday life. For example, on the Coromandel Penisula growing numbers of holiday-home owners are placing increasing and seasonal demands on the infrastructure of the district. It is unclear how much of the pressure felt at peak times is due to tourism and how much to ratepayers. The same applies to other services such as roads, shops, hospitals, and public toilets. The complexity of the relationships between tourism and the host community and the blurred lines between tourism and other activities often make it very hard to make reliable links between causes and effects. This uncertainty needs to be acknowledged in planning for, managing and evaluating tourism and its environmental effects.

## Systems and Stakeholders Government System for Management

The present government system for the management of environmental effects associated with the tourism sector is assessed. This assessment is made against the broad criteria. Management of tourism and its environmental effects is not a straightforward or clear-cut matter, especially in the relationship between the public and private parts of the sector, when the latter plays such a dominant part in tourism management. The sector is characterized by a wide range of different government agencies, each with different roles, responsibilities and manadates, some of which overleap, others of which leave gaps. Some statutory non-government organizations also have relevant roles for tourism. The multi-faceted nature of the government system can lead to considerable confusion for many operators, tangata whenua and other stakeholders. Making progress, whether with a tourism development proposal, a community consultation programme, or an effort at strategic management, can be cumbersome and slow.

The range of different legislation and statutory frameworks relating to the tourism sector and the management of its environmental effects is another aspect of this fragmentation. There is often considerable variability between the provisions and purposes of different statutes, between different councils' plans and policies, between iwi resource management plans and Crown policies, between DOC's different regional CMSs and the many non-statutory programmes and initiatives that apply both for the tourism sector and for environmental management. There is no evidence of major inconsistencies between the RMA and other legislation that affects tourism management, but there are some specific areas of concern about interface issues (eg. In the areas of marine pollution, provision of public toilet facilities, legislation for recreational fishing allocation, air space control, and safety and navigation issues along lakes and rivers).

Communication and integration of policy between the different agencies and levels of authority is often less than effective. This is particularly evident with agencies that do not have tourism or environmental management as one of their primary roles. In some of these agencies, the relationship of activities undertaken to tourism is not always clearly identifiable, so those activities are not given appropriate priority or included in strategic planning from a tourism perspective. Agencies may be characterised by strong internal lines of accountability but poor links to other agencies. The wide-ranging nature of tourism activities, with well-established interdependent networks of destinations and attractions over several different regions or areas, also intensifies the need for good communication.

This analysis shows a system that performs well in parts and which is partially succeeding in managing a dynamic economic sector. Overall, however, the government system for management of tourism is fragmented, especially between agencies which promote tourism and those which manage its effects. There are few mechanisms for communication and coordination between different parts of the tourism sector.

Integration between agencies can be improved through:

- improved coordination at Ministerial or senior management level, involving primarily a core group of Tourism, conservation, Environment, Local government, Maori Affairs and Transport linked to a further group including Statistics, Health, Internal Affairs, Customs, Biosecurity and Business Development.

A greater awareness of tourism issues within various government agencies generally. For many of the relevant ministries a tourism adviser, as within Puni Kokiri, may be a suitable option. Regular liason at appropriate working levels of relevant agencies is essential, without necessarily creating new formal structures. When the different roles and responsibilities relating to tourism and its effects are combined within the one agency, other problems arise. Earlier we discussed some of the difficulties for agencies with marketing, policy, and operational roles. This mixture of responsibilities can mean that it is difficult to give adequate consideration to environmental issues. Even when efforts have been made to deal with these issues, there can be distrust or a lack of support from communities and stakeholders, because of their consciousness of the agency's dual or multiple roles, and the perception that other concerns are outweighing the public or stakeholder interest.

From the perspective of central government decision-making. the tourism sector is characterized by unusual diversity of government policy purchase. This diversity, and the differences in scale and resourcing of the various agencies, has meant that the provision of policy advice has appeared to be dominate by the NZTB.

## National Agencies

*The New Zealand Tourism Board:* The NZTB has had considerable success in marking New Zealand internationally as a high-profile tourism destination, despite high travel costs from most other parts of the global and a fiercely competitive world tourism market. The NZTB's marketing work has recently been matched by constructive initiatives in other aspects of tourism development, including involvement with standards and brands development, and with regional tourism strategies. The Board's statutory objective is to ensure that New Zealand is marketed so as to maximize long-term benefits to the country. It has set the following goals for the tourism sector:

1. Continuing growth in the contribution of tourism to the New Zealand economy to achieve targets of $9 billion in foreign exchange earnings and 180000 full-time jobs (or there part-time equivalents) by the year 2000.
2. Continuing improvements in visitors satisfaction, consistent with the positioning of New Zealand as a distinct, competitive and high-value destination with authentic experiences and a friendly welcome.
3. Encouragement of industry profitability and appropriate returns on investment.
4. Any adverse impacts from tourism on the environmental attractions upon which it depends are avoided, remedied or mitigated.
5. Acceptance by New Zealand host communities of a diverse mix of visitors and tourism activities.

Some people feel that the NZTB, focus on economic measures and overseas marketing is to narrow and does not allow it to deal fully with the wide aspects of tourism development, such as tourism's associated environmental effects, or to reconcile the goals it has set.

Since the formation of the NZTB, its effective marketing activities have largely driven the New Zealand tourism sector, to an extent that may have outstripped the capacity of the sector to manage the environmental consequences of tourism growth. This may be related to the setting of NZTB objectives in isolation from more wide-ranging objectives for the sector as a whole.

The role of the NZTB, now and in the future, cannot be considered in isolation from other government agencies, notably the Tourism Policy Group (TPG) of the Ministry of Commerce.

*Tourism Policy Group:* The TPG has an important role in tourism. It provides among several other functions general policy advice to government. The TPG has also undertaken a significant amount of useful research into tourism related matters including bibliographies of tourism research, research on tourism and landscape, toilet facilities, and funding options. The TPG fulfils and essential role but is hampered by:

- its very small size, especially in relation to the size and significance of the tourism sector;
- its location as a small unit in the large and diverse Ministry of commerce;
- its relative isolation from the tourism industry.

Government requires a strong source of neutral policy advice on the development of the tourism sector, but in recent years has now retained sufficient capacity for such advice. This is a significant strategic weakness for a sector as important to New Zealand as tourism.

*The Department of Conservation*: There has been ongoing debate about DOC's role and directions in tourism management, and calls from some for DOC to have a reduced role or no direct role in visitor management. However, DOC has a unique responsibility as the Crown agency charged with administration and management of the conservation estate, which requires a the capacity to make decisions, determine strategy, establish controls and allocate resources for visitor services on the estate. At present DOC is distinctive among government agencies in its purposeful integration of conservation objectives with visitor use, through its Visitor Services Strategy and the regionally specific provisions in CMS and other management plans. Passing responsibilities for tourism and visitor management to a separate agency would only further complicate the assessment and management of environmental effects. It should be noted that any major changes to the system for tourism management on the conservation estate would require revision of the Conservation Act

## There has been debate over the provisions of the Conservation Act

Which requires DOC to "foster" recreation and "allow" tourism, to the extent that this is not inconsistent with conservation. This distinction between recreation and tourism (which in DOC's definition is tied to commercial activities) caries implications of relative value, and has been the cause of some dissatisfaction in parts of the industry. In practice, DOC's strategic approach and on the ground management are less focused on whether a visitor to the conservation estate has his or her experience facilitated by a third party in a commercial transaction, than on the effects, activities and quality of experience of their visit.

DOC's concessions regime provides a framework for the activities of commercial operators on the conservation estate and for the department's oversight of these activities. Concerns about the concessions regime have been expressed by various interested parties. Many tourism industry and business interest complain of inconsistencies in policy, charges are often seen are unrelated to the value of conservation resources being sought. On the other hand, some conservation interest argue that :

1. concession fees under value conservation resources;
2. application are not sufficiently well scrutinized;
3. consultation is in adequate;
4. monitoring is inadequate;
5. DOC is not able refuse applications which do not adequately protect conservation values.

Most concessionaries consulted in this investigation demonstrated concern for the natural sites and values on which their business depends, and an understandable interests in their maintenance. Many are calling for more rather than less stringent control by DOC, especially in setting total allowable use limits.

Under the conservation amendment act 1996 the concessions regime is an effects–based regime similar to that for assessing resource consent application under the RMA; the processes for application and assessing environmental effects are also similar. For concession applications, environmental effects are assessed on the basis of conservation values, rather than sustainable management of resources. However, a significant difference is that for concession applications, the assessment of environmental effects is made on the basis of effects on conservation values, not in terms of sustainable management of resources. As under the RMA, it is very difficult to assess cumulative effects on a case by case basis. Monitoring of long-term ecological effects, and determining carrying capacities or acceptable thresholds of use, will be very important.

On balance, the need for DOC to retain a visitor services role as part of its statutory responsibilities also requires its oversight of the concessions process. The concessions regime set up by the Conservation Amendment Act 1996 is still new and being refined. Principles for further improvement of the system include consistency between conservancies, and better communication between concession holders and DOC.

On the conservation estate, DOC has the primary responsibility for managing the environmental effects associated with tourism.

It is appropriate that the Department of Conservation should retain responsibility for visitor services, including concessions management, as part of its management responsibilities.

**Local Government**

While all local authorities contacted during this investigation have welcomed tourism for its economic potential, their performance in the management and monitoring of tourism effects has been variable. This is obviously influenced by the resources available to them, which vary greatly even on a per capita basis. Variability in performance is also related to the conceptual and practical difficulties encountered by local authorities in addressing tourism as a sector, under the effects-based approach of the RMA. Territorial local authorities all have district plan provisions that significantly affect tourism planning, even though most do not specifically cover tourism as an activity.

There is widespread concern about TLAs' ability to balance their different roles of tourism promotion, policy regulation and provisions of services and infrastructure. These roles are undoubtedly conflicting at times, but the real and potential conflicts of interest involved are not essentially different from those arising in a number of other council management roles. In tourism management, the separation of tourism marketing into semi-autonomous regional tourism organizations (RTOs) helps to reduce conflicts of interest, especially where there is scrupulous transparency in the structures and operation of RTO boards and other council decision-making committees.

The role and scope of RTOs vary considerably and continue to evolve. The roles and structures adopted by the Rotorua RTO are one positive example of an expansion of RTO activity beyond the primary focus on marketing and production to wider strategic considerations and issues of regional tourism development. RTOs also have a valuable role in setting standards for tourism in the region through local codes of practice and product branding schemes, some of which may have a particular environmental emphasis.

Regional Tourism Organisations have a crucial role in tourism management, which should include a strategic approach to tourism development at local and regional levels, as well as marketing. Such an approach should be linked to any national strategies.

Regional councils have little direct involvement in tourism issues, except when management of major biophysical resources of the region is involved (e.g. the management of the Rotorua Lakes District and the Bay of Plenty geothermal resource, or visitor activities in the Hauraki Gulf). Regional policy statements and plans can have an important impact on the physical and natural environment on which tourism depends, through matters such as soil and water conservations, pest control, pollution and waste management, and coastal activities. This may, at times, involve regional council liaison with RTOs on tourism planning issues.

Outside the conservation estate, local authorities have the primary responsibility for managing the environmental effects associated with tourism. Their performance in this role varies widely.

**The Tourism Industry**

The tourism industry (i.e., the private sector tourism operators) is a central player in the management of the environmental effects associated with tourism because of the direct effect of management decisions by businesses on the environment.

The tourism industry is marked by extraordinary diversity, with a large proportion of small operators, across a wide spectrum of activities and services. To those enterprises which are principally focused on tourism – notably in accommodation and food, transport, and activities and attractions – can be added an even more diverse range of businesses which provide significant products and services to tourists as part of their work with the general public, such as petrol stations, supermarkets, or entertainment providers.

Such diversity has important implications for the effective management of the environmental effects associated with tourism. It is unrealistic to expect a single consistent viewpoint or policy position from the sector. Some issues will only have relevance for particular groups. Questions of coordination and consultation within the industry will require careful attention.

There is potential for constructive industry input into local authority planning processes at an early stage, as an alternative to participation in, and possible confrontation over, individual resource consent applications. However, the many smaller businesses (over 80% of the industry) do not generally have the capacity of larger operations to deal with wider environmental management and planning matters.

In some sections of the industry, there are few barriers to entry and often relatively minimal establishment costs, leading to very competitive and price-sensitive behaviour and consequently a high turnover of businesses and operators. This has implications for the management of environmental effects through increased difficulties in developing an awareness of environmental aspects and of any industry standards and regulations.

This diversity is accentuated by the highly competitive, market-driven and marginally profitable nature of many parts of the industry. Returns on equity are strongest for the accommodation and food and transport sectors. In 1996, 21% of tourism enterprises made a loss, and a further 74.9% managed returns of less than 4%. Only 1.2% of businesses achieved a return of more than 12% in that year (NZTB unpub). Acute and diverse pressures on profitability in almost all parts of the industry suggest that, despite the desire for a quality product driven industry, much of the industry depends for its survival on high turnover at low prices. Such vulnerability is not confined to the smaller businesses. For example, Shotover Jet posted a $16 million loss in 1996, and Tourism Holdings' profit for that year ($6.9 million after tax) was just over half the previous year (*National Business Review*, 26/9/97).

This general economic vulnerability has implications for the management of tourisms' effects on the environment. Some operators have recognized potential adverse environmental effects of their operations and made positive initiatives to manage these effects. A good example is the work of the Environmental Hotels of Auckland (EHOA) group in such areas as energy and water use efficiency. But making the extra effort to accommodate environmental dimensions could seen an expensive luxury to some operators, and there are perceptions that such costs can reduce competitiveness. Some in the industry may be reluctant to support environmentally sustainable practices and standards for these kinds of reasons. This pattern is an indication in itself of the need for a more sustainable and strategic approach. It is in the long-term interests of the industry and certainly the country that longer-term environmental, social and economic viability not be sacrificed for short-term profitability.

The vulnerability of the industry can also be a constrain on tourism operators' openness with information. Information such as statistics about visitors patterns and behaviours, or details about desirable natural destinations, may give a significant competitive advantage. These factors need to be taken into account when developing more purposeful data gathering monitoring and research programmes.

**Industry Growth and Trends**

The NZTB was heavily criticized in the early 1990s when it publicized a target of three million international tourists to New Zealand by the year 2000. This target was subsequently revised to focus more clearly on the contribution of tourism to the New Zealand economy, to achieve targets of $9 billion in foreign exchange earnings and 180,000 full-time equivalent jobs by the year 2000. Although visitor expenditure per trip is growing faster than tourist numbers themselves, these targets still represent substantially increased numbers of tourists coming to New Zealand in the next few years, probably in excess of 2.5 million overseas arrivals yearly (compared with 1.52 million arrivals in 1995).

Most planning relating to tourism assumes continued growth in tourist numbers. While growth has been rapid in the past decade, the past year has seen slowing growth in overseas visitor numbers. This has been a concern for many in the industry. Factors identified as contributing to this trend include a strong New Zealand dollar, faltering emerging economies, and the emergence of other countries (e.g. South Africa) as fashionable destinations. Changing visitor behaviour, particularly a movement towards shorter holidays, is also affecting the industry.

This slowing of growth emphasizes the industry's dependence on external factors. Some reports attribute the decline to market factors, but trends affecting the tourism sector may be a consequence of remote events far beyond the control of New Zealand decision-makers, such as fluctuations in Asian or European currencies influencing those people's travel patterns. Some in the industry argue that lower profitability is the result of over-supply of services and accommodation. This has been seen, for example, in Queenstown, where new accommodation developments have resulted in lower occupancy rates and yields.

Whatever the reasons for the recent downturn, there is general agreement that the tourism sector is cyclical and subject to fluctuations and external influences. Nevertheless it must be recognized that the marketing initiatives of the industry itself have economics influence. The scale and capacity of the larger, better-established operators, and the expertise and management systems at their disposal, mean that their influence on the overall direction of the tourism sector, and on development in particular regions or areas, can be significant. The extent of this influence is important for the management of environmental effects associated with tourism, and for the encouragement and strengthening of environmental awareness in the sector.

Government agencies have very little ability to influence the direction of the tourism industry and thus its environmental effects.

## Marketing Considerations

Some discrepancies between the marketing of New Zealand tourism product and the ability of the New Zealand system to manage the resulting tourism activities have been found. Examples include:

- the Abel Tasman National Park, intensively promoted despite being one of the most congested of New Zealand's great Walks':
- promotion of alpine adventure tourism activities such as hel-skiing and snow landings, as well as traditional scenic flights, although the adverse effects of these activities on other alpine visitors are still controversial, and are perceived as unacceptable in some areas;
- images of wildeness fisheries used to attract tourists to very fragile areas, although the means of controlling effects on those fisheries and the experiences of other users are inadequate.
- Situations where marketing and industry priorities are not sufficiently integrated with environmental requirements can result either from overall growth in tourism numbers intensifying pressure on popular places, or from marketing specific to a particular place. Where the latter occurs, visitors are attracted to places where their adverse effects on the environment cannot be managed adequately, or where their experiences, and the experiences of other users, are diminished.

Management agencies may find themselves with little control over the composition, scale and intensity of the visitor influx, or the expectations, behaviour, expenditure or effects on the environment of those visitors.

A sustainable tourism sector will require closer coordination of tourism marketing (especially internationally) with the requirements of environmental management. DOC's unique responsibility for managing the effects of visitors on the conservation estate suggests that it should have a more direct role in the development of tourism marketing strategies.

The management of environmental effects in the tourism sector is more difficult because New Zealand's strategic approach to tourism has been primarily focused on maximizing the benefits from increased international visitor numbers.

**Infrastructure**

Issues related to the provision of infrastructure to cater for tourists' requirements were a common concern throughout the investigation. Some of the most significant environmental effects of tourism are associated with the provision or lack of infrastructure. Some of the infrastructure issues associated with tourism are very specific (eg. The lack of public toilets on certain stretches of state highway, and the disposal of wastes from campervans). Other issues are much more general and not necessarily tourism-specific (eg. Policy and priority for new roads, disposal and recycling of hotel wastes, seasonal demand in holiday destinations for sewage treatment and water supply).

It is frequently different to distinguish tourism infrastructure needs from those of the general public, although the submissions from some local government agencies (especially in more remote areas) noted heavy tourism road use that was different from that of the general population. Most responsibility for infrastructure provision and management now lies with local authorities. Some infrastructure needs have been identified that are specific to the tourism sector, often located only in certain parts of a district (eg certain roads or the provision of water and sewerage on the Hauraki Gulf islands).

In other areas, overall increases in usage result in a demand for improved infrastructure, but many residents, particularly those unhappy about growth in their neighbourhoods, perceive this demand as being driven only by tourism growth (e.g road usage on the Coromandel Peninsula). This situation is compounded in areas where there is a large seasonal population of temporary New Zealand residents (holiday-home owners and tourism workers). Local authorities also have to accommodate conflicts between constituencies. Building public toilets or upgrading a scenic route may divert resources from upgrading rural roads or suburban car parking facilities.

As noted, tourism can sometimes have a positive effect in improving infrastructure for residents. However, such improvement can have a 'ratchet' effect, attracting still more tourists or residents and thereby creating adverse environmental effects.

The discussion of specific infrastructure issues related to human waste disposal indicates some persistent systems failures which result in a number of specific problems. Provision of public toilet facilities should be regarded as a public health and amenity measure and as essential infrastrucutre, like rest areas and road signs. Joint ventures between local authorities and Transit New Zealand are a practical approach. It may also be appropriate for industry operators or groups of operators to be involved. Regarding campervan wastes, adequate legal, financial and technical incentives to dispose of wastes appropriately are an obvious priority, as is education of campervan users.

Issues related to the provision of roads featured strongly in written submissions to the investigation. The Land Transport Pricing Study, a Ministry of Transport initiative to reform the management and funding of New Zealand's road network, is due for government decision at the end of 1997. Government has made a commitment that roads will not be privatised. New or upgraded roads primarily for tourism use may have adverse effects, as was claimed to be the case in the Coromandel Peninsula. However, this need not be the case; for example the upgrading of the significant tourist route through the Waipoua forest in Northland was carried out with careful attention to environmental values.

Tourism traffic will continue to be an issue as the greenhouse gas emissions debate continues. The tourism industry is hugely reliant on fossil fuels, both for bringing tourists to New Zealand and for their movement around the country. Longer-term implications for the environment of investment in road infrastructure, and dependence on carbon fuel-driven transport will need to be considered, acknowledging that the greatest share of transport fuel is used by New Zealanders for personal transport purposes.

On the question of costs for tourism infrastructure, some local authorities have commitments additional to those required by the resident population. Instances where local authorities have most trouble providing infrastructure for visitors are where:

- there is a large tourism sector in a district with a small resident population (eg Queenstown-Lakes, Far North, Kaikoura and Buller Districts).
- There is a large crown estate used for an attracting tourism and a low rating base (eg Buller district);
- Tourism is highly seasonal so infrastructure cannot cope with demand in peak times or is under-utilised for much of the year (e.g., Banks Peninsula, Thames-Coromandel); and
- There is significant tourist traffic passing through a sparsely populated district and requiring basic infrastructure like water, toilet and waste facilities (e.g., Waitomo Caves, Clutha and Mackenzie Districts).

**Access and Visitor Management Issues**

Specific issues in visitor management include debate whether it is environmentally more desirable to concentrate or disperse visitors. There are some areas that do require intensive management input, often the most popular 'icons' of New Zealand's natural areas. It would be unacceptable (and disastrous for the industry) for these areas to become regarded as 'sacrifice areas' where visitors are concentrated beyond the capacity of the area, and it may be necessary to divert people away from such places to less popular places, as is done in many national parks in the USA. This approach may not always solve problems in the long term. For example, the Kepler Track in Fiordland was developed, with industry assistance, largely to relieve the pressure on the Milford and Routeburn Tracks. It has absorbed large increases in use and now has overuse problems of its own.

Controlling access to prevent detrimental environmental effects is acknowledged as a significant issue for tourism. However, access issues are controversial (Sowman 1994), and closely related to funding issues. Some people feel that increased tourism on the conservation estate is eroding New Zealanders' statutory rights of free access to all public conservation land, including marginal strips. Such views are mainly expressed by conservation and recreation groups and concern access for tramping, mountaineering, fishing and hunting. The legitimate desire of New Zealanders for guaranteed access may require closer control over access, for example by quota or booking systems.

There was widespread acceptance expressed during the investigation that limits would need to be placed on access and use in some natural areas. Operators generally concurred, but with the caveat that limits be imposed fairly, and that they be enforced. One suggestion for setting access limits is to use a public process resulting in a management plan so there is public consensus on those limits.

**Funding**

An assessment of government funding for the management of the environmental effects of tourism is complicated due to the:

- difficulties in identifying the component targeted for management of tourism-related effects within overall environmental and conservation allocations;
- difficulties in identifying the component targeted for management of environmental effects within overall tourism allocations;
- difficulties in identifying the tourism component in allocations made in related sectors like transport, public health and safety, border control and general business development; and
- significant spending at regional and local levels on both promotion and management.

Private sector investment in tourism effects management, within the context of investment in activities, facilities, promotion and development is another dimension altogether, and equally difficult to quantify with any precision.

The multi-faceted nature of the tourism sector and its various effects result in considerable uncertainty over exactly what direct and indirect government spending is relevant, and what trends may be evolving. The lack of precise data reflects and is closely intertwined with the difficulties of distinguishing tourism activities and their effects on the environment from more general public uses and effects. Such uncertainities can only be resolved through purposeful research and monitoring to track spending, target the tourism component in more general allocations, identify relationships between expenditure, demands and returns, and more clearly determine the full range of contributions that are being made to the tourism sector.

Given this present lack of clarity about details, there are three broad areas where the adequacy of current funding levels are of greatest concern in terms of their implications for the management of environmental effects associated with the tourism sector. They are:

- management of both physical and social effects associated with tourism on the conservation estate:
- provision of infrastructure for tourism, especially in smaller communities; and
- gathering of data for tourism management, especially regarding tourists' activities, expectations and actual levels of effects.

The investigation found common and consistent perceptions among communities of imbalances between funding for tourism marketing relative to funding for the management of environmental effects associated with tourism. Also widely evident were specific concerns and perceptions of inadequate overall funding for DOC, the adequacy of DOC's allocations for management of the effects of visitors on the conservation estate, and the implications of the funding of DOC's visitors services responsibilities for its other conservation functions.

Since DOC's inception in 1987, its funding for various visitor-related activities has declined in real terms, while the numbers of international visitors to the conservation estate has at least doubled and domestic use also increased significantly. There was also concern expressed at the level of funding for protection of natural places and values outside the conservation estate, and the resources available for compliance monitoring for tourism developments.

Many of the people consulted felt there is a need for additional money for managing the environmental effects associated with tourism, especially in relation to natural areas and infrastructure. No attempt has been made in this investigation to quantify the funding requirements for effective management of tourism's environmental effects, to identify specific areas where funding imbalances and other difficulties could be resolved, or to assess the extent of such possible resolutions.

Such an exercise was outside the terms of reference and would need more intensive and comprehensive study than has been possible in this investigation. However, some work was done in the early 1990s, on options for funding visitor services and tourism. Reports include those by Ernest and Young (1994), Deloittee Tuche and Tohmatsu (1994) and a paper on New Zealand Conservation Estate and International Visitors (DOC and NZRB 1993). These studies considered, from the perspective of that time, a range of mechanisms for allocating funding to tourism, visitor use of natural areas, and the management of effects on the environment. Some of the options are:

*User Charges.* These already apply to some extent on the conservation estate in the charges made for facilities and services. Fees for huts and carmpsites are not a charge for access per se. which would conflict with governments' consident policy and New Zealanders' strongly defended expectations of free public access to the public estate.

Re-prioritising within the present Vote: Tourism, specifically from marketing to other management activities.

Re-prioritising from other government revenue streams,

especially from the GST revenue arising from the tourism sector. The GST from international tourists' spending is estimated to yield between $395 and $520 million annually, depending on estimates of tourist expenditure (NZTB unpub).

General charges or levies. These can take a number of forms, including the 'green tax' levy on overseas visitors.

Options for more effective funding delivery will need to evolve as part of the development of a wider strategic approach to tourism and management of its effects on the environment.

In some areas funding issues need attention. The most significant are: the management of tourism effects on the conservation estate; provision of infrastructure at the local level; and the gathering of data for tourism management. Research and analysis are needed to determine accurately the current levels of investment by government agencies in the tourism sector, and appropriate means of targeting resources to ensure effective management of the environmental effects associated with tourism.

**Community Attitudes to Tourism**

It is widely acknowledged that host community acceptance of tourists and tourism is an essential part of sustainable tourism, but influences of visitors, and the developments that accompany them, can cause considerable tension. This investigation has established that peoples' concerns about the social effects of tourism, and their perceptions of the impacts of tourism on their communities and lifestyles, may in many cases be as significant as the actual physical effects.

Many communities welcome tourism, seeking its economic and other benefits. Councils and community groups actively encourage the development of tourism opportunities, viewing tourism as a non-consumptive utilization of their local natural resources. Other communities feel overrun and overwhelmed by tourists and tourism. This investigation has found strong strands of distrust and suspicion of tourism and its practitioners running through a wide range of community groups, recreation and environmental NGOs, iwi and hapu, planners and land managers, and within the tourism industry itself.

The difficulties many groups and individuals encounter taking part in statutory planning and decision-making processes add to their dissatisfaction. Such attitudes are often based in the bitterness of loss or irretrievable degradation of a once-loved natural place, the resentment of exclusion from a favourite place by crowds of visitors, or feelings of helplessness in the face of change. These attitudes could be potential obstacles to the development of a truly sustainable tourism sector in New Zealand. Community support, both at the national and local levels, is vital to the sector. The NZTB's goal of acceptance by host communities of a diverse mix of visitors and tourism activities, implicitly recognizes host community resistance to tourism as a serious potential threat to the country's tourism industry. An official commented during the investigation that:

> There is a lack of public participation in the tourism industry at present and tourism is essentially an introduction of visitors to the community. If that community is not involved at the beginning, then tourist developers should not be surprised if the community resists their development proposals (Ministry for the Environment official).

Host communities generally want the benefits of tourism but also want its negative effects minimized. Many communities, iwi and hapu, and interest groups are concerned about their inability to take part in decision-making on tourism issues, and seek better involvement in planning and managing the effects of tourism in their area.

**Issues of Concern to Maori**

Maori have an interesting many of the resources used by the tourism industry, both directly and indirectly. The most obvious resource is land, but geothermal resources, marine mammals, other wildlife, takes, caves and rivers are all fundamentally important to tangata whenua. Many of these resources are under claim to the Waitangi tribunal; both in the process of negotiating claims settlements. And through other legal cases, Maori are asserting their interest in these resources and their potential for tourism. Tribunal hearings commenced in September 1997 for the WAI 262 claim for indigenous flora and fauna and matters of intellectual and cultural property. This claim could have significant implications for the conservation and management of indigenous natural resources and cultural heritage and their uses, with consequent implications for tourism management.

These issues need to be considered within the wider contexts of:

- the Treaty claims settlement processes and other political processes;
- the development by Maori of practical mechanisms for the expression of kaitiakitanga systems; and
- the statutory requirements for formal recognition of the principles of the Treaty in management of natural resources.

There are strong statutory requirements in environmental management law for the principles of the treaty and Maori interests to be incorporated in decision-making and management of natural resources and places. These statutory requirements place a particular onus on the tourism sector, which relies heavily on both the natural environment and Maori culture. However, there is widespread feeling that Maori are still marginalized in the tourism sector, and their involvement in policy and decision-making processes is often less than satisfactory.

Increasingly, Maori are looking to develop their own tourism opportunities. This is seen as a constructive way to resolve the current pattern of disparities in the tourism industry, where Maori are frequently confined to service and interpretation roles, jobs which are largely unskilled, poorly paid, part-time and seasonal. The use of cultural images, or images of natural taonga that may be associated with a particular tupuna, iwi or hapu, is also a question of grave concern to Maori. By maintaining control as managers of tourism operations. Maori can also exercise control of the environmental and cultural aspects of their tourism product.

There are various ways in which Maori participation in the tourism sector can be more effective both for Maori and for tourism. Concern for the protection of natural resources by interest groups can run counter to tangata whenua opportunities to develop their lands. Improving understanding of the roles, expectations and values of the respective parties through an ongoing process of dialogue is fundamental. Greater awareness and clarity about the systems and how they operate, and about the issues at stake, whether ecological, cultural or traditional, will help reduce confusion and misunderstandings. Maori must have a leading role in developing ways to improve their participation and recognition of their particular interests in tourism's utilisation of natural taonga.

There has been insufficient opportunity for tangata whenua to participate in policy and decision-making for the tourism sector. Improved understanding and communication would help in achieving better environmental outcomes, more satisfactory integration of Maori values and priorities, and fulfillment of the requirements of the legislation regarding the principles of the Treaty of Waitangi, Maori must have the primary role in determining appropriate ways to achieve this.

## Communities and Local Government Systems

The investigation encountered considerable concern from environmental and community groups about what they perceive as a general culture of permissiveness to development, including tourism developments, without adequate regard to sustainable management.

It is clear from the district profiles that communities, or groups within communities, often believe that the social and cultural effects of proposed tourism developments will be significant and adverse. Naturally they look to local authorities to resolve these issues. One of the greatest difficulties for councils appears to be accommodating these kinds of perceptions within their various statutory processes, while at the same time attracting tourism investment. When a council is unable to do this satisfactorily, this affects community attitudes to development generally and engenders cyncism about local government, skepticism about the provisions and capacities of the legislation (in particular the RMA) and disillusionment about community participation in resource management processes. Councils' systems and structures, and the political factors involves in decision-making, are commonly perceived as hostile to community interests and good environmental management. The difficulty that some groups have mentioned dealing with DOC on tourism-related matters is a variation on this theme.

There are also concerns from various sections of the tourism industry about local authorities' ability to handle tourism issues effectively and to recognize the characteristics and needs of the industry. These concerns are not dissimilar to those expressed by operators in other resources management sectors.

One way of constructively addressing community objectives and concerns is through community participation in tourism planning. However, as the district profiles show, there is great variability in the success of consultation under the RMA. Other statutory processes are not open to public input (e.g. development of criteria by CAA for airspace exclusions. Factors cited as reasons why communities are constrained from effective participation in the processes that are open to them include lack of resources, the complexity of the process, and inability to access the information and advice needed (PCE 1996).

Although communities are varied and have diverse and sometimes conflicting goals and objectives, they can be involved in tourism planning and are a useful source of knowledge. The challenge for decision-makers involved in managing the effects of tourism and related development is to ensure open dialogue between communities, the tourism industry and themselves, and to be committed to implementing the outcome.

## A Strategic Approach

Many agencies and groups within the tourism sector have developed strategic approaches to tourism and its effects on the environment, whether for local communities or for particular areas of activity. Some of these initiatives have been successful, and are outlined here.

Some local authorities have developed are developing strategic plans and non-statutory tourism management plans, such as:

Queenstown-lakes District Strategic Plan;

Waitomo District Strategic Plan;

Local initiatives using community planning processes such as charettes; and

Vision Hauranki.

Such approaches are usually a useful way of increasing understanding and acceptance of resources management issues and liaising between different interested agencies, but to be fully effective they need to be incorporated into statutory planning documents. Vision hauraki is significant for coordinating the efforts of a large number of agencies.

The main responsibility for coordinating and encouraging strategic development and raised standards across the tourism industry lies with the New Zealand Tourism Industry Association (NZTIA) and its constituent groups. The NZTIA has recently been at the forefront of some significant initiatives for sustainable tourism management, including:

development of codes of practice and industry standards;

a lo—year National Tourism Strategic Plan for the industry;

substantial work towards a research strategy for the tourism sector;

involvement with a Ministry for the Environment project on sustainable management, in association with the forestry, agribusiness and chemicals industries;

extending the Environmental Hotels of Ackland (EHOA) project nationally; and

establishing or revitalizing sector groups and sub-groups within the industry.

DOC's Visitor Service Strategy provides another framework for managing tourists and other visitors to the conservation estate. The strategy is the result of a lengthy process of public and interest group consultation. DOC is now moving into implementation of the strategy in conjunction with the provisions for visitor services set out in each regional conservancy's statutory Conservation Management Strategy. Detailed studies of priority sites and pressure points will be mapped to form a comprehensive basis for visitor management and practical business planning.

The NXTB has worked on strategic processes for tourism on StewartIsland and in Northland, and during the course of this investigation released its draft Southern Lakes Tourism Strategy.

The TPG has identified the following projects in its 1997/98 Purchase Agreement:

- a strategy relating to the sustainable management of tourism growth in natural areas (including the conservation estate);
- a series of tourism sector forums on issues such as research needs, the investment environment, and human resource development;
- tourism infrastructure responsibilities of central, regional and local government; and
- tourism research generally.

Despite these initiatives, a continual concern emerging through this investigation is the lack of a generally agreed strategic direction for the sector as a whole. Many stakeholders hold the perception that New Zealand tourism has little clear direction. Such perceptions are a factor in much of the criticism and resistance to tourism in key communities and community groups discussed above.

There is an almost unanimous desire for tourism in New Zealand to be 'sustainable'. This is recognized at a number of levels, such as the reference in the Coalition Government agreement to 'quality, sustainable tourism,' and the policies and published statements of key agencies. There is a general understanding throughout the sector and amongst the public that New Zealand will be marketed as a quality tourism destination using our 'natural clean-green' image. However, although there is now a large international literature on the subject of sustainable tourism, so far there have been few contributions to such a debate in New Zealand outside of academic circles (Human 1997); Page and Thorn 1997; Kearsley 1997), except for a 1992 discussion paper from the Ministry of Tourism.

It is widely acknowledged that New Zealand tourism relies on the natural environment, and that this resource is vulnerable to exploitation. Some models, most notably eco-tourism provide a framework for more environmentally sensitive tourism. Recent assessments of the less positive status of much of New Zealand's environment in particular the first comprehensive report ion the state of New Zealand's environment (Ministry for the Environment 1997) are seen as potential threats to this image and our capacity to attract international travelers.

There is widespread agreement that tourism in New Zealand should be managed sustainable and marketed on the basis that New Zealand is a high-quality, product-led tourist destination. Tourism's reliance on the quality of both the natural environment and visitors' experiences is also generally recognized. However, there are systemic problems which hinder the achievement of this goal.

There has as yet been insufficient discussion on what is meant by 'sustainable tourism' in New Zealand, and what it would involve for the tourism sector. This chapter has explored the principal characteristics of the sector and the industry, the implications of these for effective management of tourism's effects on the environment, and the various often uneasy relationships of tourism with communities, with Maori, and with particular interest groups.

# STRATEGIC MANAGEMENT FOR SUSTAINABLE DEVELOPMENT

Sustainable Development Strategy provides an excellent opportunity to further institutionalise sustainable development in Environment Canada's decision-making processes, while supporting and encouraging others to do the same. While making a renewed commitment to some of the same fundamental directions outlined in the first Strategy, this second SDS focuses on commitments that have the potential to be further reaching in their impact.

Environment Canada's updated Strategy more clearly articulates goals, objectives and targets that we believe will enable the Department and Canadians to better judge where progress is being made. This SDS has been shaped by a number of factors. It reflects the results of an internal management review that provided lessons learned from the first Sustainable Development Strategy, an issue scan undertaken to identify specific challenges and opportunities for the Department, and an extensive consultation process. It also builds on the Department's commitment to expanding the capacity for innovation in Canada. Environment Canada believes that long-term effective management of environmental issues requires innovation in three areas; increasing and sharing the spectrum of knowledge upon which decisions are based; providing new incentives and tools to more fully integrate environmental and economic decision making; and forming new partnerships to both define and help deliver our mandate.

The result is a Sustainable Development Strategy that is focused on four themes:

- Knowledge for Decision Making;
- Incentives;
- Partnerships and Sustainable Communities; and
- Managing for Sustainable Development.

These areas of focus enable the Department to both build on its strengths and address some areas of weakness. The SDS reinforces Environment Canada's key role as a knowledge-based department that seeks to build upon our understanding of environmental problems, and assists in devising solutions that take into account environmental, economic and social considerations. At the same time, the Strategy will encourage the Department to more fully examine the range of tools and incentives that it uses to manage environmental problems and to build on and strengthen existing partnerships with communities and other sectors of Canadian society. Finally, it will encourage Environment Canada to renew its efforts to be a model in its operations and in managing for sustainable development. The Strategy does not attempt to reflect everything that Environment Canada does or could do, to promote sustainable development. It is a strategic document that lays out an agenda for innovation necessary to achieve long-term goals. It is intended to provide guidance to the Department, and to highlight for Canadians key directions and priority commitments that Environment Canada will pursue over the next three years to make progress on sustainable development.

## Approach to Sustainable Development

Our science, our community engagement and our work on issues such as climate change, endangered species, contaminated sites, toxics and ecosystems are primarily focused on understanding, preventing and solving environmental problems. As we better understand the interconnectedness of environmental issues and the linkages among different social, environmental and economic factors that affect our well-being, we recognise that longer term success will depend on an ability to find creative solutions that contribute not only to a healthy environment, but to a prosperous economy and a vibrant and just society at the same time. Allowing these different factors to be considered in an integrated way in decision making demands some systemic changes and innovative approaches.

By improving EC's capacity to integrate social and economic concerns into environmental decision making, we will be more successful in the long run in protecting and conserving the environment. This understanding is reflected in Environment Canada's mission statement, which *is to make sustainable development a reality in Canada by helping Canadians live and prosper in an environment that needs to be respected, protected and conserved.* While focused on environmental goals, these goals are pursued in the context of sustainable development.

Such an integrated approach to policy and programming decisions is increasingly evident in Environment Canada's work. Three current examples include:

*Climate Change*: Sustainable development was reflected in the process that Environment Canada, other federal departments and provinces engaged in to develop a National Implementation Strategy for Climate Change. Through a series of issue tables, governments, public interest groups and the private sector worked in partnership to examine the costs and benefits of a wide range of greenhouse gas reduction scenarios. Based on the work of these issue tables, decisions were made about how to most effectively implement the Kyoto Protocol. The National Implementation Strategy on Climate Change and the First National Business Plan were released in October 2000.

*Canadian Environmental Protection Act (1999)*: CEPA reflects a commitment to sustainable development in several ways. Its goal is to protect not just the environment but also the health of Canadians from toxic substances and other pollutants. By focusing on pollution prevention, the *Act* is moving away from dictating specific solutions. Rather, it encourages companies to systematically examine their production processes to identify the best method for them to prevent pollution. This allows Environment Canada to stipulate environmental results but also allows companies the flexibility to define ways and means. The *Act* also provides for substantial public involvement.

*Canada's Strategy for Protecting Species at Risk*: Canada's strategy for protecting species at risk adopts a long-term sustainable approach that considers social and economic issues alongside environmental issues. It focuses on (1) building partnerships with provinces and territories through the Accord for the Protection of Species at Risk, (2) promoting stewardship and incentive programmes to assist private landowners, citizens, Aboriginal peoples and organisations that are helping to protect species and habitats, and (3) regulating where necessary through legislation.

It is clear, however, that if Canada's environmental heritage is to be sustained for the benefit of present and future generations, support for sustainable development must be built across government and throughout Canada. Decision makers at all levels and in all sectors of society need to consistently integrate environmental concerns along with economic and social concerns in their decisions. Environment Canada has an important advocacy role to play in this regard.

Making the right decisions for the longer term requires innovation in thought and implementing these decisions requires innovation in practices and techniques. Environment Canada's Sustainable Development Strategy advances an agenda for innovation by focusing on priority areas and setting longer term goals for the Department. The great potential offered by innovative approaches will only be realised by working with others.

In this context, Environment Canada sees its two primary ongoing roles as:

Showing leadership by example by ensuring departmental operations, management practices, policies and programmes support sustainable development; and

Building capacity and commitment to sustainable development with partners in the public and private sectors, and with Canadians, by providing information, tools and other support.

The SDS provides Environment Canada with an opportunity to regularly review progress toward sustainable development and to consider, in a strategic way, how best to move forward over the short term (the three-year period of the Strategy) while supporting innovation in the longer-term. The Strategy is both an important guidance document for the Department, while also highlighting for Canadians some of those things that we commit to doing differently as a department to promote sustainable development. While much of EC's ongoing work already makes an important contribution to sustainable development, the purpose of the Strategy is to highlight a selected number of new directions and new opportunities that the department intends to pursue.

The commitments for the period 2001-2003 build on the work undertaken through our first SDS of 1997. They reinforce our department's commitment to providing strong leadership by moving toward integrated decision-making in our own policies and programmes and managing our operations in an environmentally responsible manner, and to helping guide others describes an agenda for innovation that we believe will help steer the transition to sustainable development.

Environment Canada believes in the need to adopt government-wide approaches to meet the sustainable development challenge. By its very nature, sustainable development implies the importance of working across departmental boundaries. Much of EC's effort in recent years has focused on developing this horizontal approach – and a commitment to moving forward with a government-wide sustainable development agenda–as outlined in Support for Government-wide Sustainable Development Initiatives of this Strategy.

At the same time, Environment Canada has its own priorities and opportunities for moving the sustainable development agenda forward, given its unique departmental responsibilities and activities. These priorities can be addressed alongside government-wide priorities in a coherent, mutually reinforcing manner by focusing the updated SDS on the following four themes:

- Knowledge for Decision Making:
- Incentives;
- Partnerships and Sustainable Communities; and
- Managing for Sustainable Development.

These four areas are important in moving toward sustainable

development, and are fundamental for delivering on an agenda for innovation. They are areas where the Department has some strengths and opportunities that it can build on at this time. Of course these areas represent only a small number of a much larger set of issues that need to be addressed at a variety of levels (local, national, international) in order to move forward on sustainable development. By being selective, however, we hope to ensure success in these areas, and thus build a strong foundation before moving on to new challenges.

We have intentionally used the Sustainable Development Strategy as a means to try new approaches, and to focus our efforts on those areas where we believe we can make the greatest difference in promoting sustainable development. For each of these four theme areas, a small number of goals, objectives and targets have been identified. The eight goals reflect the longer-term outcomes we are working toward beyond the three year life of this Strategy. The objectives under each goal state more specifically what we would like to achieve in the three year period of this Strategy. And finally, the targets represent even more specific commitments for the short term, to serve as progress markers in meeting our objectives.

## Knowledge For Decision Making

One of the key ingredients in being able to make wise decisions about the environment or any other issue is the knowledge that we have and can use, in decision making-having the right information, at the right place, at the right time. Canada's current sustainable development information and knowledge base is inadequate to provide the foundation for informed public debate and knowledge-based decision making. Environment Canada believes there are a number of things we can do to enhance the sustainable development knowledge base within the Department and in the country, and the communication and use of that knowledge.

Science is an essential piece of the knowledge base for sustainable development. It is science that has enabled our understanding of the mutually dependent relationships between human activities and environmental quality. As a science-based department, science is one of EC's strengths, yet there remain opportunities for further consolidation, enhancement and improved access.

In order to ensure that Environment Canada's science and knowledge base is as comprehensive and accessible as possible, a more robust environmental information system is needed. While EC already reports to Canadians in a variety of ways, including through weather and environmental prediction services, the National Pollutant Release Inventory, the National Environmental Indicators Series, and the annual report on the status of migratory birds in Canada, our information and reporting roles could be strengthened. Building a more comprehensive Canadian Information System for the Environment would help to (1) enhance accountability to Canadians through better reporting on progress in addressing environmental concerns; (2) provide information to Canadians and organisations that would enable them to take action to contribute to environmental protection; and (3) provide a basis for sound public policies. A stronger information system would also increase the visibility of environmental issues relative to other national issues.

Environment Canada also needs to improve how it uses knowledge and information in its own decision making processes. For example, while our policies and programming have historically been based on western scientific knowledge alone, we recognise that Aboriginal peoples have practiced sustainable development for thousands of years, and that their traditional economical knowledge should be incorporated into our decision making processes.

The Department is also committed to a more consistent consideration of social and economic impacts in our decision making (such as considering the impacts of our policies on different populations), but needs the tools and training to further this goal. Research to better understand sustainable development and the relationships among environmental, economic and social conditions would help with the challenge of integrated decision making. For example, building a better understanding of the linkages between environmental deterioration and human health is one area where further work is required.

Another priority issue for Environment Canada is improving knowledge and awareness of short-term weather hazards and longer-term changes in environmental conditions. Improving our predictive capacity and the access of Canadians to that information is of primary importance to ensuring that they can take appropriate steps to protect themselves and their businesses from severe weather and environmental hazards.

In order to address these priority concerns about improving knowledge for decision making, EC is committed to working toward the following goal, and over the period of this Strategy, to meeting the objectives and targets described below.

*Targets:*

* Develop an EC Monitoring Strategy by end of 2002.
* Explore with the environmental science community and others, ways of enhancing the effectiveness and efficiency of scientific research through networking and partnership opportunities, and report by end of 2002. An interim report on opportunities for strengthening Canadian environmental sciences through new networking and partnership initiatives will be prepared for the EC Science and Technology Advisory Board by end of 2001.
* Provide new knowledge to support decision making for sustainable development through implementation of EC's Nature, Clean Environment, and Weather and Environmental Prediction research agendas.
* Develop and implement an integrated Business Plan on Science and Technology for Sustainable Development with the five federal natural resource departments.
* Complete the final report of the Canadian Information System for the Environment Task Force (outlining environmental information and knowledge requirements, the status of existing data and knowledge systems, and investments needed to meet these requirements), by end of 2001.
* Ensure that EC's communications and outreach activities reflect a sustainable development approach to the issues, and where appropriate adopt the use of social marketing

tools to encourage more sustainable lifestyles and practices.

* Renew the Green Lane by the end of 2001, to ensure it has up-to-date, easy-to-find, reliable content based on an in-depth understanding of audience needs and reflective of departmental priorities.
* Establish, by end of 2001, a multi-disciplinary Sustainable Development Policy Research Programme that enhances our understanding of sustainable development and informs decision making and public debate.
* Undertake a study on Canadian values and on techniques to influence behaviour change towards sustainable development in communities by end of 2001, and use results to inform EC's community initiatives and communications strategy.
* Develop an EC policy, by end of 2003, on how to incorporate traditional ecological knowledge in departmental decisions.
* Develop and pilot a sustainability assessment tool for EC policies and programmes by end of 2003.
* Co-ordinate policy and strategic approaches for climate change and clean air initiatives in key sectors such as electricity and transportation.
* Improve lead-time for extreme weather forecasts/warnings.
* Put proper mechanisms in place, through work with community partners, to make warning information accessible to individuals in time for them to take action.
* Develop and implement new warning products.
* Make data on weather, climate and water quantity more accessible to industry and other uses.
* Build awareness of special weather forecast products that can assist targeted client groups in adopting sustainable practices (such as advisories on pesticide spraying).
* Introduce the forecast of particulates into regional smog forecasts by end of 2001.

One of the critical challenges of sustainable development is ensuring we get the signals and incentives right to encourage activity that will conserve and protect our environment. Traditionally, this has been done through government regulation and indeed, environmental regulations will continue to be essential. However, there is growing recognition of the need to expand the risk management policy choices and to shift the balance towards economic instruments.

Given the need to encourage significant behavioural change at the individual, corporate and community levels, market-based incentives are increasingly viewed as one of the most efficient means of ensuring appropriate levels of investment in our natural capital.

Natural capital includes environmental assets such as forests, land, mineral and energy resources, as well as ecosystem components such as water, air, the atmospheric carbon cycle, oceans, wildlife habitats and wetlands. Our natural capital makes a substantial contribution to the Canadian economy, and provides necessary life-support functions for citizens. The better known economic uses are for agriculture, mining and forestry. In addition, nature-related recreation such as canoeing, fishing and swimming contribute substantially to the Canadian GDP ($12.1 billion in 1996). Life-support functions range from the health benefits of cleaner air (such as lower incidences of asthma and bronchitis) to the water purification functions of wetlands. Investing in natural capital means restocking forests, conserving soil, maintaining or improving air and water quality, and restoring Canadian wetlands and other wildlife habitat. Where, how and when we invest in natural capital is the result of countless daily decisions by individuals and organisations, as we respond to a variety of signals or incentives put before us.

Key among these signals are market-based incentives; the prices of goods and services and the cost of capital and labour. The market is good at sending the right signals for human and man-made capital. However, it does a poor job of reflecting the true value of natural capital, because there is no market for its services (such as improved air quality or habitats).

While Environment Canada recognises that economic instruments are only one of an important mix of policy instruments, the department believes that the Sustainable Development Strategy provides an important opportunity for focusing attention on advancing our capacity to use these instruments.

Environment Canada will work with the Department of Finance and other appropriate government departments to further explore and encourage the use of incentives. Some specific areas of interest include:

- Evaluating the wide range of subsidies throughout the Canadian economy which may have an unintentional but negative impact on the environment and need to be re-considered;
- Exploring the use of incentives for companies which invest in new technologies or approaches that reduce pollution or conserve natural resources;
- Examining the use of charges for activities that are the source of an environmental problem such as pollution emissions, inputs to production, or final products;
- Reviewing systems of tradeable permits or emission rights (for example, domestic emissions trading for greenhouse gases); and
- Exploring broader use of deposit-refund systems where money is reimbursed to consumers when they return an item such as a battery or waste lubricating oil to a collection point.

Environment Canada will also examine opportunities including the use of incentives, to encourage Canadian industry to become more eco-efficient. Eco-efficient practices are innovative ways to: reduce material requirements, energy intensity and toxic dispersion; find value-added uses for material wastes and produce goods that are durable and reusable, while contributing to productivity gains, reduced costs and lower liabilities.

## Partnerships and Sustainable Communities

As the complexity of environmental and sustainable development issues continues to increase, more partners than ever must be involved in developing solutions and implementing them throughout the economy and society. New approaches are needed that help leverage the greatest possible collective impact from action by business, non-government organisations, universities, Aboriginal people, provinces, municipalities and citizens. Achieving results through innovative partnership arrangements is both a requirement and a critical opportunity in the transition to sustainable development.

We believe that some of the most important opportunities for partnerships are at the community level. Many communities are undergoing unprecedented change. They face complex social, environmental and economic challenges (*e.g.*, downturn in rural communities, loss of traditional industries or way of life, environmental degradation, out-migration, seasonal unemployment, urbanisation) and emerging opportunities (*e.g.*, information and other technologies, value-added industries, tourism, community renewal).

Across the country, citizens and the voluntary sector are becoming more proactive in addressing these issues through community-based initiatives and comprehensive planning. Municipal governments, led through the Federation of Canadian Municipalities, are actively pursuing environment and sustainable development agendas. As communities make the connection among economic, social and environmental pressures, they look for similarly integrated support and responses from government (not centrally developed solutions). They also seek a more meaningful interface with governments through partnership approaches.

A more integrated approach to bringing communities information and expertise and delivering federal programmes and services will empower both communities and the Government to identify and respond to sustainability goals and objectives.

At Environment Canada, we have been working to enhance community sustainability through our programmes and services for some time (*e.g.*, through our regional ecosystems initiatives and our education and communications efforts). We have focused considerable attention on building partnerships at the community level which bring together a broad range of government, private and voluntary sector organisations, and on providing vital knowledge, tools, information and funding to enhance the ability of communities to promote sustainable development. As a department, we draw on our partnerships in and with communities to help carry out our sustainability mission, and to address key issues of concern to Canadians such as clean air, clean water, nature, climate change and weather at the local level.

Despite the many community-level programmes and services offered by EC, it continues to be a challenge to successfully engage Canadians in their communities in efforts to move toward sustainable development. By focusing part of our updated Sustainable Development Strategy on building partnerships with communities, we believe we can improve the effectiveness of our contribution to community sustainability and help empower citizens to take appropriate action. Stronger partnerships – with communities and others – are fundamental to leveraging the greatest possible collective impact from our efforts on sustainable development.

* Put mechanisms/strategies in place (including Internet and more traditional means) to ensure that stakeholders partners and other communities of interest have regular opportunities to put forward their ideas, concerns and perspectives on community sustainable development issues.
* Increase involvement of Aboriginal people in migratory bird management and other conservation initiatives.
* Enhance community access to EC science that is "useable" and that meets community needs, through pilot projects and government-on-line initiatives.
* Assist the Department of Indian and Northern Affairs in 2001 with the implementation of the Environmental Capacity Development Initiative to build First Nation, Innu and Inuit capacity in environmental stewardship and to strengthen partnerships.
* Provide support for environmental education and training to Indigenous youth beginning in 2001.
* Build the capacity of youth to provide policy input and support environmental action by providing support to youth groups to develop a governance framework, create a fundraising strategy and develop a youth network across the country.

* Develop, with partners, a national strategy on environmental education and an action plan for its implementation, and submit these to the UN Commission on Sustainable Development by spring 2002.
* Strengthen the Ecosystems Initiatives to be more effective delivery mechanisms for sustainable communities, through the integration of social, economic and environmental considerations in programme objectives and implementation.
* Implement the North American Bird Conservation Initiative by 2002 – a regionally-based, biologically driven, landscape oriented bird conservation initiative that will work closely with landowners to inform and influence land use practices.

## Managing for Sustainable Development

We believe that Environment Canada has a responsibility to show leadership across the federal government on sustainable development. In order to be successful, internal operations, procurement and management practices must support and promote sustainable development.

Greening operations and Environmental Management Systems (EMSs) are examples of areas where EC has a great deal of expertise and where concrete steps can be taken over the short to medium term to promote the Department's sustainable development agenda. Environment Canada must be a leader in this area, and continue to build on past successes in solid waste management, green laboratory operations and energy conservation and conversion.

Environment Canada supports current efforts to build a coordinated, government-wide approach to sustainable development in government operations. A guidance document released in June 2000 with suggested targets and performance measures was an important first step in building a greater capacity to report government-wide progress in greening operations. This kind of coordinated approach will be helpful to departments as they plan improvements in their environmental performance and to Canadians who want to monitor the Government's progress.

Key challenges for EC in its own operations include: continuing progress in implementing the departmental EMS; developing appropriate performance indicators for greening operations; and making progress on greenhouse gas reductions from its facilities. Environmental accounting is one of the tools that could help the Department to move toward its operational goals by encouraging better integration of its environmental management system and its financial information system. A closer integration of these two systems would enable the Department to report on both the financial and the environmental costs and benefits associated with its operational decisions. This kind of more integrated accounting would help to promote sound management, reduce environmental costs and foster greater awareness and accountability among managers for operational decisions.

In addition to work on greening its operations, in order to truly show leadership across the federal government on sustainable development, Environment Canada also needs to develop effective human resource strategies that ensure the Department has the critical knowledge and skill sets required to deliver on its sustainable development goals.

A final important component under the theme of managing for sustainable development relates to how our department works with other departments across government. We recognise the need to enhance the co-ordination of policies horizontally across government departments, and see efforts to build and institutionalise that horizontal co-ordination as a key challenge of "managing for sustainable development."

It is a long-term challenge and, as with all big challenges, progress will have to be made one step at a time. The following commitments will provide the focus for EC over the next three years.

### *(1) Sustainable Development in Government Operations*

In an effort to build a coordinated approach to sustainable development in government operations, a guidance document entitled *Sustainable Development in Government Operations: A Coordinated* Approach was released in June 2000. The document recommends best practices in seven priority areas of operations – procurement, waste management, water conservation and waste water management, energy efficiency, vehicle fleet management, land use management, and human resources management. It proposes a tool box of collaboratively developed performance measures and offers a sample set of targets in each of the seven areas (see Table 8.2). By encouraging the adoption of common performance measures and targets, the aim is to further reduce the impact of federal operations on the environment and to facilitate measuring and reporting on progress across government in these priority areas.

Over the next three years, EC proposes to:

- Incorporate targets and performance measures from the guidance document *Sustainable Development in Government Operations: A Coordinated Approach* into Environment Canada's EMS aspect action plans, and work toward achieving these targets as they relate to EC's operations.

**1. Procurement**

- By March 31, 2002, adopt as the default condition the purchase of environmentally responsible goods and services, whenever available and in a manner consistent with Canada's international trade obligations.
- By March 31, 2002, PWGSC will introduce environmental specifications into all standing offers, where requested by client departments.
- By March 31, 2002, introduce environmental specifications into all appropriate sections of the *National Master Specifications*. Specifically by March 31, 2001, introduce environmental specifications into the 23 sections of the Specifications that address energy efficiency issues. This recognises the primacy of Kyoto commitments with respect to greenhouse gas emissions.
- By March 31, 2002, provide green procurement training to all personnel with purchasing responsibility.
- By September 2004, include reports based on Treasury Board's *Green Procurement Reporting Framework* in all departmental performance reports.

**2. Waste Management**

- By March 31, 2004, divert 70 percent of solid waste from landfill—thas is, 70 percent by weight of all solid waste is to be recycled.
- By March 31, 2004, develop and implement a protocol to use economical alternatives to hazardous materials and/or processes that generate hazardous waste.
- By March 31, 2001, incorporate solid waste diversion practices into all construction, renovation and demolition projects.

**3. Water Conservation and Wastewater Management**

- By March 31, 2004, implement water conservation measures at all federal facilities, when it is feasible and cost effective to do so.
- By March 31, 2001, develop and implement revised wastewater management guidelines for federal facilities.

**4. Energy Efficiency**

- By March 31, 2001, complete a study to identify cost-effective opportunities to use more efficient and environmentally responsible energy sources in Crown-owned buildings.
- By March 31, 2004, implement in Crown-owned buildings energy conservation measures associated with the Federal Buildings Initiative and other programmes, when an energy assessment has demonstrated that it is cost effective to do so.
- By March 31, 2001, Introduce enhanced energy efficiency specifications into the 23 sections of the *National Master Specifications* relating to equipment that uses energy.

**5. Vehicle Fleet Management**

- By September 2002, include report on compliance with Treasury Board's *Motor Vehicle Policy (1996)* and the *Alternative Fuels Act* in all departmental performance reports.

**6. Land Use Management**

- Continue to assess all proposed projects to determine if they are considered projects as defined by the *Canadian Environmental Assessment Act (CEAA)*.
- Continue to comply with the CEAA for any proposed activity considered a project as defined by the Act.

- By March 31, 2001, identify and prioritise federal contaminated sites, and prepare action plans.
- Continue to remediate and monitor Crown-owned contaminated sites as determined by action plans.

7. **Human Resources Management**

- By March 31, 2002, establish and implement environmental training plans commensurate with operations.

*(2) Federal Sustainable Development Strategy for the North*

During consultations for the last round of Sustainable development Strategies, Northerners expressed a desire for a more coordinated approach across government to sustainable development issues in the North. As a result, an effort is currently underway to prepare a single coordinated Federal Sustainable Development Strategy for the North. The aim is to develop and adopt a strategy that:

- identifies goals and actions of federal departments that will contribute to sustainable development in the North;
- establishes linkages and coordinates activities; and
- uses consistent approaches to consultation, and involvement of Northerners in its implementation.

Several departments and agencies are participating in the development of this coordinated strategy. Two phases of consultations have been undertaken. The first phase in November 1999 provided the opportunity for departments to report on progress on their 1997 strategies and to discuss key issues with Northerners. Based on feedback, a second round of consultations was held in the spring of 2000 to discuss possible actions. Departments are currently working on drafting a strategy. Given that the Federal Strategy for Sustainable Development in the North has not yet been completed, it is too early to outline all of EC's northern commitments in our Strategy at this time. It is possible, however, to describe some of the areas in which EC is working to build support for coordinated work across departments in the North.

For instance:

- Communicating with Northern communities about the Kyoto

Protocol commitments, their implications for Canadians and specifically how Northern communities can contribute to these commitments;

- Providing Northern communities with waste management information and tools (*e.g.* guides to recycling, composting, green procurement) as it applies to remote communities, including those with only air of sea lift re-supply;
- Advancing knowledge, tools and awareness of the response of Northern ecosystems to major drivers of change in the Canadian North through the Northern Ecosystem Initiatives;
- Incorporating Aboriginal traditional knowledge in the development of Environment Canada legislation policies and programmes by developing an Environment Canada traditional knowledge policy, and training staff in the application of the policy;
- Participating in and/or leading in the development of a government-wide approach to traditional knowledge;
- Developing a Cumulative Effects Monitoring and Assessment Framework for application to all types of Northern development projects;
- Undertaking a literature review on the issue of valuing country foods in the North; and
- Developing a Land Claims Agreement familiarisation programme for environment Canada staff by September 2001, that is piloted within Environment Canada by December 2001 and delivered to 50% of Environment Canada staff managing or delivering Northern programmes and policies by 2003.

*(3) Productivity Through Eco-efficiency*

Improving the capacity of Canadian industry and small business to develop and use eco-efficient practices that improve their environmental performance is recognised as an important element of making progress on sustainable development. It is also an area in which several federal departments have a significant role to play. As a result, an interdepartmental working group has been established to develop a framework and identify potential initiatives that could be pursued in a coordinated way. There are three key areas in which work is being considered:

- strengthening research and development to address the need for trained people to work for industry to identify and implement eco-efficient practices;
- working with industry, particularly small and medium-sized enterprises, to help them identify and implement eco-efficient practices and tools; and
- developing performance measures and benchmarks to quantify both environmental and productivity benefits of eco-efficiency.

As part of its contribution to this horizontal initiative, EC proposes to:

- use the pollution prevention provisions in CEPA and voluntary initiatives to encourage companies to systematically review their operations and identify opportunities to address environmental issues in an efficient and effective way; and
- work with small and medium-sized enterprises to increase the number identifying and implementing eco-efficient tools and practices (*e.g.*, through the expansion of programmes like Quebec Region's Enviro-Club programme).

### *(4) Knowledge and Information/Sustainable Development Indicators and Reporting*

Departments recognise the need to build a stronger foundation of knowledge to support more integrated decision-making and informed public debate on sustainable development issues. They also recognise the need to develop a set of indicators and a process to report regularly to Canadians on the state of sustainable development in Canada. These are both efforts that require inter-departmental collaboration.

Key efforts to enhance knowledge and information include:

- developing a plan to address knowledge and information gaps related to sustainable development through the government's Sustainability Project – a policy research initiative;

- establishing a Task Force on a Canadian Information System on the Environment, that will cover all aspects of knowledge management related to the environment; and
- establishing an environment and sustainable development research programme with the academic community.

Departments intend to work together to develop an appropriate framework for sustainable development indicators, and a set of national indicators. These would then be submitted to the National Round Table on the Environment and the Economy who have been tasked with building a national consensus around a set of sustainable development indicators for Canada.

As part of its contribution to this coordinated effort, EC proposes to:

- ensure the final report of the Canadian Information System for the Environment Task Force (outlining environmental information and knowledge requirements, the status of existing data and knowledge systems, and investments needed to meet these requirements), is completed by end of 2001.
- establish a multi-disciplinary Sustainable Development Policy Research Programme by end of 2001 that enhances our understanding of sustainable development and informs decision making and public debate.

*(5) Sustainability in Communities*

The aim of the sustainable communities initiative is to better integrate the delivery of individual federal programmes focused on community issues in order to maximise their impact within the context of community economic, social and environmental development.

In order to integrate the delivery of these programmes and ensure a consistent focus on sustainable development issues, a federal framework on sustainable communities will be developed in collaboration with other government departments and partners. The framework will describe the federal government's vision, guiding principles, strategic approach, mechanisms, and tools and a process for evaluation and reporting. In addition, an action plan will be developed which draws on the strengths of programmes across departments to apply the framework at the community level.

Progress to date includes:

- interdepartmental working group on sustainable communities established;
- National Rural Conference held in April 2000;
- research and analysis on sustainable community development commissioned through the government-wide Policy Research Initiative's Sustainability Project; and

  informal dialogue with multi-sectoral community and sustainable development experts held to scope issues and a broader policy framework for sustainable community development.

As part of its commitment to this horizontal effort EC proposes to:

- develop and implement, with partners, a federal framework on sustainable communities;
- explore the feasibility, with partners, of applying a sustainable communities approach through selected pilot projects (including those in aboriginal communities), using Federal councils as a catalyst where appropriate; and
- develop and implement government-on-line projects to support the delivery of sustainable communities initiatives and related federal programming.

## Measuring Our Performance

A critical component of the Sustainable Development Strategy process is a strong focus on implementation. Environment Canada has been making efforts to close the gap between commitments and implementation in a number of areas (*e.g.,* improving our tracking and implementation of international commitments and agreements), and sees measures to ensure effective implementation of the Department's Strategy as equally important.

Environment Canada will measure and report on its performance in implementing its SDS on an annual basis. Through the annual Departmental Performance Reports, progress at the level of goals as outlined in this Strategy will be examined, through the use of the performance measures as defined.

There is an ongoing challenge associated with reporting at the level of results, as opposed to reporting on activities undertaken. Environment Canada will work toward measuring the results of its actions, though in many cases the longer term changes we are intending to contribute to can be difficult to measure in the shorter term.

Annual reporting through EC's Departmental Performance Reports will enable us to check whether we are on course, and identify any corrective action needed during the three years period of the Strategy. We would anticipate making any necessary adjustments to our goals or targets through the Department's Annual Report on Plans and Priorities.

# 6

# POLLUTION CONTROL AND SOME RELEVANT ACTS

## Noise

The intensity of noise being propagated due to different factors/ agencies such as industries, vehicles, public address system, radio, TV, religious congregations, social functions and construction activities till the year 2000. As a result this menace has gained such a proportion that in metropolitans and other urban areas it is getting on every one's nerves. The increase in proportion of noise pollution is undoubtedly a fall out of modern civilisation and urbanisation. In some cases, the noise generated becomes both a public and private nuisance and it even goes beyond individuals tolerance levels and thereby becoming a source of health hazard. Noise was included as a pollutant in the Air (Prevention and Control of Pollution) Act, 1981 when it was amended in 1987. To achieve the objective of public enjoying the noise free environment, the Constitution of India made provisions under sections 268 and 290 as part of "Public Nuisance" of the Indian Penal Code. In addition, Section 133 of the Code of Criminal Procedure Act also confers sufficient powers to the District Magistrate of the area concerned to abate the public nuisance or to remove the public inconvenience. The Motor Vehicle Act, 1939 has also certain provisions to enforce the 'killing noise' generated through varying types and of different intensities of horns fitted with all sorts of vehicles plying on our roads. The authorities concerned can take note of such vehicles creating public nuisance by violating the provisions of Motor Vehicle Act and can accordingly be punished. In those cases where the noise being generated crosses the decent limits and thereby is an unreasonable interference with any individual's use or enjoyment of his property or some right over or in connection with it, then he can resort to legal remedy under the 'Law of Torts' against those responsible for it (directly or indirectly). Public nuisance under this category is the undesireable noise generated on the occasion of Indiam marriages which to most people in urban India mean traffic jams, bhangra, pop, unending merrymaking in the form of ladies sangeet, music night with DJ and other music instruments, etc.

The courts have taken note of an instance where the noise generated by setting up of a flour mill resulted in interfering with the physical comfort of certain people living in the area. The court considered setting up of the mill as a nuisance and issued prohibitory orders restraining the owner of the flour mill from running it in the locality which was already considered to be too noisy (Radhey Syam v Geer Parsad, AIR 1978 Allahabad, 86). Similarly, the court endorsed the decision of the Commissioner of Police banning the use of electric loudspeaker for calling the 'Azan' five times a day as it disturbed the people living in the locality due to the noise created by the use of loudspeaker. The defendant took the plea that the use of loudspeaker was for religious recitation of 'Azan' and the ban imposed by the Commisioner as unjustified. The court held that the ban imposed on the use of loudspeaker as legal. The court also pointed out that the religious faith or belief are subject to public order, morality and health (Masud Alam v Commissioner of Police, CWN 293 and 353-354). In Church of God (Full Gospel) in India v. K.K.R. Majestic Colony Welfare Association and Others (AIR 2000 SC 2773; Supreme Court's Initiatives, 2001 AIR Journal/56II), an appeal by special leave was filed against the judgement and order passed by the High Court of Judicature at Madras. The Honb'le Supreme Court of India rescued the captive audience which was intermittently exposed to roaring decibles of noise on the ground of religion. K.K.R.Majestic Colony Welfare Association and Others made a complaint to the

Tamil Nadu Pollution Control Board against Church of God (Full Gospel) who recited prayers with musical instruments such as drum sets, triple gango, guitar and other sound producing instruments which caused noise pollution, disturbed and caused nuisance to the normal day-to-day life of the residential colony. The church authorities while contending the case in the High Court of Judicature at Madras took the plea that the petition has been filed with an oblique motive in order to prevent a religious minority institution from pursuing its religious activities and the court cannot issue any direction to prevent the church from practicising its religious beliefs.

The orders issued by the court resulted in dharnas and demonstrations by the minority community. The trouble began during midday namaz when azan (call) was given on loudspeakers and a Bench of the High Court comprising acting Chief Justice Mr Justice Nagendra Rai and R.S.Garg, which was in session, took notice to it and questioned the use of loudspeakers despite an undertaking by the mosque authorities not to use the public address system while the court was in session. A few years ago also, the court had directed that the public address system would not be used during the court proceedings till 4 pm.

Following directions of the Himachal Pradesh High Court, the state government has issued a notification banning the use of pressure horns and the manufacture, sale and use of firecrackers generating high noise levels in the state. A division bench of the court directed the state government as well as the authorities concerned to ensure strict compliance of notification. Writing for the Bench, Chief Justice of Himachal Pradesh High Court observed that noise pollution was a grave social menace, adversely affecting the quality of life, and the issue of controlling it needed to be handled carefully. The court had referred the case to a committee of experts to give suggestions on checking this social menace. The state government issued a notification for implementing Section 5 of the Environment Protection Act, 1986 and the Noise Pollution (Regulation and Control) Rules 2000. The notification says that no public address system (microphone) shall operate for any time in the silence zones, which includes a 100-metre radius around hospitals, nursing homes, educational institutions and courts. However, restrictions around schools, colleges and libraries will be operative during working hours. Loudspeakers can only be used with the permission of the local police, the Subdivisional Magistrate or the District Magistrate. The authorities have to ensure that sound limiters are fixed on loudspeakers. Loudspeakers used at religious places shall maintain the ambient air standards. Permission has to be obtained from the authorities concerned to use microphones at such places. For public address. The notification says that night-time cultural or religious functions should be organized in a temporarily covered area with sound-absorbing material. The government has fixed the sound limit as per the noise pollution rules, 2000 at 75 dB/Leq during daytime (6 am to 10 pm) and 70 dB/Leq during night-time (10 pm to 6 am) in industrial areas and 65 db/Leq day-time and 55 dB/Leq for night-time in commercial areas. The sound limit fixed for residential areas is 55 dB/Leq and 45 dB/Leq for day-time and night-time respectively. The notification states that no permission will be given to openair functions three days before important examinations, including school or college examinations, entrance test at the state level or any other competitive examinations conducted by the Himachal Pradesh Dtate Public Service Commission and the Union Public Service Commision at the state or national levels till the examination are over. The use, sale and manufacture of firecracker generating noise level exceeding 125 dB (AI) or 145 dB pk at a four-metre distance are prohibited. The use of other firecrackers or other fireworks is prohibited in the silence zones, and except from 6 pm to 10 am.

In response to a petition filed by residents of Phagwara in Punjab alleging noise and air pollution due to the presence of industries in a residential area, the Punjab and Haryana High Court on 10th November, 2002 ruled that either residences or industries will have to be shifted. According to the directions issued by the court:

" The claim of the petitioner is that they have constructed houses after getting necessary sanction from the Municipal Committee but neither the Pollution Control Board nor the Punjab State Electricity Board was taking steps to check noise and air pollution in the residential area is apparent from the existing situation in the locality that the residential houses shall have to be shifted for which the respondents shall have to bear necessary expenses for re-location, besides compensation for the constructed portions. Or in alternate, the industries causing pollution in the locality shall have to be closed or shifted."

The Delhi High Court directed the Ministry of Environment to finalise the noise standard for generator sets before 22nd February, 2000. The order was passed while hearing two public interest litigations, seeking prohibition of the use of unauthorised generator sets in public places, markets and residential areas in the city as they cause air and noise pollution (Times of India, 18.XI.1999). The generator sets installed are violating the standard guidelines under section 21 of the Air (prevention and control of the pollution) Act 1981 which is punishable with imprisonment for a term not less than one year but may extend up to six years with a fine. The CPCC under section 31A of the act is also empowered to issue directions for stoppage of electricity and water supply to the unit. As per the Environment Protection Rules 1986, there should be a mandatory acoustic enclosure for the stationary generator sets of 5 KV and above. The manufacturer should offer to the user a standard acoustic enclosure of 25 decibles and also a suitable exhaust muffler with insertion loss of 25 decibles. A proper routing and preventive maintenance procedure for the generator set should be set and followed. In Chandigarh, especially in sector 9 and 35, generator sets installed by SCO owners in the open area of rear portion are source of causing noise and air pollution. Such generators have been installed without the consent of CPCC. The Haryana Pollution Control Board launched drive w.e.f 30th September, 2004 against those who have installed generator sets above 62.5 KVA without acoustic chambers to control the noise level.

The Ministry of Environment and Forests, Government of India has notified the Noise Pollution Rules, 2000, under the Environment (Protection) Act, 1986, for preventing adverse impact of noise on human health, including harmful psychological effects. Through these rules government has taken steps to regulate the level of noise pollution in urban areas, including metropolitan cities, from various sources. These include a ban on the use of loudspeakers and generator sets without prior written permission from the concerned authorities. According to these rules the loudspeakers and public address systems can only be used in closed premises like auditoriums, conference rooms, community halls and banquet halls between 10 pm and 6 am. In other public places, these can only be used after seeking permission from a competent authority. The notification also puts ban on the use of musical vehicular horns, public performances like beating of drums and use of any sound amplifiers in silence zones, that is, in areas upto 100 metres around hospitals, educational institutions and courts.

**Fires**

It is observed that more people die in fires than in cyclones, earthquakes, floods and all other natural disasters combined. Heating sources are often cause of Fire. Space heaters, electric heaters and fireplaces should be used with caution. Cooking accidents are a major cause of home fires and cause us a lot of concern. Fires can result due to unattended cooking or due to mechanical failure of the stove or any cooking equipment.

Electrical wiring can cause a fire if it is not large enough to carry the load being supplied. Overheating of electrical appliances, poor wiring connections, use of unauthorised appliances, multi-point adaptors can result in fires starting.

Rubbish and Waste Materials that are left of accumulate can easily contribute to the spread of fire; they are also a place for malicious fires to be started. Make sure that you remove all waste materials from the workplace on a regular basis and place them in a suitable container located in a safe position outside the building premises. Do not burn rubbish on bonfire, even if it is thought safe to do so. They can easily get out of control and spread fire to nearby buildings or structures.

Hazardous Materials such as paints, solvents, adhesive, chemicals or gas cylinders should be kept in separate storage areas and well away from any sources of ignition. Smoking is also a major cause of fire.

Some Safety Measures for prevention in home

- remember basic fire safety rules and your evacuation route;
- don't keep highly flammable liquids in the house;
- when you leave your house, make sure to shut off all electrical and gas applications;
- don't plug several devices into one socket;
- A smoke filled corridor, crawl on all fours or on your ally as the smoke is less on the floor.

## Smoking in Public Places

In response to a public interest litigation (PIL) filed in the Supreme Court of India by Murli Manohar Deoria from Mumbai, the apex court in its decision on 2nd October, 2001 banned smoking in all public places (hospitals, health institutes, public offices, court buildings, educational institutions, libraries and auditoriums) and public transport, including railways with immediate effect. The Court asked the commissioners of police of Delhi, Mumbai, Chennai, Kolkata, Bangalore and Ahmedabad to inform it about the action taken against cigarette manufacturers violating the advertising code. It also asked the customs department to inform it about the steps taken to check smuggling of foreign cigarettes. The governments of Delhi, Goa and Rajasthan have already enacted laws banning smoking in public places, while the Centre is in the process of enacting an anti-smoking legislation. It is reported that at least three million people die annually in India due to tobacco related diseases, and the number may rise to seven million.

**Gutka and Pan Masala**

*Gutka*, Mainpuri, Mava, chewing tobacco and *pan masala* are household industries in several parts of Uttar Pradesh, Bihar, Madhya Pradesh and Tamil Nadu. Those manufacturing these do not realise and understand the implications and fall out of the stuff they are handling. Small affordable pouches of these were introduced in the market in 1985 and these are readily available in the *pan* shops by paying just one rupee. Young school going children have fallen victim of these and use of these was on the rise among them. The name gutkha was used for the first time in 1971 for *pan masala*, illachi and supari. Inspite of the fact that the sale of *gutka* is not permitted within a distance of 100 metres from any school or educational institution, these are being sold without any inhibition due to government rules not being implimented strictly. Similarly, sale of *gutka* is not allowed at the shops or by the vendors at the railway platforms. However, one can comfortably buy such packets at any and every railway platform. As a result, there are increasing incidence of mouth and throat problems varying from simple laryngitis to cancer. Doctors pin the cause of oral cancer (mouth cancer) and throat cancer on a range of habits like smoking, chewing *gutka*, paan and tobacco, anaemia, voice abuse and even long telephone conversation. Cases of mouth and throat cancer being caused due to gutka are being reported amongst youth between the age groups of 18 to 24 from different parts of Maharashtra, Bihar, Tamil Nadu and other parts of the country. Such cases of mouth cancer had not earlier been reported from the population younger than 35 years of age. In addition, there is an alarming increase in the incidence of sub-mucous fibrosis (inability to open the mouth) because of the indiscriminate use of *gutka* and *pan masala*. To overcome this menace amongst youth of our country, especially school going children, it is necessary that the young children are educated about the ill effects of gutkha on their health. The existing laws also need to be strictly enforced against the sale of gutkha to young school going children who may fall easy victim to its ill effects. If needed, the government may pass new legislation for a total ban on the sale of *gutka*, *pan masala* and other forms of chewing tobacco which are alarmingly increasing the incidence of victims falling prey to these, particulary among the youth in country. The Tamil Nadu government has announced a five-year ban on manufacture, sale and distribution of *pan masala, gutka* and chewing tobacco with immediate effect (Times of India, 20.XI.2001, p.1). The Maharashtra government imposed ban on the manufacture and sale of *gutka* w.e.f 1st August, 2002 for a period of three years. The Maharashtra Government also requested other states all over the country to impose similar ban on the sale and production of *gutka*. Following a notification of the Bihar Government, the sale and consumption of *gutka* have been banned in the state w.e.f. 1st April, 2003. According to the notification, anybody found selling *gutka* would be imprisioned for three months to three years.

According to Neeta Pradhan and Preeti Gopalkrishna (INDIA TODAY, April 2, 2001 Issue, p. 50): "The West gave the world chewing gum. And India gave the world *pan masala*. In fact, *pan parag* has become synonymous to the generic product. The band is not only popular across the length and breadth of India but has crossed boundaries to find a huge market in the US, Europe, Middle East, Australia and many other countries" Commenting in INDIA TODAY on the young boys getting addictive to *pan masala*, M.M.Kothari, Chairman, KPL observed: "People consuming pan masala with zarda (tobacco) can get addicted, but *pan masala* by itself is not addictive. But, it should be consumed moderately and merely as mouth freshner. Too much of anything is harmful to health."

A Division Bench of the Kerala High Court in its ruling on 19th December, 2001 quashed the notification issued earlier on May 31, 2001 (to be effective from July 1, 2001 for one year) by the Director of Health Services prohibiting manufacture, storage, distribution and sale of *pan masala* containing tobacco or any other ingredient injurious to health. The Bench quashed the notification while allowing a petition by some tobacco merchants challenging the notification. The Bench held that in the absence of any rules, the Director had no jurisdiction to issue a total ban of *pan masala*.

The Supreme Court of India on 5th August, 2002 stayed the Allahabad High Court order issued on 18th July, 2002 banning the sale and manufacture of *pan masala* and *gutka* in Uttar Pradesh. At the same time the apex court issued notices to the Centre, Andhra Pradesh, Dental Council of India and two major *pan masala* manufacturers on a plea seeking a ban on the sale and manufacture of *pan masala* and *gutka* across the country. The Society for Cancer in Oral Cavity Protection filed the plea against the Andhra Pradesh High Court order rejecting a PIL seeking the ban order. On April 23, 2002, the HC had said it could not interfere with the state government's policy matters. The SC bench also issued notice to the UP government, which had issued a notification banning the sale and manufacture of *pan masala* and *gutka* in line with the HC order. The order came on petitions by the largest *pan masala* manufacturers – Kothari Products Ltd, Dharampal Satyapal Ltd and K.P Pan Flavour Pvt Ltd – who sought an interim stay on the ban order.

The Madhya Pradesh High Court at Jabalpur in its directions issued on 2nd August, 2002 asked the Government of Madhya Pradesh to impose ban on the production and sale of gutka in the state with immediate effect.

The Zafrani Zarda and Pan Masala Association of India opposed the ban on *gutka* and *pan masala* on a plea that it would jeopardise limited livelihood options of 23 million people directly or indirectly associated with the industry who would get jobless. They also pointed out that the ban will increase smuggling of products and prompt manufacture of spurious products.

Commenting on the ban, Tribune in its editorial dated 23rd July, 2002 (p. 10) observed:

" The decision of the Maharashtra and Uttar Pradesh governments to ban the sale and manufacture of *gutka* and similar tobacco-based products deserves a qualified welcome. The Punjab and Haryana High Court recently imposed a ban on using public transport for advertising *gutka* and *pan masala*. The centre also intends to introduce a law for banning the production and sale of all forms of tobacco-based products. A half-hearted ban on life-threatening substances would result in the loss of revenue to the state governments without achieving the goal of protecting the health of the people."

The organisation, Guru Gobind Singh Study Circle, Ludhiana filed a public interest litigation (PIL) on 20th December, 2002 before the Punjab and Haryana High Court seeking directions for taking immediate steps to ban the manufacture, distribution and sale of *gutka*, along with other chewable tobacco products. The petitioner also sought directions for the adoption of measures to prevent irreparable damage to the health of the "future generation", including students, directions for the removal of vends near the educational and religious institutes, besides banning and pulling down of boards advertising the products on the buses and walls in public places and other means by which such messages reach children. Seeking directions for maintaining a minimum distance of 2 km between the outlets, counsel for the petitioner had added on behalf of the organisation that the products were freely available in provision stores, even at tea stalls and STD booths. In the hearing on 20th February, 2003, the health authority of Punjab Government, while admitting the various hazards to health touched upon in the writ petition lauded the objectives and the intention of the petitioner. It further pointed out that it is considering ban on the sale of these articles under PFA Act 1954. The government sought a period of two months time for taking a decision (Hindustan Times, 21.2.2003, p. 2; Times of India, 21.2.2003, p. 2 and Tribune, 21.2.2003, p. 3).

In response to a Public Interest Litigation (PIL), the Supreme Court of India in its decision on 2nd August, 2004 lifted ban on gutka and pan masala. The Apex Court struck down as unconstitutional the notification issued by Maharashtra and Andhra Pradesh banning manufacture, sale and purchase of these items. According to the Court, the state governments cannot impose such a ban under the Prevention of Food Adulteration Act (PFAA) even if the move of the states was well intended. The Supreme Court judgement points out that a total ban could be imposed only by the Union Health Ministry under Subsection 1A(f) of Section 23 of PFAA. It is reported that the Union Government has already told the Delhi High Court that it was seriously contempolating enacting comprehensive legislation to regulate the sale of tobacco products, including pan masala and gutka ( Times of India, 3.8.2004, p. 8; Hindustan Times, 3.8.2004, p. 1; Tribune, 4.8.2004, p. 17; India Today, July 5, 2004 Issue, pp. 52-55).

**Traffic Accidents**

Road network is laid for better connectivity and service but at the same time the number of accidents is also on the rise. The main causes are the violation of traffic regulations, speeding, drunk driving and poor maintenance of the vehicle and the roads. All those reasons add to the rising number of accidents and road fatalities.

Many factors govern the safety of passenger in an aircraft. It includes technical problems, fire, landing and take off conditions, the environment an airline operates in (mountainous terrain or frequent storms), factors like airport security in cases of hijackings, bombing attempts etc.

- safety Measures:
- drive only if you are competent enough;
- the best way to be safe on the roads is to follow lane driving for the your own safety.
- familiar with road markings. Road signs and honour them; while driving avoid sudden acceleration and deceleration;
- Stay claim, Listen to the crew members and do what they say. The cabin crew's most important job is to help you leave safety.
- Remember smoke rises. So try to stay down if there's smoke in the cabin. Follow the track of emergency lights embedded in the floor; they lead to an exit if you have a cloths, put it over you nose and mouth.

The most common types of rail accident are derailment due to lack or maintenance, human error or sabotage. Various type of dangerous cargo are also transported such as fuel oil products, etc. In the picture, bogies of the derailed Bangalore Express lying on the tracks near Pendakal station, 250 km south of Hyderabad, on Dec. 21.2002 20 persons were killed and 80 injured, 24 of them seriously.

India has one of the highest accident rates in the world. Every year more than 3,00,000 accidents are reported. Fatality rate is as high as 60,000. Studies on accidents, the world over, have shown that the human factor is responsible for a majority of accidents.

**Sewage and Toilet Problems**

The Supreme Court of India directed the state government way back in 1995 to make budgetary allocations for the Rs 43 crore sewerage system. Anguished at the lethargy on the part of the Orissa government to implement model sewerage system in one of the four important pilgrimage places of the Hindus, the court asked the Chief Secretary of Orissa Government and Commissioner of Puri to be personally present before it on August 29, 2001. The Apex Court also expressed displeasure on the affidavit filed by the Housing and Urban Development Commissioner-cum - Secretary saying: "It is unfortunate that notwithstanding the orders of the Supreme Court sine 1995, the matter is dragging on." It may be pointed out that the National Environment Engineering Research Institute (NEERI) had approved a project envisaging refurbishing of the entire sewer system and setting up a sewer treatment plant (STP) at Puri, the seat of Lord Jagannath. The environmental experts pointed out that discharge of untreated sewer into the sea was polluting it.

Acting on a petition seeking directions to the State of Punjab and other authorities concerned to take immediate steps for the disposal of sewerage and rainwater in Nayagaon, the Punjab and Haryana High Court on 28th January, 2003 directed that the same should be done within a period of eight months. The petitioner contended that the contaminated water collected in the Janta Colony was causing damage to about 10,000 houses of slum dwellers and other residents of the localities.

Times of India (7.X.2004, p. 10) in its editorial published under the title "Nation without toilets" made the following observations: "Fifty seven years after independence, Union Minister of State for Urban Employment and Poverty Alleviation Selja's statement that over 70 crore Indians do not have access to proper toilet facilities does not come as a surprise. On the contrary, this reveals the gross failure of successive governments at the Centre and in the states to provide basic sanitation to most people. The country has no dearth of programmes and committees on how to improve sanitation. But what has been lacking is the political will to achieve this objective, most people are forced to defecate in the open in the absence of toilets. This is particularly devastating for women as it severely hurts their self-esteem, dignity, safety and indirectly their literacy and productivity. Studies reveal that poor women in most states, without access to toilets, try to avoid their use by not drinking water when thirsty or eat when hungry. This, in the process, has affected their health. According to a study, over 180 million man days – equivalent to Rs 12 billion – are lost every year because of sanitation-related diseases. The Central Rural Sanitation Programme (CRSP), launched in the 1980s, failed. Though the CRSP was scrapped, it raised the sanitation coverage to 14 per cent in the 1990s from almost zero in the 1970s. Organisations like Sulabh International have proved that affordable and sustainable toilets can be built for various categories. More NGOs should come forward to supplement the government's efforts to meet what is the basic human need."

**Solid Waste**

The Supreme Court of India, in its ruling in the case Almitra H.Patel Vs Union of India (Civil writ petition no 888/96) issued directions to the government and local bodies (municipal corporations) of the country to manage their waste. The Court also instructed the government to form a committee to look into the matter and formulate procedures by which the waste generated in the cities could be converted into useful products or be safely disposed off. The committee submitted its report in March, 2000, after which Municipal Solid Waste Management and Handling Rules were notified in September, 2000. According to the directives, the corporations of the country have been given time till December 31, 2003 to provide facilities to either incinerate, peletise or use the waste for any other useful process.

To curb the growing tendency amongst residents of Chandigarh, Panchkula (Haryana), Mohali (Punjab) and other cities and towns in different parts of the country to throw malba (building material refuse) a strict law need to be enforced to overcome the environmental hazard being posed by such a practice. The building contractors and residents throw/dump malba in any open space they come across. In most cases, municipal corporation or other administrative body removes such a malba at their own cost and fine is imposed on the defaulters which hardly is a deterrent. In Chandigarh, the city administration has earmarked spaces for malba dumping in largely low-lying areas, which need to be leveled. By dumping malba at such sites, a dual purpose is served. In addition to getting rid of the building material waste, it acts as land-fill. It is reported in a section of media that the Chandigarh Administration is contempolating to enforce Section 144 of the Code of Criminal Procedure (CrPC) to ensure that city residents do not throw malba in the open spaces. If imposed, Section 144 of the CrPC gives powers to the District Magistrate (DM) or the Deputy Commissioner (DC) to issue order in urgent cases of nuisance. The DM can ask any person to abstain from carrying out any act if he deems it to be a danger to public health, or disturbance of public tranquility (Chandigarh Tribune, 20.3.2004, p. 2).

A petition was filed in the Punjab & Haryana High Court on 23rd September, 2004 by advocate Amar Vivek of Chandigarh who launched a save Rose Garden campaign seeking directions for shifting the venue of rallies and dharnas from the road dividing Sectors 16 and 17 to some alternate site, besides maintaining the cleanliness of Rose Garden and Shanti Kunj in Sector 16. In his petition, the advocate had added that the authorities should be directed to provide amenities like water and mobile toilets to the agitating farmers. Taking up the case, the Bench of the High Court had asked the authorities to inform the court about the steps being taken for preventing further damage to the gardens.

**Deforestation**

The Supreme Court of India in a landmark judgement has banned all non-forest activities (including felling of trees, closure of saw mills, veneer or plywood mills,mining and also transportation of timber or wood by any means from the seven north-eastern states) in the forest areas and directed that Forest Conservation Act, 1980 be applied to all forests irrespective of ownership or classification. The ban imposed by the Supreme Court of India on logging, augurs well for the country's forest. The interim order banning the felling of trees from all forests has virtually brought to a standstill extraction of wood and veneer mills under the state governments, making central clearance mandatory for their operation. The Supreme Court of India has also directed ban on transportation of timber and cutting of trees from the north-east to the rest of the country. It has also asked the state governments to workout a regulatory system to harvest wood from private plantation. The ban imposed by the Supreme Court of India has given the forests a respite. The Court has also issued directions to other states (J & K, Himachal Pradesh and Tamil Nadu) asking them to stop felling of trees with a view to protect and preserve the forests (T.N.Godavarman Thirumulkpad V Union of India (1997) 2 SCC 267 and (1997) 3 SCC 312).

Some of the directions issued earlier by the Supreme Court of India were subsequently modified by the Court. The Ministry of Environment and Forests came forward with the perception that in view of the local people of the North-Eastern States having dependence on the forest resources in the region, it may not be desirable or even feasible, to completely ban running of timber or wood based industries. Appreciating the perception of the Ministry of Environment and Forests, the Supreme Court of India issued directions for complete moratorium on the issue of new licenses by the state governments or any other authority for the establishment of any new wood – based industry for the next five years after which the situation will be reviewed. In another case, the Supreme Court of India restrained the state government and its functionaries to restrain from cutting any tree/trees till further orders, even if it was found to be diseased tree. These directions were issued in response to a petition whereby it was pleaded that under the garb of removing infected trees, trees having no disease were also being cut. The Court has also issued directions for constituting an independent commission comprising of a police officer not below the rank of I.G. and Director, Indira Gandhi Forest Academy, Dehradun with a view to get a complete picture of the deforestation and extent of illegal mining done, damage caused to the hills and forests and to identify the culprits as also the manner of restitution and reforestation (T.N.Godavarman Thirumulkpad V Union of India (1997) 5 SCC 760; 7SCC 440; 10SCC 775; (1998) 6 SCC,190; 9 SCC 632 and 660).

According to the analysis of the satellite imageries of last few years pertaining to Arunachal Pradesh it has been noticed that this region has lost 1,417 square kilometers of forest area during the period 1996-2000. Studies of such imageries from other states such as Uttar Pradesh, Himachal Pradesh and Jammu & Kashmir also indicate similar position. Such a problem had primarily arisen because of the indiscriminate felling of trees by unscrupulous timber contractors and saw mill owners.

Several states had been diverting the money generated from diversion of forest land for non-forest activities. Only a part of the money thus generated was being used for afforestation purposes. The defaulting states (West Bengal, Orissa, Bihar, Jharkhand, Gujarat, Kerala, Karnataka, Andhra Pradesh, Haryana and Himachal Pradesh) were reportedly achieving the "felling targets satisfactorily but were far behind in achieving the regeneration targets." The compensatory afforestation funds (CAF) to which some the state governments were entitled to receive in lieu of the diversion of the forest area for non-forest purposes was either not being realised or not being spent. The Supreme Court of India in a landmark judgement delivered in early November, 2003 observed that the states were either not realising the CAF or were not "utilising the funds for the purpose for which these were being generated." The apex court has also revised the net value of the forestland to be diverted for non-forest purposes. According to sources in the Ministry of Environment and Forests the quantum of unutilised or unrealised CAF runs into several hundred crores as the states have no mechanism to ensure proper utilisation of funds so generated. In view of the observations made by the apex court that in a number of states the regeneration of compensatory afforestation does not commensurate with the actual felling, the Union Ministry of Forests and Environment has has directed the defaulting states referred to above to temporarily suspend all approved working plans, which include logging of trees. However, other related works, including regeneration and protective afforestation, will continue as before. In fact, the ministry has already suspended working plan of compensatory afforestation of Himachal Pradesh and Haryana.

### Wetlands

This decision brought to an end the plunder of wetlands, homes of migratory birds in the Gujarat State. According to the directions given by the court, the State Government of Gujarat is to set up a Gujarat Wildlife Advisory Board (GWAB) comprising of 20 members (10 representatives from the government and 10 other people). The proposed GWAB is expected to look after and decide on matters related to water bodies and bird sanctuaries in the state as prescribed under the Wildlife Protection Act, 1972. Commenting on the judgement, Lalsinh Raol, an Ahmedabad-based ornithologist said: "It is a landmark judgement that will go a long way in saving wetlands." Timely intervention by the Gujarat High Court in August, 2001 has helped rescuing a wetland and practically thwarted a bid by builders to construct residential buildings on Gopalnagar lake near Kalol, 30km from Ahmedabad.

INDIA TODAY, in its edition dated Ist September, 2001, made the following comments (p.30): "The 2.5 sq km lake is home to a large number of migratory species. Apart from the 5,000-odd flamingoes that inhabit the lakes for up to seven months a year, pelicans, Brahmani ducks and Iranian geese from around the world visit the lake. The issue of its conservation, however, came into the limelight only in March last year when Biren Padhya, a young birdwatcher, took on the might of the constructors' lobby which was keen to build residential quarters after drying the lake. He filed a petition challenging the builders and the state Forest Department for being hand-in-glove with them. At the same time, another bird watcher, Sandip Brahmbhatt, also approached the court. The builders...............claimed that for years the lake had been part of an agricultural land and that the area figured in the Ahmedabad Urban Development Authority's (AUDA) residential plan. But people living around the lake contended that Gopalnagar lake was perennial till last year, when the builders closed all water inlets to the lake, drained it and gave it for cultivation. Padhya and Brahmbhatt, who painstakingly gathered facts on the lake, produced satellite pictures that showed the presence of lake. The judgement has now brought into focus the dubious role of government agencies like the Forest Department and urban development authorities. The question this case has raised is whether the Forest Department is doing its duty of protecting the environment or whether it has become a handmaiden to land sharks...............The court has now directed the state government to ask AUDA to revise its development plans in order to ensure the safety of the wetlands. It has ruled that the revised plans should undergo the scruitiny of GWAB, which has to report on the Gopalnagar case to the court within two months. Ahmedabad has 125-odd lakes 40 years ago, of which only 12 remain. But their plunder has continued, particularly after the January 26 quake when more than 100 buildings either collapsed because they were built on soft surfaces created after reclaiming lakes or were demolished later for safety reasons. The decision augurs well for the protection of what is left in the state, which none other than Salim Ali – India's most famous ornithologist- called the 'kingdom of migratory birds'."

The arificially created Sukhna lake of Chandigarh had been losing its depth and shrinking in its area due to deposition of silt and other sediments being brought from the surrounding fragile hills which constitute part of the Siwalik Group of rock formations consisting essentially of sandstones, shales and conglomerates. In the controversy pertaining to the decision of UT Administration Chandigarh to raise level of the Sukhna lake Chandigarh by 2 feet, the Punjab & Haryana High Court on 26th July, 2003 directed the Chief Engineers of Punjab, Haryana and the UT Administration to ensure that the water levels of the Sukhna lake does not rise beyond the level stipulated by the BBMB. This decision of the court was welcomed by the citizens of Chandigarh keeping in view the safety and future of the lake as the raising of the crest level of lake by 2 feet could pose a danger to the whole structure. The raising of the crest level could also result in increase in silt deposits on the bed of the lake. The existing (designed) pond level of the lake is 1159 feet, whereas the level at top of the gates of the regulator is 1160 feet. Commenting on the subject, A.S.Prashar Wries (Tribune, 29th July, 2003, p. 3): "In the case of Sukhna lake, the administration has been toying with different solutions, including desilting operations through manual operations, mechanical desilting, wet dredging and finally, raising of the crest by about 2 feet on which the radial gates of the lake rest. When the administration announced the plan to raise the crest, objections were raised by experts besides a great hue and cry by the ge neral public who pointed out that this was not a safe way because it could endanger the safety of the wall and other structure. But the administration went ahead and spent about Rs 15 lakh to build the crest. The high court verdict means that all that money has been spent for nothing."

## Mining

The indiscriminate mining and quarrying activities in different parts of the country, especially in the Himalayas has its impact on ecology and environment degradation. People have been approaching the government and judiciary from time to time complaining against the excessive mining or over exploitation of mineral resources under the pretext of development and economic growth by adopting unscientific techniques and thereby disturbing the overall ecological balance of the regions involved in such mining activities. It has also been pointed out through petitions and Public Interest Litigation that the state governments concerned are not taking serious note of the disturbing ecological balance and are not observing the directions given to them by Directive Principles of the State Policy (Article 48-A, etc). In addition, these activities are having heavy toll on the forest wealth in the form of deforestation, soil erosion, polluting the river and underground water, drying up of natural springs, causing instability to the hill slopes resulting in large scale landslides. Such mining activities have also left imprints of many other kinds having direct and indirect affect on the environment of the region affecting the day to day life of the local inhabitants of the area. The conditions were getting bad to worst with increasing limestone mining and quarrying activities, both legal and illegal, in the Dehradun-Mussoorie areas of Uttaranchal and adjoining Sirmour District of Himachal Pradesh. The environment and ecological balance of the entire region was getting disturbed. A group of citizens and the Rural Litigation and Entitlement Kendra wrote to the Supreme Court of India against the limestone mining activity pointing out its adverse affect resulting in denuding the hills of the famous tourist resort of Mussoorie. Removal of trees and forest cover resulted in increased soil erosion and landslides. The petitioners brought to the notice of the court the fact that the mining and quarrying operations being carried out in the entire Dehra Dun-Mussoorie hill range are having adverse impact on the ecology and environment of the entire region and pleaded for the directions for these operations to be stopped immediately to protect the healthy environment of the region and to safeguard the public health of the people living in this area. This letter was treated as writ petition by the Court under Art.32 of the constitution in view of the fact that the mining activity affecting the ecology, environment, etc. involves violation of right to life and personal liberty under article 21 of the constitution. In this case which concerned primarily regarding the working of the limestone quarries in the Dehradun-Mussoorie areas, the Supreme Court of India constituted an expert committee (Bhargava Committee) to assist the court on some technical issues raised in the petition. The Court on the basis of report submitted by this committee ordered the closure of a number of limestone quarries and observed (Rural Litigation and Entitlement Kendra, Dehradun V State of U.P., AIR 1985, SC 652-53 and 1259):

"This is the first case of its kind in the country involving issues relating to environment and ecological balance and the questions arising for consideration are of grave moment and significance not only to people residing in the Mussoorie Hill range but also in their implications to the welfare of the generality of people, living in the country. We are already of the view that so far as the limestone quarries classified in category "C" in the Bhargava Committee Report are concerned which have already been closed down under the directions of the Bhargava Committee should not be allowed to be operated. If the lessee of these limestone quarries have obtained any stay order will stand dissolved and if there are any subsisting leases in respect of any of these limestone quarries they shall stand terminated without any liability against the State of Uttar Pradesh. If there are any suits or writ petitions for continuation of expired or unexpired leases in respect of any of these limestone quarries pending they will stand dissolved (AIR 1985, SC 955 at 1654 para 4)."

As a consequence of the orders passed by the court large number of persons working in the limestone quarries had to lose their jobs due to closure of limestone quarries. The unemployment thus created posed serious hardship to the lessees. The Court was conscious of this fact and as such stressed the need of reconciling the development versus conservation of environment. While issuing directions for the closure of various limestone quarries, the Supreme Court kept in view the good and healthy environment of the area as can be made out from the following observations of the Court while issuing orders in the petition referred to above (M.K.Ramamurthey, "Environment as a Public Interest Cause: The Case of Doon Valley" in Bandopadhyay et al. (Ed.) India's Environment: Crisis and Responses, 241-44, 1985):

"this would undoubtedly cause hardship to them, *but it is a price that has to be paid for protecting and safeguarding the right of people to life in healthy environment with minimal disturbance of ecological balance and without avoidable hazard to them* and to their cattle, homes and agricultural land and undue affectation of air, water and environment".

In addition to the above, the Court made following observations in its orders reflecting its concern towards ecological balance of the region under reference and also stressing the fact that development is not antithetical to environment:

" We are not oblivious of the fact that natural resources have got to be tapped for the purpose of the social development but one cannot forget at the same time that tapping of the resources have to be done with requisite attention and care so that ecology and environment may not be affected in any serious way, there may not be depletion of water resources and long term planning must be undertaken to keep up the national wealth. It has always to be remembered that these are permanent assets of mankind and are not intended to be exhausted in one generation."

Commenting on the hardship to be caused to the workers of the quarries to be effected by the closure order, the Court observed (p.656):

"The consequence of this order made by us would be that the lessees of limestone quarries which have been directed to be closed down permanently under this order or which may be directed to be closed down permanently after consideration of the report of the Bandopadhayay committee would be thrown out of the business in which they have invested large sums of money and expanded considerable time and effort...... However, in order to mitigate their hardship, we would direct the Government of India and the State of Uttar Pradesh that whenever any other area of the state of Uttar Pradesh is thrown open for grant of limestone or dolomite quarrying, the lessees who are displaced as a result of this order shall be afforded priority in grant of lease of such areas......We are conscious that as a result of this order made by us, the workman employed in the limestone quarries which have been directed to be closed down permanently under this order or which may be directed to be closed down permanently after consideration of the report of the Bandyopadhyay committee, will be thrown out of employment and even those workman who are employed in the limestone quarries which have been directed to be closed down temporarily pending submission of schemes we would, therefore, direct that immediate steps shall be taken for reclamation of the areas forming part of such limestone quarries with the help of already Eco-task force of the Department of Environment, Government of India and the workman who are thrown out of employment in consequence of this order shall, as far as, practicable and in the shortest possible time, be provided employment in the afforestation and soil conservation programme to be taken up in this area."

In M.V.Sharma V Bharat Electricity Ltd (AIR, 1987 SC 1792), the Supreme Court of India laid down guidelines for the protection of workers health and held that living in polluted environment endangers the very life of human beings, animals and plants. The Supreme Court of India has ordered the closure of certain limestone quarries on the ground that there were serious deficiencies regarding safety and hazards in them, that mining activity has to be carried on to the extent it is necessary in the economic, interest of the defence of the country as also for safeguarding on the foreign exchange position (Rural Litigation and Entitlement Kendra V State of U.P., AIR 1987,SC 359).The observations made by the Court as referred to above clearly reflects its concern for sustainable development.

In addition to the above the Supreme Court of India also directed the government to file affidavit of responsible authority as to whether keeping in view the broader principles of environment, ecology, environment protection and safeguards, anti-pollution measures, it is in the interest of the society that the economic and defence requirements should be met by import or by tapping other alternate indigenous sources or mining activity in the area should be permitted to the limited extent (AIR,1987 SC.2426). It may not be out of context to refer to the case Ambika Quarry Works V. State of Gujarat, AIR 1987, SC 1073 where the court dealt with the question as to " how to strike balance between the need of exploitation of the mineral resources lying hidden in the forests and the preservation of the ecological balance and to arrest the growing environment deterioration."

In another case (Rural Litigation and Entitlement Kendra V State of U.P., AIR1988 SC 2187and AIR 1989 SC 594), the Supreme Court of India imposed total ban on the operation of mining activity in certain areas of Dehradun-Mussoorie region on the ground of environment protection. In an exceptional case, the Supreme Court of India (AIR 1991 SC 2216; (1991) 3 SCC 347) allowed a mine to operate until the expiry of lease as exceptional case on undertaking by the lessee that land taken on lease would be subjected to afforestation by him. The lessee violated the directions of court regarding afforestation and damage caused to the environment of the area affected by mining activity. Keeping in view the principle of ' polluter pays' the Court directed the lessee concerned to pay Rs.Three Lacs to meet the expenditure towards afforestation program of the area damaged by the lessee. The Court also issued direction for the supervision of the afforestation program by the monitoring committee which had earlier been constituted by the Court.

The orders imposing ban on the limestone quarrying had its impact on the cement factory of the Doon Valley. The Supreme Court did not permit this cement factory to run in this valley as it had directed to restore the Doon Valley to its original character and for its declaration as non-industrial. However, the court asked the government for providing an alternate site for the shifting of the cement factory of the petitioner from the Doon Valley.

A public interest litigation was filed in 1987 in the Himachal Pradesh High Court by an illiterate housewife (Kinkari Devi) belonging to Ghato village in Sangrah valley, about 62 Km from Nahan in Sirmour District of Himachal Pradesh for the closure of mines in the Sangrah valley. In her petition, Kinkari Devi alleged that heavy unscientific and uncontrolled limestone quarrying being carried by more than 100 lessees and some illegal persons in the Sirmour District has caused considerable damage to the hills of the region and is posing danger to its ecology and environment. The petitioner requested the court for issuing of direction for stopping the limestone mining operation by blasting of the hills in the Sirmour District permanently as this is polluting the entire area and is proving hazardous to the adjoining lands, water resources, pastures, forests, wild life, ecology, environment and inhabitants of the area. According to the petitioner thousands of the trees in the area have been cut, water-borne and other diseases have increased in the region and even birds and animals, including livestock, were perishing. Citing the case of Sangrah valley, she pointed out that as a consequence of unscientific blasting and mining activity undertaken by eight mines located across the valley, the entire region was experiencing frequent landslides, mountains were getting denuded and water sources polluted. I The petitioner also requested for the appointment of a commission to assess the damage caused to the environment, ecology, natural resources and to the inhabitants of the area as a consequence of the uncontrolled quarrying of the limestone by the respondents who may be directed to pay the compensation to the affected persons. The state government conceded the fact that the mining operations, are in fact, disturbing the environment of the area where quarrying is being carried out. The Himachal Pradesh High Court constituted a high powered committee to visit the area affected and to submit report within stipulated period. The author (VJG) happened to be non-official member on this committee. The committee after visiting all the limestone mines in the Sirmour District submitted detailed report to the Court. On the basis of this report and keeping in view the judgement of the Supreme Court of India in the Dehradun-Mussoorie area, the Himachal Pradesh High Court pointed out that the limestone mining in the area under reference will involve violation of articles 14,21, 48-A and 51A(g) if a just balance is not struck between development and environment by proper tapping of natural resources. The High Court observed (p.8):

"There is both a constitutional pointer to the state and the constitutional duty of the citizens not only to protect but also to improve the environment and to preserve and safeguard the forests, the flora and fauna, the rivers and the lakes and the other water resources of the country. The neglect or failure to abide by the pointer or to perform duty is nothing short of a betrayal of the fundamental law, which the state and indeed every Indian, high or low, is bound to uphold and maintain."

The Court issued an interim direction to the State Government to set up a committee to examine the issue of proper granting of mining lease and the necessity of granting leases keeping in view the protection of environment (Kinkri Devi V. State, AIR 1988 H.P. 4). The Court issued directions that mining operations should be stopped immediately and no lease be either granted or renewed till the committee submits its report.

The Himachal Pradesh High Court on 19th May, 2003 took a serious note of the allegation of illegal mining being done in Jandur village of Baijnath subdivision. Taking action on the letter written by the president of the Mahila Mandal, Jhandpur, and representatives of some panchayats, the High Court issued notices to the Secretary Home, Director of Industries, Deputy Commissioner, Kangra, State Geologist and District Mining Officer, Kangra, and directed them to file a reply within five weeks. The petitioner had alleged for extraction of sand and grit in illegal and unscientific manner in connivance of the Mining Department.

In a significant decision taken on 5th September, 2003, the Himachal Pradesh Government accepted the recommendations of the committee constituted by the government under the regional controller, Indian Bureau of Mines, Dehradun, to study the environmental impact of mines falling in the unsuitable zones of Sirmour district. The government also decided to reopen limestone mining in the district after strict compliance of the norms and measures suggested by the committee.

Expressing her anguish over the illegal mining being carried on by the mining mafia despite court ruling said (Hindustan Times, 22.3.2004, p. 12): "In blatant violation of the Himachal Pradesh High Court's stay order in 1966 the mining mafia began reckless blasting in the fragile environs of the Trans-Giri just two months after the ruling......people need to come forward to fight against the mining mafia. I want to see the mines closed".

The Himachal Pradesh High Court in its decision on 2nd June, 2004 issued directions to all District Magistrates, SP's and mining officers of the state stating that they would be held responsible if illegal, unscientific and indiscriminate mining took place in their respective districts. A Division Bench of the Court further directed that the policy formulated by the state under the directions of the High Court be implemented in letter and spirit. The order came on a petition filed by the Bhakra Beas Management Board (BBMB) for the management of silt and other environment related issues. The Court had earlier directed the Central Pollution Control Board to constitute a committee to suggest an action plan for the management of silt and other environment-related issues with respect to the hydel project of the BBMB. Following the directions, a committee was constituted, that submitted its interim report and sought time till October, 2004 to submit its final report. Taking serious view of unscientific mining the Court observed that if any incidence of illegal mining, was brought to its notice, DMs, SPs and mining officers would be liable to be procceded against for contemt of Court.

Sub-Divisional Magistrate (SDM), Kharar in the Ropar District of Punjab reported illegal mining of sand along the Siswan rivulet (stream) to the Deputy Commissioner, Ropar.The stream passes through villages of Sohali, Rakoli, Teur, Jhingra, Kherpur, Mullanpur and used to wreak havoc along its course due to overflowing in rainy season. To deal with this natural calamity and to prevent destruction of its banks, the government had constructed strong bundhs (kutcha dam - Siswan Dam) on the northern and southern ends of the Siswan stream at the distance of 700 metres. To earn revenue under provisions of the Mining Act, the Mining Department of the State gives annual contracts for mining of sand, stones, minerals from the river bed produced from natural resources. Illegal mining of sand from the root areas of the dam resulted in causing major breach in Siswan rivulet bundh near Thhaska village in August, 2004 leading to heavy loss in several villages of Kharar sub-division. This breach had also led to increase in flow of water manifold in SYL canal, which had developed major breach near Rajpura in Patiala causing heavy destruction. It may be pointed out that mining within the radius of 200 feet of the rivulet/dam was prohibited by the Deputy Commissioner and to check illegal act of mining, mining guards were deputed on the sites. In his report, the SDM established that presently the Siswan rivulet was flowing along the southern end and the area from where mining contractor was undertaking mining of sand falls within 200 feet radius, following which the bundh has weakened posing flood threat in the area thereby causing heavy loss in the affected villages. SDM held Mining Department responsible for allowing the continuation of the illegal act and recommended the cancellation of contract of mining contractor involved in illegal mining.

The excavation of 'Cheja Pathar' from the area falling within the limits of 'protected forest land' was considered by the Rajasthan High Court as non-forest activity. According to the Court any activity which involved cleaning of forest land or portion thereof for any purpose other than afforestation is a non-forest activity. The Court agreed with the decision of the Forest Department in stopping the lease holder from excavation of 'Cheja Pathar' from the mine situated within the forest area (Ratan Lal Sharma v Forest Department Rajasthan and others, AIR 1987 Raj 129).

The decision regarding refusal for renewal of mining lease for minor mineral (black trap) at village Morai of Taluka Pardi in the Valsad District of Gujarat by the Forest Department was upheld by the Supreme Court of India as the renewal of the lease was likely to lead further deforestation of the area (Ambica Quarry Works v State of Gujarat Air 1987 SC 1073). In a similar case the Andhra Pradesh High Court upheld the decision of the Forest Department in refusing renewal of mining lease to excavate iron ore in one of the village of Kukool District of Andhra Pradesh (B.V.Joshi v State of Andhra Pradesh, AIR 1989 AP 122). In another case Andhra Pradesh High Court made it clear that neither the State Government nor any other authority has powers to accord permission for use of any forest land for non-forest activities without the prior approval of the Government of India (Anupam Minerals Ltd v Union of India AIR 1986 AP 225).

Another glaring example of vandals being busy blasting our mountains can be observed within an hour's drive from New Delhi – Surajkund and the hot water springs at Sohna in Haryana. The boulder-strewn beauty with thorny flowering bushed of rocky escarpment (Aravalli hills) of Sohna are no longer visible. The hills of the area have been dynamited and reduced to rubble.

The Supreme Court of India directed the Government of Rajasthan not to permit degradation of natural environment by authorising the mining operation in the protected area of 'Sariska Natural Forest' (Tarun Bharat Singh v Union of India and others AIR 1992 SC 514).

In a case pertaining to stone crushers situated in the 'abadi area' resulting in causing potential health hazards, the Punjab & Haryana High Court held (Ishwar Singh v State of Haryana, AIR 1996 P.& h 30):

" (i) The stone-crushers must be shifted from abadi to earmarked areas within a period of one month positively failing which business may be closed down and licences may be withdrawn/cancelled by the State Govt.

(ii) That the citizens of the area are authorised to prefer

their claims for grant of compensation if they have suffered any harm or loss due to the pollution caused by the crushers in the area."

In 2001, citizen's organisaions moved the Supreme Court of India and got an order to ban the destruction of Aravalli range – the oldest range of hills in our country and home to hundreds of species of flora and fauna. The court passed strictures against the state governments concerned, named firms and people in powerful positions responsible for defiance of orders.

The vast cave created by mining in the world famous Makrana marble mines is posing serious problem for the residents living above the famed mines as they are beginning to find themselves perched atop the cave created by unscientific mining and improper waste disposal. The people living in 1500 houses in a colony built over the exploding marble mines of Makrana suffer from strange infirmity as they reportedly experience ten to fifteen earthquakes daily, all caused due to illegal underground mining being carried out at a depth of 50 to 70 metres. At most places mining has been done by undercutting and there are large overhangs, which makes them very unsafe. The miners dig verically to a certain depth, then allegedly dig horizontally as a result of which houses built above the cave caused due to mining have begun to crack. The mining at places is reported having reached just below the Jodhpur-Delhi railway track which is being used by several superfast trains, including Jaisalmer-Delhi Intercity Express, Palace on Wheels, Jodhpur-Sawai Madhopur Intercity Express etc. It may be pointed out that violation of mining norms had earlier led to collapse of the Makrana-Parbatsar railway track a few years ago. According to Railway and State's rules, mining activity is not to be permitted within a distance of 45 to 50 metres of the railway track. In contradiction to these norms and rules, the mining at Makrana has reached to within 8 metres of Jodhpur-Delhi track in some places. Moreover, the method adopted by quarry operators does not comply with the Metalliferous Mines Regulations (MMR), 1961 which are applicable to every mine of whatever description other than a coal or an oil mine. The inquiry instituted by the State Department of Mines and Geology found two mines (which fall in the Brown Range) violating prescribed norms and concluded that a tragedy was waiting to happen on these tracks. According to D.M. Surana, MBM Engineering College, Jodhpur, whenever, the State Directorate of Mines and Geology (DMG) had ordered closing the mines either due to unsafe conditions or because of close proximity to the railway track, the mine owners have gone to courts and "in certain cases stay orders have also been granted" (Sunday Hindustan Times, 27th July, 2003, p. 11).

Rattan Singh and two others of Dev Dhae village in Yamunanagar district of Haryana filed petition against Union of India, State of Haryana and Director of Mines & Geology, Haryana and others, seeking directions for cancellation of lease for mining of minor minerals adjoining the Yamuna river banks up to Kalanaur village. In his petition, the petitioner submitted that if mining were not stopped, it would destroy the greenery and the agricultural land in the area. The petitioner also pointed out that the illegal mining threatened villages near the embankment of the river (Times of India, 25.3.2003, p. 6; Hindustan Times, 25.3.2003, p. 2; Tribune, 25.3.2003, p. 4). It may be pointed out Aravalli range constitutes a 'water-shed' and is the source of 'several seasonal streams'. The mining in the entire belt has adversely affected the natural drainage system, recharging of the ground water table, rapid dwindling of trees and an increase in the pollution levels in the area. A survey conducted by the London-based Environmental Investigation Agency has revealed that the key tiger habitat in Rajasthan's Jamwah Ramgarh Wildlife Sanctuary is under serious threat. In addition, quarrying for talc and marble in the area is also causing severe hardship to local farmers (Tribune, 20.3.2004, p. 10).

An editorial published under the title "Plunder of Aravalli Hills" pertaining to banning of all mining activity in the eco-fragile Aravalli range made the following observations (Tribune, 22.XI.2002, p. 10):

"The Supreme Court has banned all mining activity in the

entire Aravalli range falling in Haryana and Rajasthan. Welcome as it is, the order will hurt the well-entrenched business-political interests, particularly in Haryana where the government had not just failed to stop the widespread mining, much of it being illegal, but actually defended it. The reason was the mining mafia engaged in the cash-generating business included powerful politicians of all shades. A large part of the Aravalli area has forests protected by the Environment (Protection) Act. The Act provides that the forest land cannot be put to any non-forest use like mining. The mine-owners used to get permission for mining in a small part free from forests and then ransack the entire area in the absence of any monitoring agency. From New Delhi to Mount Abu the Aravalli hills have been denuded of vegetation and plundered indiscriminately for sand and silica, which are used in construction activity. The the Gurgaon-Manesar-Faridabad area a boom in construction activity had fuelled stone and sand mining. A concerned Supreme Court had on May 6 this year (2002) slapped a similar ban on a 5-km stretch in the Delhi-Gurgaon area and appointed a committee to study and repair the damage to the hills and the environment. The SC-appointed Bhure Lal committee recommended 'tighter and constant monitoring of the area by a central government agency" as highly placed and powerful individuals were involved. This was a well-deserved indictment of the Haryana Government.

The Haryana claim that the ban on mining will cause immense financial loss is based on short-term considerations. The social and environment costs of mining are no less significant. A study of the Central Pollution Control Board has found that mining has lowered the watertable in the affected Delhi and Haryana areas. The shrinking forest area of Aravalli will disturb the environmental balance. The quality of air goes down, affecting the health of the residents in the area. The noise pollution caused by stone crushers and blasters is beyond tolerable limits. Besides, trucks carrying construction materials like sand and stones and driven by ill-trained drivers are serious traffic hazards. So indifferent has been the state administration to the environment and health aspects of mining that it sleeps over reports of massive mining going on right under the nose in the Ghaggar river bed. The minimum that the state government can do is to undertake without delay water-harvesting measures in the areas where the watertable has declined alarmingly."

The Supreme Court of India took umbrage at the Haryana Government's order issued on 29th November, 2002 confining the ban on only the notified forest areas in the hill range and the state government was forced to issue an order imposing a blanket ban on mining being carried out in the Aravalli range. The Apex Court took exception to the Haryana Government's interpretation of its directive and asked the government in its directions on 9th December, 2002 to implement the blanket ban on mining in the Aravalli within 72 hours and file a compliance report in the court.

The Supreme Court of India in its decision on 16th December, 2002 amended its earlier order that had imposed a blanket ban on all kinds of mining activities in the 250 km in the Aravalli mountain ranges of Rajasthan and Haryana. The court has now allowed legal mining operations in Rajasthan's Aravalli area but the stone quarrying and crushing operations in Haryana would remain suspended. According to the decision mining in Rajasthan would be permitted in areas where specific prior permission had been obtained under the Forest Conservation Act and the Environment Protection Act. After the modification in the court orders, mining activities in Rajasthan were resumed as also the seven quarries (Ferozepur Rajput, Bajida Pahari, Begawali, Godawali, Ransika, Sarohi and Khori) in Faridabad district which did not require the mandatory Environment Management Plan (EPM). Sand, silica and stone are now being quarried from several small hillocks in the remote villages of Faridabad to feed the huge construction industry in the Faridabad, Gurgaon and the Capital region of Delhi. These quarries were earlier regarded as minor by the mining industry, but gained importance following the modification of the Supreme Court order. As a result of the large scale quarrying activity in the region, one can see the gigantic scars in the Aravalli mountains. Till recently, what were once hills about 2 km in diameter and hundreds of feet high have now turned into pits filled with water. It may be pointed out that the Punjab Minor Mineral Concession Rules, 1964, as applicable to Haryana, provide that if sny minor mineral not specified in the lease is discovered within the lease area, the lessee shall report about the discovered mineral without delay to the government and shall not sell such mineral without obtaining the lease thereof. If he fails to apply for a lease within six months of the discovery of the minor mineral, the government or its authorised officer may give the lease in respect of such mineral to any other person. But this rule is applicable to only those mines which are given on lease and not auctioned.

The Supreme Court of India took a serious view over the continuing mining operations in the eco-fragile hills in Haryana and warned the state and the contractors of "serious consequences" if such activities were carried on despite its order imposing a complete ban. It took exception to the fact that the high-powered committee assigned the task of filing a status report on the ground situation could not do so for failure of authorities concerned in Haryana to provide relevant documents. A Bench comprising Justices Y.K.Sabharwal and H.K.Seema on 24th January 2003 said: "We are extremely concerned that illegal mining activities, both major and minor, are going on unabated till Sunday last. We are stll more disturbed by the fact that this is happening despite ban order imposed on November 25 and December 16 and affidavits filed by the Deputy Commissioners of Gurgaon, Faridabad and range police officers stating that no mining activity was going on in the prohibited areas of Aravakki hills. If the Court orders were not implemented in letter and spirit, serious consequences will follow."

Perturbed at the statement of lawyer Ranjit Kumar, who is assisting the court in the matter, that around 6,000 truck loads of minerals have been transported out of the state after the ban was imposed, the Court asked the state government to file a status report on the ground situation within two days i.e by 26th January, 2003.

The Centre on 5th March, 2003 informed the Supreme Court

of India that it has withdrawn the power it had vested in the Haryana and Rajasthan governments to grant and renew mining leases for mining major minerals exceeding five hectares in Aravalli hills. Henceforth, all mining leases for areas more than five hectares would be granted and renewed by the Union Government with mandatory clearance under the Environment (Protection) Act, 1986. The Apex Court was also informed that power for mining leases for areas below five hectares would still vest with the state governments.

The Supreme Court of India in its directions on 16.4.2003 sought two investigative reports on the status of mining in Gurgaon and Faridabad districts of Haryana filed by the Ministry of Environment and Forests and the Central Mine Planning and Design Institute Limited. These reports were sponsored by the Central Pollution Control Board. Relying on these reports, the government told the Apex Court that it had no objection in allowing operations in most of the mines as they complied with the guidelines issued by environment protection authority. Despite agreeing that a comprehensive study of the Aravalli hill range was required due to its ecological importance, the Centre said 71 mines in Gurgaon and 10 in Faridabad could be allowed to resume operations as they have complied with most of the stipulated conditions. Of the 71 mines, 17 were within a five-km belt of the Delhi-Haryana border. The other mines were divided into four more categories and the government said that they could be allowed to operate if they meet the requisite guidelines.

The Supreme Court of India on 1st March, 2003 rejected the Haryana Government's request for an interim direction to its forest and revenue departments for identifying the land to be covered under the foreign-aided plantation projects in Faridabad and Gurgaon districts affected by unregulated mining which has caused havoc on environment. Rejecting the plea by Haryana Government counsel, a bench of the Apex Court said: "You want the court to come to the aid of the state to legalise something without having anything on record. Who knows how much plantation has been done and how much money spent. It has become a lucrative business. Whether the money has been properly spent or has been pocketed by someone else, there is nothing to show it". While reserving its order on public interest litigation (PIL) on the issue of alleged illegal mining in Faridabad and Gurgaon areas, the court said the project for which about Rs 80 crore had been recived from foreign countries, had been going on for the past nine years but the state had failed to put material about it on record. The state is reported to have carried out the plantation work without preparing the records.

A mafia is allegedly making an attempt to undermine the ban imposed by the Supreme Court of India on the mining activity in the Aravalli range falling in Faridabad and Gurgaon districts. As already referred to earlier in the preceeding pages, the apex court, which had initially imposed a blanket ban on all kinds of mining activities in the Aravalli range, had llater modified its orders to allow mining from those areas which did not require the mandatory environment management plan (EMP). In view of the amended Supreme Court orders, the mining activities in Rajasthan restarted, but in Faridabad and Gurgaon districts the mines remained closed. It is reported that seven quarries (Ferozepur Rajput and Bajida Pahari located near Palwal, Begawali, Godawali, Ransika, Sarohi and Khori) in Faridabad, which did not require the EPM, also reopened. These quarries were considered to be unimportant and minor by the industry before the Supreme Court imposed the ban. However, these quarries assumed importance after the apex court modified its orders. It may be pointed out that the Punjab Minor Mineral Concession Rules, 1964, as applicable to Haryana, provide that if "any minor mineral not specified in the lease is discovered within the lease area, the lessee shall report the discovered mineral without delay to the government and shall not dispose of such minor mineral without obtaining a lease thereof. If he fails to apply for such a lease within six months from the discovery of the minor mineral, the government or its authorised officer may give the lease in respect of such mineral to any other person." However, in case of these quarries which are not given on contract (against the system of lease), the rules do not provide for allowing the contractor to take out any minor mineral which is not specified in the contract.

The Punjab and Haryana High Court on 13th May, 2003 directed that a team be deputed to assess the loss caused due to illegal mining undertaken in Angpur village of Faridabad district from 1989 to 2001. The HC also directed the Haryana DGP and Secretary of State Mines and Geology Department to file affidavits detailing the efforts made to take action against persons responsible for illegal mining in Anangpur village. In their detailed orders, the Judges observed:

"In compliance with the earlier orders, the agency has submitted an investigation report. It was opened in the presence of the counsel for the parties and the report has been pursued. We have also heard the submissions of counsel for the agency Rajan Gupta and Investigating Officer Ajit Singh. The Officer states that he had contacted the Institute authorities for the evaluation of the loss caused on account of illegal mining in the village between 1989 and 2001, but due to some reason the authorities have not been able to make assessment. In view of the fact that the state exchequer has been put to loss of hundreds of crores of rupees due to illegal mining, urgent action is required to take in the matter in our opining irreparable damage has been caused to the environment and ecology of the area. Therefore, we deem it proper to request the Director to get in touch with the Dhanbad Institute head"

In a public interest litigation (PIL), an environment activist lawyer pointed out that the Apex Court had put a ban on mining activities and pumping of ground water in and from an area up to 5-km from the Delhi-Haryana border in the Haryana side of the ridge and also Aravalli hill region following the report of Environment Pollution (Prevention and Control) Authority (EPPCA), headed by Mr Bhure Lal. It is true that the haphazard mining in the fragile Aravalli hill region of Haryana and Rajasthan comprising Gurgaon, Faridabad and Alwar districts, had badly affected the natural drainage system and the ground water table of the entire region. This has been stated in a study report on the impact of mining in the

Aravalli range on ground water, placed before the Supreme Court of India by the Chandigarh-based Western Region Central Ground Water Board which conducted a repeated survey of the entire area on court's direction. Taking a serious view of the Haryana Government allowing large scale illegal mining in Faridabad and Gurgaon districts, a Bench of the Supreme Court had directed the Union Ministry of Environment and Forest, to place before it by April 24, 2003, the two other study reports about the impact of mining in the region. The Bench was not also satisfied with the affidavit of the Union Environment and Forest Ministry, which said the "mining operations may be permitted subject to imposition of additional conditions by the CGWB wherein clearances have been issued by the Union Ministry of Mines and the state government". The study by the institute was ordered by the Apex Court in sponsorship with the Central Pollution Control Board to assess the impact of large scale illegal mining on environment, ecology and ground water table. The Environment Ministry has stated that the Ministry of Mines in 2001 had delegated its powers to states for granting approval of mine plans and renewal of mining schemes for 29 categories of non-metalliferous mines.

The Supreme Court of India on 18th March, 2004 declined to vacate its stay on haphazard mining activities in the region, including an area up to 5 km from the Delhi-Haryana border. The court appointed a monitoring committee to assess the overall impact of legal or illegal mining in the region and the ways to restore ecological balance in the area. The Court in its directions said: "The (stay) order of May 6, 2002 as clarified herein cannot be vacated or varied before consideration of the report of the monitoring committee". The bench also said that it would also consider a total prohibition on mining activities undertaken under stringent conditions in certain areas if the committee ultimately found that it led to an adverse and irreversible effect on the ecology (Hindustan Times, 19.3.2004, p. 3; Tribune, 19.3.2004, p.2). Despite a ban imposed by the Supreme Court of India, illegal mining was reportedly going on in the mountainous area in village Ferozepur Rajput, Tehsil Hathin in Faridabad district of Haryana. In response to a

PIL seeking directions to quash the contract given by the Haryana government to a contractor for mining in this village, the Punjab & Haryana High Court issued notice Haryana Co-Operation Minister Kartar Singh, contractor Ram Avtar and Others on 16th September, 2004. seeking response to the petition where it was alleged that the Haryana Government had by granting the contract for mining, sought to jump the ban imposed by the Apex Court,

The three public representative members of the monitoring committee appointed by the Supreme Court of India, to report on illegal mining in Aravalli hills have strongly opposed the reopening of the mines in specified areas keeping in view the fragile nature of the region (Faridabad, Gurgaon districts of Haryana and Alwar district of Rajasthan). The Committee sent its report in this regard to the Apex Court in early September, 2004. The three members recommended that Union Environment and Forest Ministry's notification regarding saving the Aravalli Hills be extended to the whole of the region to save the fragile hills. According to the three panelists (Tribune, 4th September, 2004, p. 2): "We have seen the bomb-scarred mining landscapes of Faridabad and Gurgaon with their 'horror impact' on this land. We believe it is the duty of all parties concerned to restore these lands to their original shape and look........The money for the restoration of environment of the region should be mobilized from the mine owners and work on the project should be started immediately by involving them." The report of the monitoring committee was considered by the Supreme Court on 2nd September, 2004 and it sought replies from the government agencies and other parties within four weeks.

Commenting on the ban imposed by the Supreme Court of India and the plundering of Aravalli ranges, Ruchika M.Khanna made the following observations (Tribune, 19.X.2004, p. 6):

"Despite the Supreme Court ban on mining in the Aravallis, the mining mafia operating here (Gurgaon and Faridabad districts) is plundering the 250 km long Aravalli mountain ranges, causing irreversible loss to the ecology of the land. Though the officials in the Department of Mines and Geology, Haryana, deny that any illegal mining is taking place, a visit along the Aravalli mountain range, falling in the districts of Gurgaon and Faridabad, reveals otherwise. The mining mafia is undermining modifications in the initial order of the apex court with regard to allowing mining in certain areas, which do not require the mandatory Environment Management Plan (EMP). The mine owners obtain approval for a certain stretch, and then mine indiscriminately. The political patronage to the miners, remote terrain, and dependence of local population on mining as employment, makes monitoring difficult. Several small hillocks in the remote villages in Gurgaon and Faridabad are being plundered for their sand, silica and stone, in order to feed the gigantic construction industry in the two districts of the state, and the national Capital. Till a few years back, what were once hills, hundreds of feet high, are now pits filled with water. All along the mountain range, these deep pits mark the mountain face. It may be noted that the Aravallis form a small watershed in the area. They set off several seasonal streams, which helps recharge the ground water. Indiscriminate mining over the years has led to a sharp fall in the water levels of the area surrounding the Aravallis. The miners operate here in broaddaylight, and a steady fleet of trucks can be seen ferrying the sand, silica and stones from near the narrow roads in the villages of Kotla and Kansali in Gurgaon and Mathepur and Ferozepore Rajput in Faridabad. The flora and fauna on the Aravalli Hills is also a casualty. The forest cover created by the state Forest Department by years of plantation on the Aravallis has almost vanished as a result of illegal mining."

Mining in Khanak quarry of Bhiwani in Haryana was banned on 1st December, 2001 by the district administration. In a letter sent to the Mines Department, the Forest Department has clarified that the hill areas of Khanak -Dadam and Riwasa, etc have not been declared unauthorised for mining works. Earlier the Forest Department had prohibited mining operations in Rawaldhi, Nauranghabad, Loharu, Tosham, Jhumpa, Kairu, Kakdoli sardara, Khariawas, Bhiwani and Zonepal in compliance with the orders of the Supreme Court of India. The largest mining area of Khanak was not included in this prohibition. However, in spite of no prohibition on mining, the district administration had banned operations on December 1, 2002 in this area and appointed duty magistrates to enforce orders. Khanak quarries opened for operations on December 24, 2002.

Holding "uncontrollable greed" responsible for environmental degradation in Rajasthan, the High Court has castigated the pollution control board for hurriedly approving operation of thousands of mines that had been flouting norms all these years. The 23,000 mines of which 18,000 have maximum one acre of area, could operate only after a Supreme Court order in 2002, which recorded no objection given by the Union government, Rajasthan government and environment empowerment committee. They were, however, directed to strictly enforce the environment protection laws. In fact, Chief Justice Anil Dev Singh's judgement reveals that the SC judgement was also violated both by the mine operators and the government in Delhi and Jaipur. It warned "The present generation cannot be allowed to rob nature and deprive the future generation of its bounties." Anguished over the defiance of laws, the bench passed directions to restore the fundamental rights to life and pollution free environment, denied to the citizens due to "illegal" mining (Times of India, 2.XI.2004, p. 4).

The Supreme Court of India on 25th January, 2005 lashed out at the Haryana government for its "complicity" in the unabating illegal mining in Gurgaon district and Aravalli Hill ranges of Haryana despite repeated orders banning such activities in eco-sensitive areas by mining mafia. The apex court issued contempt notices against two senior state government officials. Turning its focus to the Haryana government, the Bench said on November 25, 2002, it was made clear by the court that the DC and IG would be personally responsible for implementation of the order. The Supreme Court Bench asked the counsel to convey to the state government: "even if it wished to protect those indulging in illegal mining activities despite repeated court orders, they will be dealt with". The Bench observed: "Do not force us to deploy paramilitary forces in the area to implement our orders. Despite its clear orders banning all mining activities, the court has been taken for a ride as its order was being defied with the connivance of state government officials. There is limit to tolerating such action". The court also asked the Chief Secretary and the two contemnors to file within three weeks an affidavit stating as to what action had been taken against those who actually carried out the illegal mining rather than the arrest of poor and helpless labourers working at these sites. The Bench asked for giving detailed report as to what "concrete action has been taken against the real responsible persons violating the court order". Warning that strict action would be taken against the two officers if they fail to take corrective measures, the court directed them to file their replies to the contempt notices within three weeks. They were reminded that the responsibility to implement the May 6, 2002 and March 18, 2004 orders imposing ban was cast upon them. When the counsel said no illegal mining was going on, an enraged Justice Y.K.Agarwal pointed at the photographs annexed with the plea showing mining activities on in full swing. Stating that he had seen blasting going on in the area himself while passing through the Delhi-Gurgaon road recently, Mr Justice Agarwal asked: "How can the mining go on without the connivance of officials? Who will check it if they don't take action and implement court orders?. Noticing defiance of its orders and pulling up the Union Environment and Forest Ministry for not filing its report about the "impact" of illegal mining on the ecology of fragile Aravalli Hills, the Bench asked: "Should not such officers be put under suspension? If this is the attitude of officials to the apex court, what could be the state of affairs in implementing the lower courts' orders". Rejecting the contention of the Haryana Government that over 600 FIRs had been registered against persons found violating the court order since November 25, 2002 till date, the Bench said: "prima facie it seems true that illegal mining activities are going unabated and the constitution of a committee to stop it, as mere paper work ". The Aravalli Hills, which extend from Haryana to Rajasthan, act as a natural buffer stopping the Thar desert from expanding towards the northern agricultural plains.

The range has been termed by experts as an eco-sensitive area.

In a petition filed by 20 residents of Naurangpur village against the revival of stone-crusher units which, the petitioners said, had been closed as per a High Court judgent of 1995, a division bench of the Punjab & Haryana High Court while dismissing the petition held: "We've concluded that the writ petitions have not been filed in good faith to genuinely redress any grievance of the inhabitants of Naurangpur village. In another petition, the Punjab & Haryana High Court dismissed petition challenging the operation of stone-crushers in Gurgaon region, outside the Notified Crushing Zone. While dismissing the petition the court observed that the petitions seem to have been filed merely to stall the setting up of new crushers within the given parameters, without genuine grievance. The petitioners in their petition had said that they were aggrieved by the operation of the crushers which posed a threat to environment.

An NGO by the name Wildlife First succeeded in winning a historic and hard battle to safeguard the Kudremukh National Park, by appealing to the courts. In a landmark decision, the Supreme Court of India upheld the sanctity of Kudremukh National Park , saying mining operations of Kudremukh Iron Ore Company Limited (KIOCL) should be wound up by July, 2004. The apex court gave the ruling after hearing the matter at length and on the basis of recommendations of the Central Empowered Committee. The campaign against mining in these rich tropical rainforests, located in one of the world's top biodiversity hotspots was initiated in 1984 through a wildlife survey by scientist Ullas Karanth who detected significant population of globally-threatened lion-tailed monkeys in Kudremukh, leading to the notification of the National Park by Karnataka in 1987. The mining has been destroying the ecosystem by polluting the air and causing damage to the land and water in addition to distrubing the animals.

The Himachal Pradesh High Court in its directions given on 17$^{th}$ September, 2003, directed the state government to close down all the stone crushers in the state. The order came following the failure of the state-level committee to find zones for stone crushers in the state. A Division Bench of the court while taking this decision observed that in past four months the committee even failed in checking or regulating large-scale pollution, of air and noise. On 22nd September, 2003 the H.P.High Court constituted a committee under the chairmanship of a former Chief Secretary of the state, Mr B.C.Negi, to find out whether stone crushers in the state are functioning as per the norms laid down by the state government. The court also directed the Secretary Industry of H.P. to file an affidavit by 24th September, 2003 explaining how many stone crushers are working as per norms. The court directed the committee to give its report within three weeks. The court made it clear that if any stone crusher was found violating the norms, it would not hesitate in closing down such a unit permanently. It may be pointed out that the court had earlier directed the state government to close down 314 stone crushers in the state in the wake of failure of the State Monitoring Committee to submit its report in time before the court. These orders were passed by the court on a public interest litigation.

The H.P.High Court on 24th September, 2003 framed guidelines for the functioning of stone crushers in the state. The court directed the state level five-member committee to look into the guidelines framed and other aspects such as minimum distance conditions from educational institutions, health institutions, district headquarters and national and state highways. A Division Bench of the court directed the crusher owners to approach the Deputy Commissioner of their respective districts in this regard. The Bench also directed the Deputy Commissioners to check the no-objection certificates and lease obtained by the crusher owners. After satisfying all the standards, the Deputy Commissioners would permit the functioning of these units. The Himachal High Court in its orders issued on 20th May, 2004 directed the state government to ensure that not a single stone crushing unit was allowed to operate in the state which was violating the pollution laws as well as other laws. The Bench of the Court directed the Secretary, Industries, to file the compliance report by 18th August, 2004.

The Himachal Pradesh Forest Department and the BBMB have not in a position to resolve the issue over the controversial muck dumping issue in the Suketi khud which falls in the forest area as per provisions of the Indian Forest Act and the law laid down by the Supreme Court of India in various judgements. According to the officials of the state Forest Department, the BBMB is violating the provisions of the Forest Conservation Act, 1980.According to the provisions of this Act, no silt/muck could be dumped in the forest area without the permission the Central Government. However, the BBMB had been throwing silt in the khud which is part of the forest area without permission from the Central Government. In contradiction to this, the BBMB has said that the provisions of the Act does not apply to them as the project was cleared before the Act came into being. The Beas-Sutlej Link Project which was commissioned in 1977, had been throwing silt in the khud by conducting a dredging operation at the balancing reservoir at Sundernagar. The silt-free water is used in the Dehar power house. The silt flow into the Beas after covering 24 km area of khud passing through the Balh valley. The residents of this valley have been complaining that their fertile land is getting destroyed by the silt.

In Punjab, illegal mining by stone crushers in the Gurdaspur district is continuing blatantly, endangering ecology of the area. There are reportedly hundreds of stone crushers in this district and the mining was continuing on both sides of the border of Punjab and Himachal near Pathankot. Most of these crushers are located near or in the Beas and Chaki river beds. According to the mining rules, the stone crushers can only mine stones lying in the river beds. Contrary to these rules most crusher owners are digging the river beds. As a result land along the Beas in Mirthal area is getting eroded and the river is changing course endangering the national highway along the Mukerian – Pathankot road which runs just 200 meters from the Beas banks near Mirthal. Farmers of the area have also been complaining that fertile land was being washed away by the changing course of the river due to mining along the banks. According to the Environment Protection Act, 1986, no stone crushers could be set up within 250 metres of an environmentally sensitive area which includes the natural river banks. However, certain stone crushers are operating right on the river banks or even in the river beds in the case of the Chaki river. One can observe huge trenches (in some cases extending for more than 30 to 40 metres) having been dug up along the banks of Chaki river by the stone crusher owners along the road leading to the new airport of Pathankot, the military hospital and the Air Force station. There remains an earth wall of 3 to 5 meters between the Chaki river and the said installations thereby posing a serious threat of these installations getting flooded in the event Chaki river gets flooded.

It may, however, be pointed out that hardly any of the above referred norms are being observed by the stone crusher owners. It is reported in the media that the police has registered cases under Section 188 of the CrPC against owners of 11 stone crushers carrying out illegal mining in the Chalki river of Gurdaspur district. According to the Chairman of the Punjab Pollution Control Board (PPCB) violation of pollution norms set by the board are being checked (Tribune 1.X.2004, p. 20).

The Jadugoda Uranium Mines of Jharkhand are being exploited for Uranium mining since 1958. These mines provide Uranium to 12 nuclear reactors in the country. Uranium Corporation of India (UCIL), a PSU, extract uranium from these mines at Jadugora. The toxic wastes from mines are dumped near the tailing ponds which have become a source of radiation problem for the people living in the area. Villagers living around such tailing ponds in which uraninite waste is dumped have complained of an increase in cancers, still births and deformities. Approximately 30,000 people (mostly tribals) live in the 15 villages in and around these mines. Many persons from these villages are reported to be suffering from the "radiation - related problems." The Jharkhand Organisation Against Radiation (JOAR) has raised the issue of radiation due to uranium mining in the area and its impact on the environment, health and safety of Jadugora area. The JOAR claims to have organised a health survey of the people of the area living within 11km radius of the tailing dam in the year 1998. It is reported that the results of the survey showed that 47 per cent of women reported disruption in their menstrual cycle and 18 per cent of them stated that they had suffered miscarriage or given birth to still-born babies during the five years period (1993-1998). According to Mr Ghanshyam Birulee, the President of JOAR, "33 women of Talaitand village are reported facing problems in conceiving due to radiation. Children born with deformities are being noticed here." In addition, there are also reports having been published in the media regarding calves born without tails, babies born with deformed limbs and kendu and papaya plants in the area without bearing seeds. This issue is also lying pending before the Supreme Court of India where the state-owned Uranium Corporation India Ltd (UCIL) has filed a counter affidavit denying any health hazards and environmental decay caused due to radiation from the nuclear waste in and around Jadugora (Times of India, 18.4.2000,p.12). A team of scientists from Bhabha Atomic Research Centre (BARC) visited Jadugoda area to study the impact of radiation on people due to mining activity of uranium. According to Dr N.K.Prasad, Civil Surgeon of East Singhbhum District, "BARC has pointed out that levels of radiation in that place is not alarming" (Hindustan Times, 23.5.2000). Commenting on the subject, an editorial published in Times of India under the title "High-risk Radiation" points out (5.X.2001, p. 8):

"We have seen such exposes from time to time – Jadugoda is an example, but such is the mystique and secrecy which surrounds our nuclear establishment that no one dares to demand corrective action. The horror of Jadugoda has been documented extensively. Children in the 15 villages.surrounding the uranium mines show signs of genetic mutation and over 60 per cent of the workers manning the tailing ponds are afflicted with serious ailments like bone, blood and kidney disorders, brain damage, cancer, paralysis, tuberculosis and nausea. Not surprising considering that workers manually handle uranium slurry. Heart-rending pictures of deformed children have been carried in a number of periodicals ans papers, but the management dismisses all this evidence as the fabrication of anti-development lobbies."

The Uranium Corporation of India Limited (UCIL), a nodal government undertaking entrusted with the task of mining uranium for India's nuclear programme, is not functioning in conformity with any national or international safety environment norms. In East Singhbhum district of Jharkhand more than 50,000 persons are reported having been directly affected by high dosage of radioactive contamination. The radioactivity levels in the area is 100 times the laid down standards and thousands of people in the region are suffering from birth defects, congenital deformities, tuberculosis, cancer and other ailments directly associated with exposure to high levels of radioactive radiation. The contamination in the area is at three levels i.e air, water and soil.

It is reported that the Uranium Corporation of India Limited (UCIL) is planning to set up a uranium mining and processing project in Nalgonda district of Andhra Pradesh. Uranium mill tailings and radon (due to decay of Uranium 238) may pose serious health hazards for the workers and residents living in and around the project area. The inevitable discharges from the mine area is likely to harm the Nagarjunasagar and Akkampally reservoir and Gandhi National Park. It may be pointed out that in the US, mill taillings located at active and inactive mill operations are considered to be potential and significant health hazards. Commenting on radioactive spectres that haunt Andhra as Nagarjuna Sagar awaits Uranium mine, S.Anant states (Outlook, September 22, 2003, pp. 32-34):

"Having left a trail of deformed children and unexplained deaths of miners in Jaduguda, Jharkhand, the nuclear establishment is all set to spread the radioactive threat to hundreds of villages in the southern state. The Uranium Corporation of India Limited's (UCIL's) hydro-metallurgical plant in Nalgonda district has attracted the ire of environmentalists who say its proposed open-cast mine abuts the massive Nagarjuna Sagar reservoir. It is feared that radiation – and heavy metal – contaminated storm water run-off from the Uranium mines would find its way into the reservoir. This is likely to impact the entire downstream of the Krishna river basin which caters to over six districts. The processing of the Uranium ore mined at Lambarpur–Peddagattu will be done 18 km away, in a mill at Mallapuram that sits 4 km from another water body, the Akkampally reservoir. The Andhra Pradesh government is laying huge pipelines along a 130 km route to supply water from this reservoir to Hyderabad–Secunderabad and 600 villages most of whose inhabitants are affected by flurosis caused by excessive presence of fluoride in potable water. Having a tailings pond-where radioactive and chemical waste from the mines and the mill will be dumped – close to the rreservoir can be dangerous, fears Eavi Rebbapragda of Mines, Minerals and People, an NGO working for people who inhabit areas with mines. A United Nations Environmental Programme Report of 2001 lists 221 tailings dam 'incidents' the world over. Says M.V.Ramana, research staff member at Princeton University's Programme on Science and Global Security: 'In Jaduguda, Uranium mill tailings have been used to construct houses and roads; UCIL auhorities have not warned the people that these emit radioactive radon and are therefore harmful to the health'. Besides the tailings, the 'rock overburden' – the pressure of tonnes of rock piling up as a result of mining – poses an environmental problem. In Jaduguda, radon-emitting tailings pond was perceived as the key hazard to the villages that surrounded it. Uranium mining generates massive amount of low-level radioactive waste. Once mining begins in Lambarpur – Peddagattu, UCIL also intends to open up Chitral, right in the middle of the tiger reserve. But if J.Rama Rao is to be believed, 'this is against the guidelines of the environment ministry for location of industrial and mining activities around the protected and ecologically sensitive areas, and the provisions of the Wildlife Protection Act, 1972, and Forest Conservation Act, 1980'. The reserve is 6 km away from the proposed mining area and the law prohibits such activity within 25 km of a notified sanctuary."

Reportedly permission for uranium mining near the Rajiv Gandhi Sanctuary will not only contaminate drinking water, but may also lead to further erosion of the tiger's habitat.

The Rescuers can use the skilled manpower if available and also take the help of the local community if required.

Sometimes these rescue materials are not available to the rescue team at the site of emergency. Therefore the rescuers use locally available resources like carrels, tinned cans, tubes etc.

There are various other methods, which would be useful for rescuing the victims, the adequate method of rescue is to be determined depending upon the nature of the casualty, the nature of the injuries and the position in which the casualty is found.

If the community does not have a recent experience to recollect, but still is a potentially vulnerable area the incidence of nearby areas should be discussed. Local knowledge to cope up with the disaster should not be overlooked during these discussions. It is essential to tap information and take it forwards towards a meaningful process during the next step of analysing situations. The important task here is to mobilize community participation through awareness generation techniques by various options. It consists of local elected representative, grass root level government functionaries. NGOs, CBOs, youth clubs and members form the Mahila samities, mobilizing the community for the preparation of the Disaster Management Plan.

# COASTAL ECOSYSTEM AND ENVIRONMENT

Farm pollution of rivers rose in 1988 to a record 4,141 cases reported in England and wales according to a report by the Water Authorities Association and the MAFF, Animal slurry, the main form of farm pollution, is more than 100 times more damaging then untreated sewage, while the liquid from silage is 200 times more damaging. In November 1988, a £50 million package of grants was announced by the Agriculture Minister for stopping farm pollution. Farmers can claim up to half the cost of building or improving facilities for the storage, treatment and disposal of slurry and village effluent.

India has a coastline of more than 7,500km influencing the lives of almost 370 million coastal people with high productivity due to its rich biodiversity and a variety of ecosystems like mangroves, coral reefs, sea grasses, salt marshes, sand dunes, estuaries and lagoons. Oceans are fabric of life and hold the key to sustained life on earth. They are not just treasure of fishes, life saving drugs, new hydrocarbon sources, minerals or other resources but are greatest treasure for harnessing wealth on God's Earth. Main pressures on the coastal zones originates from industry, tourism, urbanisation, aquaculture, fisheries, and growing movement of population of large number of cities and towns along the coastal areas in recent years. The population influx in the coastal areas and anthroporaphic impact has damaged the coastal ecosystem.

Major part of Indian coastline is considered crucible of life as pollution problem along the coastline is more severe due to the megacities (Mumbai, Calcutta, Chennai, Mangalore, Kochi, Vishakhapattnam, etc) where a huge amount of municipal waste (including garbage) is generated because of the high population density and this waste reaches the sea through creeks, streams, rivers, underground acquifers and even pipelines. In addition, coastal pollution is also caused through air in the form of acid rain, auto pollution, industrial pollution, particles from air borne heavy toxic metals and organic chemicals (including fertilisers, pesticides, herbicides, etc). In Mumbai alone, 1600 million litres of untreated sewer reaches the sea everyday. This in turn affects various species of fish, molluscs, algae and other marine resources that play a vital part in the Indian economy. Ecology of oceans and coastal areas depends on how we use waters and rivers. According to the National Institute of Oceanography, fish, prawn and shrimp yield across the Kerala coast has declined by 25 per cent due to coastal pollution. We should stop over fishing and make efforts to protect fish habitat in oceans. Petroleum and industrial hazardous waste being discharged into oceans are one of the main causes that adversely affect the sea life. Oil drilling along the coast or off-shore regions need to be stopped. There seems to be an invisible destruction along Indian coasts due to shrimp farming for export. The other anthropogenic factors which have impact in disturbing the coastal ecosystem include disposal of untreated domestic and industrial wastes, development activities like construction of ports, harbours, beach resorts, dredging for navigation, ocean traffic, exploration of minerals, oil and gas, and natural phenomena. Increasing flows of sewage and industrial wastes are destroying fishes and killing entire biological communities. In addition, rapid development in India and adjoining countries of South Asia (Pakistan and Srilanka) have also affected coastal resources, leading to negative trends in the long term with regard to their sustainability. Nearly 228 million people sustain themselves on fishing and agriculture along the 7,500km of bountiful sundrenched land. A paper published in the British weekly *Nature* (Times of India, 30[th] June, 2000) by a group of scientists from United

States, Scotland, Sweden and the Philippines have warned that aquaculture is a "contributing factor to the collapse of fisheries stocks worldwide." According to them fish farming, promoted as a smart way to help feed the worlds surging population, is having a disastrous impact on the environment and on stocks of wild fish. They are of the opinion that this is mainly because huge amounts of seafish, especially anchovies and mackerel, are being scooped from the oceans and ground up into meal to feed penned fish. As a result, the farms, especially those specialising in carnivorous fish and shrimp, are themselves facing serious environment consequences. They destroy habitat in fragile tropical areas, devastation non-native species, encourage the spread of fish disease and cause pollution, in the form of fish effluent.

According to Ramasamy (2002): "Coastal zones always remain active as multivariate geologic/geomorphic processes viz. Tectonic, riverine, coastal and aeolian act in varying degrees and duration in space and time. As such various processes act in different permutations and combinations in different segments of the coasts where various landforms are in the process of evolution. Further, as the coastal zones form the junction between the continents and the oceans, even mild land movements cause visible modifications in the land-water distribution in the coastal zones. As such coastal geomorphic features stand as a testimony for such geologic/ geomorphic processes, past sea level changes, palaeo-flood cycles etc. Therefore, the geoscientists always have a great attraction for studying the coastal zones. Of course, the optimal utilization of the coastal resources by providing sustainable development and protection from natural disasters is one of the driving forces for man's interests in the coastal areas."

The saltiness of the ocean water has been attributed as a result of several natural influences and processes, including the salt load of rivers (no river is free of it). Ever since the first rains descended upon the young earth hundreds of millions of years ago and ran over the land, the natural geological process had their impact in breaking up the rocks and transporting the debris, sediments and their minerals to the seas resulting in oceans becoming salty. As the things stand today, rivers carry an estimated four billion tonnes of dissolved salts to the ocean annually. Salts become concentrated in the sea because the sun's heat distils or vapourises almost pure water from the surface of the sea and leaves the salts behind.

Deteriorating marine environment resulting in increasingly polluted oceans, the world over has become a subject of discussion internationally. It may, however, be pointed out that the discharge of any type of sewage (municipal, industrial or otherwise) into the sea or any act by which water gets polluted would appear to be actionable at Common Law, that is the Law of Torts in India. People are beginning to wake up to the hard facts of its threat to marine life, resulting in fish getting contaminated with poisonous matter. Consumption of such contaminated fish may cause diseases of spinal cord. In addition, oysters (shellfish) collected from water polluted with petroleum waste has been found to contain potential carcinogens. Among the pollutants causing serious damage to marine environment include petroleum (including oil spills), industrial hazards, urban waste, agricultural pollutants, organic wastes, synthetic organic chemicals, inorganic chemicals, mineral substances, radioactive materials and sediments. Consumption of sea food by humans from the contaminated ocean waters is reported to be the cause of large number of hazardous diseases (numbness, giddiness, gastrointenstinal disturbances, incoherence of speech, paralysis of the respiratory muscels and all types of deformities). An article published under the title "Diving into Marine Life" in the Hindustan Times of 18th September, 2000 has made the following observations:

"..........Nations dump their toxic wastes in oceans without the slightest flicker of guilt. Statistics are alarming. The estimate of the World Bank is that each year about 550 tonnes of pesticides from the agrarian sector reach the Mediterranean. The North Sea is afflicted with 1.5 million tonnes of nitrogen and 100,000 tonnes of phosphorus. It is known that the toxic waste produced in the northern countries is dumped in the southern seas. Fury was whipped due to the discovery that radioactive thorium waste was dumped in Malaysia, while the Bayer chromium plant near Mexico or the mercury pollution in Nicaragua's Lake Managua became dumping grounds of the US Pennwalt Corporation's chlorine plant. Effluents from Swiss wineyards flow down the Rhine to the Mediterranean Sea and from the Hungarian Chemical Works down the Danube to the Black Sea. The recent oil spill in Brazil that led to about 4 million litres of oil seeping into the Iguazu River was as horrific as the spill created in Iraq War when oil refineries in Kuwait were destroyed and it took months to contain fires and save the waters and its lives. If one were to walk a kilometre along Antarctica's shoreline, one would find sticky black tar, broken bottles and soaked cigarette butts. And next to them on the ground, in a frantic attempt to survive, are ulcerated fish and poisoned sea birds. Cancers and tumours in aquatic life have become a major epidemic in the highly polluted waters like Europe's North Sea.

English novelist, Joseph Conrad sums it very aptly: "We cannot control the sea, but we can abuse it. It is a shame that the oceans, from where it is said life originated are being blantantly used to kill life as well! At the same time, in Russia, women are being encouraged to deliver babies in water for saline water is the cleanest form of water. But humans in the greed for health and their own self gratification are not observing any marine laws."

Russian nuclear submarine *Kursk* was in news in August, 2000. This submarine while carrying out naval exercises in the Barents Sea of the Arctic Ocean on 12th August, 2000 lost radio contact with the Russian North Fleet Command. On 13th August, the submarine was located on the sea bed at a depth of 108 meters. 118 crew members of the submarine lost their lives in this incident. The exact cause of the accident has not been made public. According to scientific experts this might have been due to explosion of a torpedo in the forward compartment of the submarine or the submarine might have collided with the sea bed or another submarine or surface ship. A nuclear submarine is powered by a small nuclear reactor that enables it to stay underwater for several months. Besides the loss of human lives, it is feared that the leakage of the radioactive material out of the reactors of the submarine may contaminate the sea/ocean water and endanger the marine life living therein. It may, however, be pointed out that the *Kursk* mishap is the world's six such fatal tragedy involving nuclear submarines. Sailors jokingly refer to nuclear submarines as "Iron Coffins". This incidentally proved to be correct for the 118 sailors of the *Kursk*.

The Coastal Regulation Zone (CRZ) notification which is the most important instrument to protect India's coastal wealth is facing hostility. This notification has not been seriously implemented inspite of the fact that it was finalised in 1991 and is not very comprehensive. Among the crucial provisions of the notification includes that "no developmental activity within 500 metres of the high-tide line on the seashore and 100 metres of rivers, creeks and estuaries." Inspite of the above provision in the notification, hotels, industries, aquaculture and housing estates all along the coasts brazenly violate the CRZ, greatly accelerating the destruction of the coastal ecology. In addition, business sharks have been trying to encroach the coasts for shrimp farming, chemical industries and luxury tourism. The fallout of government supported damage and waste dumping continues all along the Indian coasts unabated in violation to the provisions of the notification.

At times, making noise about environmental atrocities pays off since the masses get involved, bettering chances of averting impending disaster, e.g. many prawn and shrimp exporters who had set up base in coastal areas were forced to close shop when their pollution and environmentally unfriendly production technologies were highlighted by environmentalists.

Thousands of industries, housing complexes and resorts – many blatantly violating coastal zoning laws- first destroy vast stretches of crucial coastal wetlands and then pour their wastes into the rivers, creeks and estuaries, crucibles of life for sea beyond. Unchecked dumping of untreated effluents and sewage – a staggering 32,000 million metric tonnes – into rivers, estuaries and inland water bodies is eventually washdown into the sea. It is now an established fact that what "flows down into the sea" will come back to us in one form or the other for the rest of our life. These effluents are a constant threat to marine life of sea and results in destroying fish-breeding areas and lowering the catch. As many as 100 cities in six states (Maharashtra, Tamil Nadu, Andhra Pradesh, Orissa, Kerala and Karnataka) discharge huge amounts of untreated sewage directly or indirectly through the coastal system into the sea. Seas of waste along coastal areas in these states portend an ecological disaster as industries and government conspire to bypass laws protecting coastal areas which are getting damaged, ruined and destroyed at a fast pace. The worst offenders are Mumbai (where 95 per cent of the sewage is not treated), Thane and Chennai. The Mumbai coast is classified as ground zero – a zone of heavily sullified lifeless waters. One could find *dolphins* in Mumbai harbour in Mid-80's. In fact they would be there all over the Arabian Sea from Aden to Mumbai. Today, there are no *dolphins* in Mumbai. As a result of all these pollutants which are discharged into the sea, the fishes in the coastal waters from Gujarat to West Bengal get poisoned – a direct result of the destruction of the complexes of life cycle of coastal wetlands. More than half of India's fish catch is picked up next to shore. Compared to the nutrients – rich coasts, the oceans are biological deserts. According to marine biologists pollution in the open sea is most visible but less worrying than pollution in the coastal zones. Open sea pollution does not extend beyond 5km from the shore-line: the seas have an immense capacity to diffuse into them. This is not so far the fragile coastal zones with ecologically intricate arrangements of mangroves, coral reefs, backwaters, estuaries, sand dunes, fish, aquatic plants and rivers, which form a tapestry of nature.

A paper published in the Journal *Science* issue of 9th January, 2001 reveals that home heating and cooking fires in India and Southeast Asia, fueled by wood dung and farming wastes, pump tonnes of pollution into air, contributing to the staining of almost 14 million square miles of the atmosphere above the Indian Ocean. Pollution from such fuels causes greater carbon monoxide concentrations in the atmosphere. Experiment, found that although

Europe and North American still lead the world in per capita release of carbon dioxide into the atmosphere, Asia is catching up. The study also points out that the nature of pollution from Asia deviates from that in Europe and North America. The study found: "Considering the population size, the situation in Asia may become more serious. This will add considerably to the global atmospheric pollution in the Northern Hemisphere. Unless international control measures are taken, air pollution in the Northen Hemisphere will continue to grow into global plume across the developed and the developing world."

Environmentalists predicted doom when the Rashtriya Chemicals and Fertilizers (RCF) ammonia-urea complex was set up on the Konkan coast. This plant which lies four kilometres from the coastline produces 4,500 million tonnes of fertilizer everyday. An ammonia unit supplies raw material and three other chemical manufacturing units join the process. In view of scientific management of the effluents being generated by the unit, the water quality of the Arabian Sea where these effluents are being discharged remains fairly unchanged.

Narmada estuary in Gujarat collects the untreated waste of 800 chemical industries as Amlakhandi snakes 27km to this estuary. Prior to the setting up of the industries in this region, the rainwaters of this quiet, unswept Amlakhadi creek which join the salty estuary of the mighty Narmada in South Gujarat used to provide nurseries of millions of fish that came to spawn from the oceans. The fish used to feed itself on microplankton that flourished in the nutrient-rich waters. The adjoining land had flourishing paddy fields and farms of sugarcane. A turgid red and black soup of heavy metals, in concentration of 100 times that of safe limit is all that is left and seen now. The fish have long gone. The farmers on the land are fighting a losing battle as the area is flushed with toxic soup when the tide comes in. As a result yields of paddy and sugarcane have gone down considerably. Story similar to that of Amlakhadi estuaries is being repeated in all other estuaries of Gujarat. In Mithapur and Porbandar, acidic waste water from soda-ash units have made the coastal waters of the area so toxic that fish fauna does not survive for more than 15 minutes in the inter-tidal zone.

**Hot Spots of the Coasts along Arabian Sea and Bay of Bengal**

**Arabian sea**— Mithapur Industrial waste; Porbandar, industrial and domestic waste; Verval, Domestic waste – Falling fish catch; Mumbai, Industrial and domestic waste – Mangrove destruction and falling fish catch; Karwar, Industrial waste; Mangalore, Industrial and domestic waste – Falling fish catch; Kotchi, Industrial and domestic waste – Falling fish catch

**Bay of Bengal**—Tuticorin, Industrial and domestic waste; Pondicherry, Industrial and domestic waste – Falling fish catch; Chennai, Industrial and domestic waste – Falling fish catch; Visakhapatnam, Industrial and domestic waste – Falling fish catch; Puri, Domestic waste – Mangrove destruction and falling fish catch. (*India To Day*, 15th March 1987, p.85)

The functional diversity which is typified by the wide range of chemicals found within marine organisms, suggest that oceans can be an important source of new biochemical products, including medicines. The medicines derived from the marine organisms include antibiotics, antocoagulants, and drugs for treating cancer and heart diseases. In addition to being a source of medicines, food and industrial products, marine biodiversity provides a range of ecosystem services essential for human survival.

India offers a diverse and rich range of beaches. Among destinations interesting from tourists point of view include beaches at Goa (Calangute, Colva and other smaller beaches all over), Kerala (Kovalam), Maharashtra (Ganpatipule, Murud and Dahanu), Orissa (Puri), Karnataka (Karwar and Marwanthe), Union Territorries of Daman, Andaman and Nicobar Islands and Lakshadweep). The number of beaches are fast diminishing and those existing are steadily being deteriorated or ruined as the water has low bacterial level along such beaches making them unsafe for swimming. A visit to some of these beaches quickly fills one with most obnoxious smell, due to sewage-filled nullaha adjacent to such beaches which at times, especially during rainy seasons often overflow into the ocean and adjoining beaches. In Goa, iron-ore rejects of the past 35 years have turned many of the once white beaches red. Nearly 15 million tonnes of mining waste has been dumped into the sea. In Pondicherry, the sea breeze is laced with the stench of chemical waste pouring into the waters from pipelines on the beach.

Satellite imagery of coastal areas reveal the extent of changes which they have undergone with time. These imageries can also be used to measure changes in the extent of the mangrove areas. India had 4,827 sq km of mangrove forests in the coastal and peninsular regions in 1997. Of this, 3,704 sq km was in the eastern coast and 1,123 in the western coast. The mangrove area in different parts of the country is getting depleted due to various reasons like pressure excerted by firewood and fodder requirements, need for construction material, insect attacks and aquaculture farms. The trees which offer high biomass, also act as a buffer against the devastating impact of natural calamities and stabilise the shore line and act as a bulwark against the encroachment of the sea. The decline of critical habitats implies that species dependent on such areas may also be in jeopardy. Change in natural vegetation cover from tall trees to agricultural crops in the coastal areas have resulted in causing great damage to such areas from high-speed winds as these areas are either devoid or have lesser wind barriers. Mangroves provide a natural barrier to the high velocity winds. Taking clue from the devastation effects wrought by the supercyclone in Orissa in 1999, the Central Government has identified the coastal areas of West Bengal, Andhra Pradesh, Tamil Nadu and Gujarat for developing "shelterbelt" mangrove plantations.

The marine ecologists are worried in particular about the likely threat to be faced by the mangroves. Ecologists are unanimous that the life-sustaining mangroves need to be protected at any cost. The highly - evolved mangrove system prevents soil erosion and protect the mainland areas, besides minimizing flash floods from cloud bursts. Further, mangroves play a crucial role in cushioning the impact and protect the shores of the island from waves, tides, fury of strong sea and sea swells, hurricanes, cyclones, typhoons and depression. Mangroves also serve as repository of biodiversity. Mangroves provide an important nutrient inputs and primary source of energy for tropical estuaries through export of organic material.

Estuarine ecosystem which include mangroves and sea grass beds, are among the most productive ecosystems on earth. Even though they generally occur in tropical waters where productivity is low, coral reefs contain the highest levels of known diversity. The mangroves provide a suitable habitat for prawns, shrimps, crabs, *oysters,* besides serving as breeding grounds for fisheries and aquaculture. Estuaries, mangroves and other wetlands act as pollution filters and interface between the land and sea, stop soil erosion, protect the mainland areas, besides minimising flash floods from cloud bursts. These serve as invaluable marine nurseries and are habitats for a significant number of marine species. More than a third of India's mangrove forests have been cleared, threatening 185 species of fish, 20 species of shell fish, 177 species of birds and various other animals, including the Royal Bengal Tiger. These habitats are often rich in food, and their shallow waters and vegetation provide shelter from predators. Three-fourths of the commercial fish catch in US waters for example, consists of species dependant on estuaries for part or all of their life cycles.

Of all marine habitats, coastal ecosystem in general - including reefs, mangroves, seagrass beds and lagoons - have been the most heavily affected by human activity – especially by development related activities along roughly half of the world's coasts. 69 per cent of coasts in Asia are most threatened by degradation. Study of the digitised map data and defined coastal zones within 60 kilometres of the coast and adjacent nearshore waters indicate:

Cities with populations of more than 100,000 captures potential threats from coastal development, sewage and industrial pollution.

Major parts measure the potential threats from species introduction through the release of ballast water, the potential for oil spills, and industrial pollution.

Road density is an indirect measure of acess to coastal region.

Pipeline density measures the potential threat of oil pollution and of spills of other industrial wastes.

Pollution density measures potential threats from coastal development and pollution.

Each of the five indicators referred to above were given equal weight in the construction of final index of potential threat to coastal ecosystem.

Coral reefs are limestone formations produced by minute organisms found in shallow, tropical marine waters. A rise in sea temperature can kill coral reefs which in turn means the loss of marine animals and plants. This disrupts ecosystem and increases damage to resources on which people rely, such as fish stocks. The rock - like substance composed of the skeletons of the dead polyps are called corals which form continuous reefs. These reefs are considered as one of the means of livelihood of people living along the coastal areas in view of their being home to a wide diversity of plants, algae and fish. There are increasing reports of dying and massive bleaching of corals, *oysters*, diseased shell fish etc. in waters of many coastal areas which are attributed to these waters having been infected with human virus as the sea level rise due to increase in sea surface temperature caused by El Nino and global warming and intensification of pollution from the land. About 10 per cent of the corals worldwide have died and if the present trends and conditions continue, another 20 to 30 per cent of coral could be lost. Coral reefs along the Indian coast (Lakshwadeep islands, the Andaman and Nicobar Islands, the Gulf of Kutch and the Gulf of Mannar) are getting affected due to bleaching and bacterial diseases caused by unchecked pollution and bacterial growth. Bleaching, which is referred to as the rapid loss of pigmentation and whitening of corals due to reduction in photosynthetic activity and loss of symbiotic algae on corals is adversely affecting the coral reefs of Andaman and Nicobar Islands. It is considered to have been caused due to environmental stress such as elevation of sea surface temperation as a result of global warming. Eighty two per cent of the corals have been bleached in Lakshwadeep, sixty per cent in Andaman and Nicobar, eighty nine per cent of the Gulf of Mannar and thirty per cent in the Gulf of Kutch. In fact, cent per cent mortality in some parts of Lakshwadeep and Malvan in Maharashtra can be observed. Dead corals along these islands can be identified by their bleached look, caused by loss of pigmentation. The damage to such coral reefs in Lakshwadeep and the Gulf of Kutch has been attributed to the bacterial diseases and siltation. A paper published in the March, 2001 issue of *Current Science* by Dr Roshan Arthur, Scientists of the Centre for Ecological Research and Conservation (CERC), Mysore states that approximately 26 per cent of the corals in Lakshadeep and 23 per cent in Gulf of Mannar are dead (Tribune, 8.3.2001, p. 11). Environmental pollution in the 21 islands along the stretch from the Gulf of Mannar to Tuticorin has endangered the coral reefs and the rare quatic flora and fauna in the region. The government has declared the islands as Gulf of Manaar Marine National Park and entrusted its upkeep with the Forest Department. According to James W.Potter, an ocean studies specialist at the University of Georgia, while presenting the results of his researches at the national meeting of the American Association for the Advancement of Sciences, the pathogens viruses, bacteria and fungi killing the coral in many cases had not been previously identified by researchers. He is of the opinion that corals are like the canary in the mine. They are telling us that the water where they live is becoming suboptimal for their existence. Porter said the "loss of coral is significant because the reef building animal is the basis for the health of the tropical seas."According to Chandralata Raghukumar of the Biological Ocenography Division of the National Institute of Ocenography: "The loss of algae is said to make corals susceptible to disease, which have increased dramatically in recent years, both in terms of outbreaks and emergence of new ones" (Times of India, 9.X.1999, p.7). Hans and Ove Hoegh – Guldberg - Head of Queensland University's marine studies center and his economic father – spent two years examing the effects of rising sea temperature on the reef for Queensland tourism authorities and the World Wildlife Fund for Nature (WWF). A report released by them on 21st February, 2003 has come out with the findings that the brightly-coloured corals that make Australia's Great Barrier Reef as one of the world's natural wonders will be largely dead by 2050 because of rising sea temperatures. The coral reef will be bleached out and replaced by ordinary sea weed, costing the tourism industry billions of dollars. Their report found no prospect of avoiding the "long term eventualities" of coral bleaching because greenhouse gases were already warming the seas as part of a process. According to the report "Coral cover will decrease to less than five per cent on most reefs by the middle of the century under even the most favourable assumptions".

The Sunderbans, the world's largest delta and mangrove gene pool, is under threat. Without remedial steps coastal West Bengal could face an ecological disaster. According to Suman K. Chakrabarti 9INDIA TODAY, November 4, 2002 Issue, pp. 62-64): A massive increase in population since 1770 and the resultant development activity is the biggest cause of ddeforestation in the Sunderbans. Vanishing mangroves are worsening the impact of cyclones in Orissa". Commenting on Sunderbans he states: "Although the Sunderbans were declared a UNESCO World Heritage Site in 1984, conservation efforts over the years have focussed mainly on the Royal Bengal Tiger. If a UN sponsored study conducted by the School of Oceanoggraphic Studies (SOS) at Kolkata's Jadavpur University iis to be believed, large parts of India along the eastern coast may be severely affected as early as 2020 because the Sunderbans – the world's largest delta and mangrove gene pool that straddles the region – is on the verge of destruction...........While the rising sea level and soil erosion would submerge large parts swathes of land rendering thousands homeless. Kolkata and other areas on the coastline would be under constant threat of cyclones, gales and storms. The diveerse marine life – river sharks, red crabs, shrimps, snakes – uniquely adapted to the saline water would be threatened drastically affecting the food chain. Entire fisheries would be washed out and consumption of prawns alone cut at least 40 per cent. The disappearance of the largest carbon sink in the region would increase global warming and ultimately change the climate of entire south-east Asia. All these portent point to the fact that a human ecosystem may not eventually be sustainable in the Sunderbans............The declining cover of mangroves – which account to nearly 90 pper cent of the marine species in India – is the main cause of increasing soil erosion and silt accretion, which in turn pose a threat to Sunderbans.........The mean sea level in the Sunderbans has shown a steady increase at the rate of 3.14 mm every year, much higher than the global average of 2 mm per year. Scientists believe that in the next 50 years a rise of even 1 m in sea level would mundate 1,000 sq km of the 102 islands in the Sunderbans............The population pressure on the Sunderbans ecosystem, which act as a pollution sink for Kolkata and as a nursery for the aquatic resources in the Bay of Bengal, has been telling. The indiscriminate ffelling of trees has created a shortage of fuel wood and drinking water".

Writing on Orissa's mangroves, Ruben Banerjee made the following observations (INDIA TODAY, November 4, 2002 Issue, p. 64):

" At first glance, the Mahanadi delta in coastal Orissa seems picture perfect – a maze of rivers and creeks cutting enchanting swathes through the mangroves. But the bauty is only skin deep. The mangroves that appear lush and dense form only a narrow strip. Though pillaging for fuel wood and fodder has been continuing for years now, the severest threat comes from the illegal prawn farms – nearly 10,000 hectares of mangroves come under prawn forms along the coast. 'The mangroves' disappearance is mankind's loss'. Says Biswajit Mohanty of the Wildlife Society of Orissa. 'Human greed is to be blamed.' Says Anup Nayak, divisional forest officer of Dajnagar division".

One of the fastest growing threats to marine environment is tourism. In 1991, the island of Mauritius hosted 300,000 visitors and their untreated sewage was dumped in the lagoons. The physical damage caused by tourists trampling on corals, diving and dragging their boats, anchoring through reefs is raising alarms in Israel, Kenya and the Maldives. Studies conducted in different parts of the world show that vast colonies of human viruses migrate regularly into coastal waters from the septic tanks. The migration of viruses from septic tanks infect coastal areas within 24 hours of being flushed down toilets. Many people get infected with such viruses picked up while swimming, wind surfing or boating in infected waters. One study found that almost a quarter of the people using marine beaches develop ear infections, sore throats and eyes, respiratory or gastro-intenstinal disease. Some of the viruses detected in coastal waters are linked with heart disease, diabetyes, meaningitis and hepatitis viruses (Times of India, 24.1.1999, p.15).

The first comprehensive assessment of bio-diversity under the United Nations Environment Programme (UNEP's) concludes that between 5 to 20 per cent of some groups of animals and plant species could be threatened with extinction in the foreseeable future. 50 per cent of the world's population lives within 60 kms of the coast, which in itself is a threat to marine life. About one billion people, mostly in developing countries depend on fish for protein, yet many of the world's marine fisheries are reported to be in serious trouble. Wars too play havoc with marine environment.

In India, nearly 150 million people are prone to water-related hazards in coastal areas, with flooding from the sea as well as from rivers due to tropical cyclones and heavy rainfall causing havoc (Prof.S.Ramachandran in German News, Vol.XXXVIII, March, 1997, p.16). Commenting on the subject, INDIA TODAY observed (February 2004 Issue, p. 24): "Given the frequent cyclones in the Bay of Bengal, the unique biogeochemical processes of the Arabian Sea and the biannual reversal of monsoon winds and currents, the Indian ocean is a complex oceanic realm".

**Mumbai Coast** (Based on *India To-Day*, March, 15, 1997)

Process Involved and its Impact on the Environment:

*Mangroves*: Along the creeks and estuaries act as filters for pollutants and nurseries for fish lost to developers, slums and industries. Mangrooves now survive only near Thane, Mahim and Vasal. The Mahim mangroves grow on black sludge of sewage and industrial waste. All marine life has been killed.

*Sewage*: Is pumped directly into the sea near Mahim, Worli and GoraL: 1,95,000 cubic metres everyday, 95 per cent of it is untreated. The creeks are clogged with sewage. This leads to blooms of algae, whose remains are consumed by bacteria that use up all the oxygen in the water, so fish die.

*Oil:* From leaking ships and storage tanks pour into sea. With lex enforcement of pollution laws, many ships dump wastes and oil during the night. Oil are a constant danger. 35,000 tankers using an international shipping lane pass 25 km from shore every year.

Industrial Unit: Pour treated and untreated wastes into the estuaries, creeks, mangrove and swamps. A variety of deadly heavy metals fill the waters, killing marine life and contaminating fish. This poison is passed on up the food chain to fish eaters in Mumbai.

Fishing Villages: Struggle for survival in Mumbai. Fisherman need to go more than 20 km further than they once did to get a decent catch. The size and quality of fish have deteriorated, and some species that breed near the coastline, like two varieties of *Hilsa* are just not found.

## Marine Algae, Biofertilizer and Natural Fertilizer

The scientists of the Bhavnagar based Central Salt and Marine Chemicals Research Institute (CSMCRI) have developed a technology to convert marine algae into biofertilizers. The Institute is planning to transfer this new technology developed by it to industries for the manufacture of biofertilizers on commercial scale. The newly developed technology may help to boost food production in the country.

A team of scientists from the National Science Foundation (NSF), led by Jonathan Zehr, a marine scientist at the University of California, have published results of their findings in the August, 2001 issue of *Nature*. These scientists are reported to have discovered photosynthetic bacteria that fixes nitrogen, converting nitrogen from the atmosphere into a form other organisms can use. Many other kinds of nitrogen-fixing bacteria have also been found living in the open ocean. Although nitrogen accounts for nearly 80 per cent of the Earth's atmosphere, most organisms can use it only when it is "fixed" to other elements, to make compounds such as ammonia or nitrate. As a component of proteins, nitrogen is essential to all known forms of life. Zehr and his coworkers found the nitrogen-fixing bacteria, which they have grown, in water samples collected from the Pacific Ocean near Hawaii. The organisms appear to belong to the genus *Synechocystis*, a group of cyanobacteria (photosynthetic bacteria formerly known as blue-green algae) that includes both marine and freshwater species. The new nitrogen-fixers are about 100 times as large as typical photosynthetic ocean bacteria. These appear to be active at greater depths (100 to 200 metres below the surface) and over longer time periods than other two known nitrogen-fixers in the open ocean. The amount of nitrogen fixation in the open ocean has implications for global warming because nitrogen stimulates the growth of marine algae, which absorb carbon dioxide from the atmosphere. The new findings suggest that the deep ocean is teeming with organisms that produce essential natural fertilizers.

Despite India's 7,000-km coastline, seaweed harvesting has not been exploited in the country so far. This is an industry waiting to be exploited especially in view of the fact that the technology used in seaweed harvesting is cheap, it is eco-friendly and easy to harvest. Moreover, this industry could create more than a million jobs. It may be pointed out that the largest producers of seaweed are far eastern countries like China and Korea, as well as the US. Japan is one of the largest markets for algae-based products (INDIA TODAY, December 27, 2004 Issue, p. 65).

### Seashore and Superceramics

While visiting any seaside during vacations or otherwise, we often come across curio shops and boutiques selling all sorts of knickknacks made of conch shells. Adam Aston has made the following observations on the remarkable durability of these conch shells (Business Week, July 10, 2000, p.101, Edited by Catherine Arnst):

"Now it turns out these elegant corkscrew shapes, with their pearlescent interiors are, are more than pretty shelf décor. They're showing the way to tougher ceramic material too. A research group at Case Western University in Cleveland has discovered why conch shells are so remarkably durable: It's thanks to their plywood-like layered composition and the way the grain in each layer is oriented. Like wood, the grain of any single layer of the conch's structure runs mostly in one direction. But Arthur H. Heuer, a Professor of Ceramics, and a graduate assistant, Shekhar Kamat, discovered that the grain in each layer runs perpendicular to the grain in the layer beside it. That makes the shell hundreds of times harder to penetrate than if it were made of an equal volume of unlayered material. The perpendicular grains seem to prevent cracks from migrating from layer to layer. If scientists can replicate these structures in the lab, the shells could lead to the development of ultratough, lightweight ceramic composition for such uses as featherweight bulletproof armor. Who could have thought a souvenir could prove to be useful."

**Land Under Sea**

India is reported to have taken decision to use Article 76 of the UN Convention of the Law of Sea which decides the outer margin of the continental shelf for the countries "in the southern part of the Bay of Bengal on the basis of sedimentary thickness" to claim one million sq km of its land submerged in the sea. This would get the country an additional one million sq km of international waters in the strategic Arabian Sea and the Bay of Bengal. This would mean that the coastline of India, the real Indian boundary would be about 2,000km away. According to the proposed shelf plan, the new boundaries would mean that in the West, Indian borders would now be adjoining the waters of Pakistan, Oman, Yemen till the Carlsberg Ridge bordering the Indian Ocean. In the East, Indian borders will be next to Bangladesh, Myanmar, Thailand, Indonesia and Sri Lanka on the southern side. This additional area could be used by the country for strategic defence operations, mining, fishing and oil exploration which is said to be one of the potential areas off the west coast of India. In addition, all the merchant ships crossing Indian waters, many of which will be from Pakistan, Afghanistan and Iran, would have to take permission from the Government of India before crossing waters.

India's initial claim of the land referred to above was based on the United Nations Survey in 1978 which had concluded that India could get at least one million sq km extra if it lays claim to the continental shelf extending from the main land mass into the sea.

If Sri Lanks also decides to make claim similar to that of India, it would be asking for waters that extend up to Indonesia on the eastern side and India on the northern side.

## Ool Spills

Oil spills are one of the worst water pollutants. Such spills from ships and tankers operating along Indian coastline are a regular occurrence and they are wreaking immense havoc to marine life and aquatic plants. In addition, oil refineries and storage tanks are also another major source of oil leakage into the ocean. Occasional spills not only paint the coast black but also leave a residue of thick oil patches sticking to reefs and mangroves and adversely affecting fish and water birds. Spilt oil choke marine life, kills local fish as oil sticks to their gills. In addition, reproductive cycle of certain species of fishes gets affected because of oil spills. Microscopic food which sustain much of marine life, mangroves and aerial roots of local plants also get destroyed. To illustrate serious impact of oil spills on marine life, case of the Gujarat's Jamnagar coastline is discussed as an example. Approximately 100,000 tons of oil gets spilled in the oceans from different sources every year.

The Marine National Park on the Jamnagar coast, which stretches over 169 sq km and has also been declared to save 200 species of rare marine life and aquatic plants, is presently sandwitched between the busy ports of Vadinar and Kandla and some private jetties. This park is, in fact, home to more than 200 species of fish, 40 types of corals, 25 types of prawns, 15 species of starfish, 150 species of aquatic animals, 90 species of water birds, the sea tortoise, sea snakes, 210 varieties of algae and many other species.

Several of these species are classified as endangered species. Unfortunately, this marine park is on the verge of being destroyed by oil spills and coastal pollution.

The movement of cargo ships in the Gulf of Kutch during the last five years where the Vadinar and Kandla ports are located, has gone up many folds. Nearly 1,000 ships pass through this Gulf every year. The oil tankers carrying imported crude pose the greatest danger in this region as oil spills occur almost once every fortnight. In addition to the oil spills, these tankers also discharge their used oil into the sea water disregarding all regulatory provisions. Small oil spills are very common in the Gulf of Kutch. One gallon of oil spill is equivalent to zero oxygen content in 5,000 gallons of sea water. According to S.K.Kotak, Port Offficer (Indian Express, 9.XII.1999, p.7): " During the receding high tide sometimes the oil slicks get diverted into the high seas. But when the spills occur and the tide is about to come in, the oil slicks touch the coast. The unfortunate part of oil spill is that unless it is spotted early, one is unable to do anything about it." Coral reefs near the Narora lagoon are under threat of extinction because of oil spills. The fisheries industries near Safaya is also getting badly affected due to oil spills.

An oil spill in waters just half a mile (800 meters) off Ecuador's Galapagos archipelago started leaking from the ship on 18th January and grew worse on 21st January, 2001, threatening to ruin the unique flora and fauna in one of the most fragile and untouched ecosystems in the world where Charles Darwin carried out crucial research to support his theory of evolution by natural selection when he visited Galapagos in 1835. Environmentalists bemoan the threat the oil spill poses to many unique species in the Galapagos Islands, situated far off the coast of South America, the sheer isolation of the islands has helped its species to evolve in unique ways. The slick caused extremely severe environmental damage resulting in the death of sea lions, pelicans and several other species of fish eating birds, land Iguanas, gigantic-tortoise and mocking birds in the islands. The Galapagos Islands (including Santa Fe island, home to the Santa Fe land iguana) are located

1,000 km west of Ecuador's coast in the Pacific Ocean and are home to hundreds of native species – including giant tortoise and iguanas – that evolved over thousands of years. The site affected by the oil spill fall near a national park (Galapagos National Park) and also a World Heritage Site. A damaged vessel, the Ecuadorean-registered *Jessica*, ran aground near the archipelago's main port, on its easternmost island of San Cristobal. It is reported that about 160,000 gallons of diesel and bunker, a heavy fuel used by tour boats that operate in Galapagos, spilled into the fragile ecosystem of the islands. The slick spread over more than 1,200 square kilometres and soaked the islands in a biting smell of diesel fuelspill had spread over about 300 square kilometers area. In a similar tragedy, the Exxon Valdez supertanker dumped 41.6 million litres of oil into the Alaskan Sea when it ran aground in 1989.

Of the latest incidence of oil spill mention may be made of the sinking of world's largest offshore oil rig owned by Brazilian oil giant Petrobras and located 125 km off Macae, the gateway to the Campos Basin off the coast of Rio de Janeiro in Brazil on 19.3.2001. The sinking resulted in killing of 10 of the 175 workers on board. At the time of sinking the 40-storey platform had 95,000 litres of oil which could spill in the ocean endangering sea birds and animals. According to environmentalists, there were 2,500 tp 10,000 sea birds around the site where the platform had sunk.

## Cyclones

Cyclones are wind-systems of low pressure areas formed in the atmosphere wherein wind spirals inward towards the center of the low atmospheric levels. These are intense atmospheric vortices (wind whirlpools) which derive their strength from warm surface waters of tropical oceans. As a result, there is a net ascent of air which is pushed upwards by converging winds. Rising air is cooled by rising to higher altitudes, where pressure are lower; hence, cloudiness, rain and snow are associated with cyclones. Cyclones have clockwise and counter-clockwise wind systems in the southern and northern hemisphere respectively. Cyclones that originate over tropical areas and contain no sharp air-mass contrasts, (or fronts) are called tropical cyclones. They affect the eastern equatorial portions of the continents. This includes the shores of the Bay of Bengal and the Arabian Sea. Every year, 6 to 7 tropical cyclones originate in the Bay of Bengal and at least one in the Arabian Sea. Of these, one or two develop into severe storms and cause widespread damage. A severe tropical cyclone is also known as a hurricane. Bangladesh was hit by the worst cyclone ever encountered in any part of the world in November, 1970 taking 300,000 lives.

Cyclones can be mild or catastrophic. Their development is governed by natural factors and their movement determined by the flow in the surrounding undisturbed atmosphere. The wind speed around the center, called the eye of the cyclone, may be 50 kmph to 400 kmph. High speed damaging cyclone winds are concentrated in a circular band which begins at the edge of the central "eye" and extends out 50 to 100 kilometers of its center (eye of the storm). Damage capacity of a cyclone is dependent on the magnitude of the low pressure generated within the whirlpool and the associated wind speed. The actual damage is caused by the strong winds, which blow at between 150-250km per hour; the heavy rainfall of 20-30cm a day and the storm surge. Wind velocity in some cases reaches above 250 kmph. When the wind speed exceeds 120 kmph, it is called super cyclone. As the cyclone approaches the coast, the level of the sea starts rising to a height of 2-3m. If the cyclone is of severe type, the level may rise to 5m or more. The rising water rushes inland submerging everything for miles around. It also makes the land unsuitable for cultivation for months or years afterwards.

Cyclones are no respecters of time or place, or of people who think "it can't happen here". On an average four cyclones of varying intensity hit some part or the other of the India's 8,000 km long coastline. The worst cyclone disaster happen in areas which are hit by cyclones once in 30 to 40 years – a time frame long enough people to forget that cyclones do occur. Some areas are more cyclone prone than others. From 1891 to 1970, the Eastern coast of India had been hit by cyclones 363 times, and the western coast, 98 times. On the western coast, coastal Gujarat is more cyclone-prone. For both coasts, the worst months, on the average, are October and November. Some cyclones move forward with great rapidity, while others move slowly or remain stationary. India's western coast of Gujarat was hit by a cyclone on 26th May, 2001 with only minor impact.

Even though weather predictions have become more accurate with the acquisition of a high-end computer system, improvements are still needed for accurate prediction of cyclones and providing necessary information to farmers and those living along or close to the coastal areas. The presently available warning systems are unable to predict accurately the landfall of a cyclone inspite of the fact that it may be possible to forecast its path three or four days in advance by constantly monitoring the formation of low pressure areas and watching their movement. However, it may not be possible to predict accurately its intensity or damage capacity. The cyclone path may be 150 km on either side of the predicted area. Even a prediction made 24 hours in advance copuld have an error of 100 km or so on the place of impact. Therefore evacuation has to be done over a swath of 300 to 400 km width along the coastline. Inspite of all such limitations, path forecast made 24 hours before the cyclone hits land is still considered as reasonably accurate. To minimize cyclone damage, the best that can be done to reduce loss to human life is to take necessary precautions. Movement of people to safer cyclone shelters is one step that should go a long way in alleviating the misery inspite of the fact that such an exercise is costly in terms of manpower and resources. With the availability of modern technology, the atmospheric conditions can be more accurately predicted by feeding the atmospheric data like pressure, direction of the wind and temperature with the help of super computers which use modelling methods. The National Centre for Medium Range Weather Forecasting is reported to be collaborating with scientists from the United States under the Indo-Us Science & Technology Forum for exchange of information, weather and climate modelling, including ways of improving global modelling forecast system. According to Dr S.V.Singh, Head of this Centre, a four-day forecast for giving information to farmers on weather would have 95 per cent accuracy during winter but only 75 per cent during summer. He stresses the need to improve this to enable the farmers to take appropriate steps on irrigation or frost.

Scientists are reportedly moving forward by leaps and bounds in their ability to predict so-called "solar storms" which can disrupt the earth's communication and power systems. According to Geoffrey H. Lindop (Tribune, 11.X.2001, p. 13): "Soon they hope to be able to forecast the sun's weather and its impact on the earth up to a month in advance. But most of the time, solar storms have little or no impact on the earth, because of its ingenious defence system. Just as the atmosphere protects us from the sun's harmful ultraviolet radiation, so the earth, magnetic field protects us from the effects of solar wind."

Orissa cyclone (categorised as a grade 5 cyclone or Supercyclone) which hit Paradip port and adjoining areas on the evening of 29th October, 1999, accompanied by 260kmph winds (according to some 350 kmph) and surges of water that swept 15 km or so inland affecting 11 of the 24 districts of the state. The super-cyclone that hit coastal Orissa on October 29,1999, devastated the Orissa coastline killing about 10,000 people and uprooting more than 1 crore 20 lakh persons, in addition to claiming about 1.80 lakh animals is considered to be the century's worst cyclone. In addition, 80 per cent of coconut trees were dead and winter and autumn crops totally damaged. It is reported that more than 8 lakh trees were lost during this cyclone. Property worth Rs1,000 crore had been damaged with near to total loss of rural and urban livelihood for about six months because of this super cyclone. The cyclone had its impact on the geography, economy and society of the entire region. Some of the psyche warped persons whose families and vocations got destroyed have still not come out of the horrors of the tragedy. The Government of Orissa found the state woefully offguard as it had no disaster management plan. It may, however, be pointed out that the adjoining state of Andhra Pradesh has constructed 1,041cyclone relief shelters, each capable of accommodating 1,000 people. These shelters are stocked with basic amenities along the coastal belt, beyond the inundation point – exclusively for those evacuated (Tribune, 18.XI.1999, p.12). According to experts, large-scale destruction of mangroves and caesarian forests and proliferation of prawn ponds along the coast helped wreck the worst-ever havoc in this super-cyclone at the expense of the thick forests. Though the cyclone affected over 250km of Orissa's 480km coastline, it was only the highly denuded patch of about 100km between Basudevpur in Bhadrak District and Astarang in Puri District through which the high tidal wave surged killing thousands of people in minutes. The core of the cyclone lay on the highly deforested Ersama block of Jagatsinghpur District, ravaging it completely. Backed by strong gale and no forest to check it, it advanced menacingly into the mainland submerging everything that came in its path. It is reported that every year an average of 2.5 sq km of mangrove forest was being destroyed in the state's coastal region.

Of all the states in the India, Andhra Pradesh is the most frequented by cyclones in view of its being most vulnerable to tropical storms. Writing under the title "Troubled Coast", Ramesh Babu Kandula from Hyderabad made the following observations (Focus, Spectrum, Tribune, 9.1.2005, p. 1):

"All nine coastal districts, alongwith four adjoining inland districts, are subject to frequent cyclones, storm surges and floods. Overdevelopment and denuding of coastal zones of their protectve vegetable belts have resulted in increased vulnerability. The deadliest disaster in the last 20 years was the November 1977 cyclone, which killed about 10,000 people. The eastern coastline has always been a trouble spot as around 80 per cent of the total cyclones generated in the region hit there. During a period of 100 years (from 1891 to 1991), 442 cyclones lashed the Bay of Bengal coast, while 117 cyclones were formed in Arabian Sea......While states on the eastern coastline are more prone to cyclones, Andhra Pradesh is the most threatened among them. The people in the state's coastal region have learnt to live with the cyclonic storms unleashed periodically by Mother Nature. Since 1900, more than 60 cyclones have hit the state. While the 1977 cyclone killed

10,000 people and affected 71 million people, the May 1990 cyclone killed 928 persons and about 24,000 cattle. The devastating cyclone of November 6, 1996 took 1,057 lives. Total economic loss caused by natural disasters in AP in 1996 is estimated at US $2 billion, with cyclone alone accounting for US $1.5 billion. The cyclone affected 9 of the total 23 districts, while the number of villages affected was 5,923. A total of about 7.8 million people were affected by the 1996 cyclone. About 827,100 houses were partially damaged while 569,000 were completely destroyed. More than 500,000 hectares of agricultural and horticultural land were affected. Stretches along the Bay of Bengal coastline have the world's shallowest waters but the relatively dense population and poor economic condition complicate the situation. The population density in some of the coastal districts is as high as 670 persons per square km."

The cyclone storm that hit Kurnool, Cuddapah, Nellore on 16th October, 2001 left a trail of destruction claiming at least 45 lives in Andhra Pradesh. In addition, 30,000 persons were reportedly marooned. It is now being considered by the people that the strong penetration of a cyclone at a velocity of 300 kmph into the mainland are the new settlers' colonies that have come up in recent times all along the coast.

At least 15 persons are reported to have died and thousands rendered homeless due to the severe cyclonic storm (at a velocity of more than 120 kmph) that crossed the Tamil Nadu and Pondicherry coast on 29th November, 2000 (evening). Pondicherry and Cuddalore were the worst effected areas due to this cyclone resulting in disruption of electricity supply, washing away of bridges, roads and other communication. In addition to the loss of life, the area is reported to have suffered an estimated loss of 250 crores. Three 'kalasams' (mini-domes) of the famous Nataraja temple at Chidambaram were blown away by heavy winds.

Coastal cities are now at greater risk from cyclones because the population growth has been greater there. To minimize the damage due to cyclones, following measures may be taken (Tribune, 18.XI.1999, p.12):

Long-term measures, which require 10 to 20 years and include building houses strong enough to withstand cyclones – this is cheaper than rebuilding destroyed houses – and land planning to keep the most vulnerable areas as green areas.

Medium-term measures, consisting of improvement in the communication network and the warning systems, and the establishment of emergency centers and cyclone shelters.

Short-term measures coming into play the moment a cyclone alert is received, including evacuation from vulnerable areas, and public health and sanitation precautions.

A severe strong cyclonic storm crossed the South Tamil Nadu coast at 3.30 a.m on 27th December, 2000. The storm lay centred 100 km east-south-east off Tuticorin on the South Tamil Nadu coast and was accompanied by copious rain and gale force winds. The authorities evacuated hundreds of fishermen and their families from the low-lying areas fearing high tide. The pace of the storm slowed down and its movement was sluggish before it reached the coast. The storm after getting weakened turned into a deep depression lying centred close to Palayamkottai. Among the districts affected by the cyclone, heavy rain and gales with speed reaching 100 kmph included Tuticorin, Ramanathapuram, Kanyakumari, Thanjavur and Nagapattinum. Several low-lying areas in these districted were inundated. More than 100 houses got damaged and some trees were uprooted in different parts of the affected districts.

In 1991, 1,31,000 people perished in the cyclone that hit Bangladesh. The northern and north-eastern port district of Trincomalee of Sri Lanka was also hit by a cyclone packed winds of 150 to 180 km an hour on 26th December, 2000 resulting in the death of eight persons. About 500,000 people were affected by the twin affects of the floods and cyclone, 75,000 families were rendered homeless while 6,600 homes were completely destroyed. The areas affected by this cyclone and compounding monsoon flood havoc included districts of Ampara, Batticaloa, Anuradhapura, Trincomalee, Mannar and Polonnaruwa. The oldest tree in the world, Sri Maha Bodhi, a *Ficus religiosa* or a banyan tree, with a recorded history of 23 centuries, survived the impact of cyclone. This tree is worshipped by more than 2,000 people daily as it is believed to be a sapling from the original tree that sheltered Buddha when he attained enlightenment in India over 2,500 years ago.

**Tsunamis**

Tsunami is a Japanese word meaning harbor wave ("tsu" meaning harbor and "nami" meaning wave). It is pronounced as su-NAH-mee and is now used all over the world to describe any powerful current. The name depicts a wave train, or a series of waves, generated in a body of water by an impulsive disturbance that vertically displaces the water column.Often the term, "seismic or tidal sea wave" is used to describe the same phenomenon. However, these terms are misleading, because tsunami waves can be generated by other, non-seismic disturbances. Although in the open ocean the wave height may be less than 1 m, it steepens to heights of 15 m or more (even upto 30 meters or so) on entering shallow water. In fact it begins to slow and grow in height as it approaches the shore. As a result of their long wave lengths, tsunamis behave as shallow-water waves which are capable of inundating or flooding as they can move inland several hundred meters past the typical high-water level. These can even travel up rivers and streams that lead to the ocean. Often the first wave may not be the largest. The danger from a tsunami can last for several hours after the arrival of the first wave. These can savagely attack coastlines, causing devastating property damage and loss of life. In fact the fast-moving water associated with the inundating tsunami can crush homes and other coastal structures. Tsunami leaves sea calm, gets rough closer to coast. Sometimes a tsunami causes water to recede, exposing the ocean floor. Large rocks weighing several tons along with boats and other debris can be moved inland hundreds of feet by a tsunami. Tsunamis can be generated when the sea floor abruptly deforms and vertically displaces the overlying water. This can be caused by tectonic coastal earthquakes, undersea landslides, volcanic eruptions, explosions, and even the impact of cosmic bodies, such as meteorites. It may be pointed out that the contributor of the world tsunami, Japan has has 20 per cent of the world's earthquakes of magnitude 6 or over. When tectonic earthquakes (earthquakes associated with the earth's crustal deformation) occur beneath the sea, the water above is displaced from its equilibrium position. The most destructive tsunamis are generated from large, shallow earthquakes with an epicenter or fault line near or on the ocean floor. These usually occur in the regions of the earth characterized by tectonic subduction along tectonic plate boundaries. Waves are formed as the displaced water mass, acting under the influence of gravity, attempts to regain its equilibrium. When large areas of the sea floor shifts, a tsunami can be created. As a tsunami leaves the deep water of the open ocean and travels into the shallower water near the coast, it transforms. The tsunami's speed diminishes as it travels into the shallower water, its height grows. Because of this shoaling effect, a tsunami, imperceptible at sea, may grow to be several meters or more in height near the coast. When it finally reaches the coast, a tsunami may appear as a series of breaking waves. Indian Ocean is reportedly having been hit by 12 deadly tsunamis between 1727 to 2004. Among the most destructive tsunamis which hit different parts of the world mention may be made of Nicaragua (1992), Indonesia (1992, 1994, 1996 and 2004), Japan (1993), Phillipines (1994), Mexico (1995), Peru (1996, 2001), Papua New Guinea (1998), Turkey (1990), and Vanuatu (1990). Amongst some of world's greatest tsunami disasters mention may be made of Aleutian Tsunamis in the Aleutian island off Alaska on April 1, 1946 and again on March 9, 1957; Kamchatka Peninsula Tsunami, Russia on November 4, 1952; Chilean Tsunami of South Central Chile on 22nd May, 1960 and Prince William Sound Tsunami off Alaska on March 28, 1964. The largest tsunami wave ever observed anywhere in the world was caused by a rock fall in Lituya Bay, Alaska on July 9, 1958. Triggered by an earthquake along the Fairweather fault, an approximately 40 million cubic meter rock fall at the head of the bay generated a wave, which reached the incredible height of 520-meter wave (1,720 feet) on the opposite of the inlet. According to a study conducted by Canadian tsunami expert Tad Murthy, Mumbai was hit by tsunami in November, 1945, after an earthquake off the Makran coast, Baluchistan (now in Pakistan) killing 4,000 people. This tsunami was severest in Baluchistan but it caused damage as far as Karachi, Muscat and Iran and waves reached 11 metres high in Kutch, but subsided to two metres by the time Mumbai was hit in the morning. For more details readers may refer to Tsunami site hosted on internet by the University of Washington's Department of Earth and Space Science.The earliest record of tsunami hitting the Indian mainland from coast was on April 2, 1727 – only five years after the battle of Plassey. An earthquake at sea, just off the Arakan coast in Myanamar, shook Chittagong. Tremors were said to have been felt as far away as Kolkata and generated tsunami that flooded Dhaka, killing 500 people. The 1737 earthquake and gigantic waves that caused great devastation could be similar to what we call in recent times as tsunami (Times of Chandigarh, 6.1.2005, p. 6). Andaman and Nicobar Islands too are no stranger to localized tsunamis. On December 31, 1881, an earthquake off the Andaman Islands led to waves lashing the Coromandel Coast and shattering installations in Port Blair. On June 26, 1941, the Andaman Islands were hit by the region's strongest earthquake which generated tsunamis invading the Bay of Bengal.

Commenting on tsunami that struck India and Sri Lanka, Tadapalli "Tad" Murty made the following observations (Times of India, 5.1.2005, p. 12):

Tsunamis are rare in these parts of the world but when it happens, it is deadly. That is the reason I have been telling professional colleagues and friends in India to have a tsunami warning system. There was a tsunami that struck the west coast of India in 1945, November 27 to be precise, following an earthquake in the Arabian Sea very close to the border of Iran and Pakistan. It was a huge tsunami and it affected what is today Gujarat, Maharashtra, Goa and Karnataka, right up to Karwar. There were three waves and the second one had the highest amplitude of 11.8 metres. I don't know the precise figures but I think the death toll was about 300. It probably did not get too much attention because World War II had just ended and the British were getting ready to leave India. Earlier, a tsunami arising from the Krakatoa volcano eruption struck India and lot of people died in Nagapattinam and other coastal towns in Tamil Nadu. Both these tsunamis were recorded in their time and form part of the historical recordd, so it is wrong to say tsunamis are new to India".

The tsunamis generated by the 26th December, 2004 earthquake of Sumatra (Indonesia) which resulted from 1200 km long ruptures in the Indian Ocean floor extending from Myanmar through Andaman-Nicobar Islands to Java-Sumatra in northern Indonesia caused considerable devastation all along the coastal areas of India, Sri Lanka, Indonesia, Thailand, Myanmar, Somalia, Malaysia and Maldives resulting in killing of more than 2,80,000 persons, injuring innumerable population and damaging property worth thousands of crores. Of these 2,28,429 people were reportedly killed in Indonesia alone. In India, about 15,000 people were killed. The state of Tamil Nadu with 7,000 persons killed in and around Nagapattinam), Andaman and Nicobar Islands (6,000 to 8,000 persons killed) were among the regions worst-hit by the tsunami. It may be pointed out that ancient scriptures and literature have evidence that waves from the Indian Ocean did hit the Nagapattinam in 900 AD and destroyed a Buddhist monastery. In Maldives, at least 42 islands were flattened with 117 people killed. In Cuddalore district of Tamil Nadu which was severely hit by the December 26, 2004 tsunami, thick mangrove forests acted as a defence against the devastating high tidal waves. In fact, five villages in this district – which were under the shadows of the mangroves like a baby in the arm of a mother – were saved from destruction. In Sri Lanka nearly 30,000 persons were killed. The other countries having impact of tsunami of 26th December, 2004 included Myanmar (nearly 90 persons killed), Malaysia (66 persons killed), Bangladesh (2 persons killed), Somalia (132 persons killed), Tanzania (10 persons killed) and Kenya (one person killed). According to some reports published in the media, the Asian earthquake and the tsunami that followed may have sunk an area in Portblair by a metre and twisted the Andaman island. Geologically, Andaman and Nicobar Islands essentially built up of coral deposits with the fragile topsoil (being largely composed of degenerated coral) trapping rainwater which occurs at a depth of two to three metres and floating over the more dense bed of saline water. The soil, which act as a sponge, is being used at an alarming rate as construction material against persistent advice of environmentalists. The exploitation of these islands was started by the Japanese during their wartime occupation for building an airstrip. Environmental damage caused to these islands has continued – the culprits being both the armed forces and the civil authorities; locals, too, have joined in this environmental mayhem. The damage inflicted by the tsunami tragedy shows how inspite of all our technological advances, humans are still helpless efore nature's fury. The tsunami waves were generated primarily due to displacement of oceanic floor which had devastating impact on the coastal areas from Indonesia to Andamans and beyond.

In addition to the loss of human lives, the tsunami of 26th December, 2004 has caused permanent damage to soil and crops in the Andaman-Nicobar Islands as the tidal waves have tyrned the soil saline thereby rendering large tracts unfit for cultivation. Another adverse impact of this tsunami is the fear that stalks Kalpakkam residents of a nuclear leak. The nuclear plant at Kalpakkam was shut down after the water from the tsunami waves had entered the nuclear plant. According to official sources, 80 people died and around 1,000 houses were damaged at the Kalpakkam complex. The walls of the complex were smashed, while some of the buildings were still in shambles (Tribune, 30.1.2005, p. 2). The fear of nuclear leak is having adverse impact on the famous tourist resort of Mahabalipuam, which by road is only 30 km away from the nuclear plant and only 7 km by sea. This tourist resort which usually teems with foreign tourists during the months of January-March, wore a deserted look with most of the beach resorts and hotel empty even more than two months after the tsunami had struck this region.

According to scientists from the Survey of India and the National Hydrographic Office, the earthquake triggered tsunami of 26th December, 2004 has caused an "anticlockwise twist" of 1.25 metres to the south-east of the Andaman and Nicobar Islands where sea beaches have vanished and land has sunk so much that it is likely to remain a part of the sea for decades to come. Giving details of the changes in the topography of these islands, Dr Prithvish Nag, Surveyor General of India said, Indira Point, the southernmost tip of the country, has got submerged under 3 metre of water. He pointed out that only a portion of the lighthouse at Indira Point is now visible (Tribune, 5.2.2005, p. 2).

It is true that an earthquake cannot be predicted, but a tsunami gives sufficient time before it strikes as the energy gets transferred from the seabed to the waves. The tsunami hit Portblair at 7.14 AM, lashing Chennai port nearly two hours later, at 9.06 AM. It hit Cochin at 11.12 AM. Nobody seems to have informed anybody despite the fact it took considerable time to travel from Portblair to Cochin. Poor communication and inadequate warning system resulted in the loss of valuable human lives. If a regional warning system had been in place in the Indian Ocean on the morning after Christmas, many thousand people could have avoided death or injury. It may be pointed out that India is vulnerable to tsumanis from three sources i.e ocean floor quakes in Myanmar-Andaman-Java-Sumatra belt, extension of Bhuj fault into the Arabian sea and landslides or volcanic eruptions.

The December 26, 2004 tsunami is reportedly having left behind vast riches on the coasts in the form of mineral deposits that have the highest percentage of titanium – the richest mineral ever. Approximately 40 million tonnes of additional deposits of illeminite have been added to the earlier estimated reserves of 284 million tones of illeminite on the coasts of Tamil Nadu (Hindustan Times, 11.1.2005, p. 7).

Commenting on the impact of tsunami on those who survived in the areas affected, Neelam Sharma observed (Chandigarh Tribune, 31.1.2005, p. 3):

"It may have taken the killer waves of tsunami a few ill-fated minutes to devastate most of the southern shores. But for many its survivors, the moments of unparallel devastation may have permanently etched in their memories, resulting in continual stress and depression. Post Traumatic Stress Disorder (PTSD), fear the psychiatrists, is the biggest challenge before the survivor-victims of tsunami, who witnessed the colossal loss of lives and belongings. In PTSD, the survivors of the tragedy continue to recall the sites of devastation and begin to live with them. This results in a state of extreme anxiety and depression".

According to Dr S.Nambi, President of the Indian Psychiatry Society (Chandigarh Tribune, 31.1.2005, p. 3):

"Previous disasters in India, including earthquakes in Latur and Gujarat, have established that the PTSD is found in 6 to 13 per cent of the victims who survive the tragedy, while in western countries the incidence is as high as 30 to 40 per cent. Tragedy affects everyone who is witness to it, be it the immediate victim or the relief workers, including the doctors and the NGO workers........Though it is common for anyone to be stressed and depressed for a short duration after witnessing mass-scale devastation, but those who are otherwise depressed due to a previous event, are likely to have depression for a longer duration".

An editorial published in Hindustan Times (28.XII.2004, p. 8) under the title "Riding the wave" made the following observations:

"The tsunami which ravaged South Asia sent out warning bells loud and clear in its destructive wake: that no coastline in the world is safe from these killer waves. Traditionally, it was the Pacific region that was supposed to be prone to tsunamis, which usually occur because of earthquakes on the ocean floors 70 kilometres deep. But in this case, the depth was just 30 kms and that too, close to the Asian land mass.....On Sunday (26th December, 2004), there was a two-hour window in which the people in the vulnerable areas could have been warned, but not because of the lack of an early warning system. The authorities should now think about establishing an advanced monitoring and early warning system for such disasters. Obviously, the Indian Meteorological Department (IMD)'s current facilities – including its three dozen seismic stations and high-power cyclone radars installed along the coastal belt – are inadequate to deal with severe quakes and tsunamis. Because of inadequate radio communications, the timely warnings issued by the IMD often fail to reach remote fishing villages and fishing boats out at sea..........Seabed sensors, for instance, can send tsunami warnings via satellite and trigger alarms within minutes. This, along with providing training and equipment to the local population, could well spell the difference between safety and devastation – or to put it simply, life and death".

Indian Government (Departments of Science, Ocean Development and Space as well as Council of Scientific and Industrial Research) has already taken decision to install automated warning system. Canadian tsunami scientist Tad Murty has suggested Visakhapatnam in Andhra Pradesh as the ideal location for setting up the tsunami warning system in view of its central positioning on the Bay of Bengal. It may be pointed out that there are 36 Indian Ocean countries and to share nformation/ to collaborate between different countries it is necessary that creation of tsunami warning system is done through the UN. Envoya from 43 countries and 13 international organizations (10 members of the Association of South-East Asian Nations – ASEAN, the Asian and African nations bordering the Indian Ocean, and major donors such as European Union, Japan and the USA) met in Phuket (Thailand) for two days (28$^{th}$ and 29$^{th}$ January, 2005) to chart a plan to create a tsunami early warning system in the Indian Ocean. Officials from dozens of Asian countries – including India, Indonesia and Thailand – failed to agree as to who should run a regional tsunami warning center. On 29$^{th}$ January, 2005, a compromise came after U.N.Secretary General Kofi Annan sent a written statement to the conference urging all nations to coordinate their regional efforts. According to this compromise, delegates at the conference decided to create several regional tsunami-warning centers around southern Asia. Earlier, at a UN conference on reducing disasters held from 18$^{th}$ to 22$^{nd}$ January, 2005 in Kobe (Japan), representatives of 150 nations participated. At this conference a consensus emerged that United Nations may co-ordinate to build a global system on a tsunami alert system in the Indian Ocean on line to the one existing and protecting Pacific Rim countries for the last four decades. The United Nations Educational, Scientific and Cultural Organization has proposed an Indian Ocean network of deep-sea buoys and communications centers that would go into operation in mid-2006. The host country Japan promised at the conference to start immediately stitching together an emergency tsunami and earthquake warning system for the Indian Ocean. Thailand wants the tsunami early warning system to be built on the existing Asian Disaster Preparedness Centre (ADPC), based in Bangkok which offers training on disaster management.

According to Science & Technology Minister Kapil Sibal, India will set up a tsunami warning system (Deep Ocean Assessment and Reporting System – DOARS) by 2007. He said that the work on system installation will start in February and key elements would be in place by March, 2006. The system would be installed using the platform of Global Ocean Observing System in the Indian Ocean, an association of marine operational and research agencies in the Indian Ocean Rim. He added that this system would be tailored to the needs of Indian Ocean Rim nations with whom the information will be shared. Member states will have to set up their own receiving stations to get networked with the Indian system. The early warning system will be set up along the fault lines stretching from Java-Sumatra to Myanmar in the Indian Ocean region and Kutch near the Arabian Sea. The system to be installed will have active inputs from Sumatra, Myanmar and Thailand and will use existing software technology for relaying timely alerts. Essentially, they depend on deep ocean sensors ( or seabed sensors) to detect seismic activity and a network of undersea Bottom Pressure Recorders (BPRs) that track a tsunami in real time. According to Kapil Sibal, UN Conference on Disaster Reduction at Kobe had endorsed the steps taken by India.

India is reported having brushed aside suggestions on an international tsunami warning system, saying it would take the lead, put its own money and set up its own network but 'share' information, or 'network', with neighbours. According to Kapil Sibal (Times of India, 26.1.2005, p. 4): "We are not joining any

UN led system ....we have no thought of an international regional consortium...There is no blanket ban, but there no blanket open door".

In Honolulu (Hawaii), The International Tsunami Information Centre (the Pacific Tsunami Warning Centre) was set up in 1965 and has almost mastered the art of forecasting destructive waves. This center has been educating the public about the threat from tsunami for the past many years. The system is connected via satellite and telephone to nearly 100 water level stations throughout the Pacific that can be used to verify the generation and possible severity of tsunami. Pacific Ocean which is relatively much bigger and has well-honed warning system and sees on an average by eight tsunamis a year – is still plagued by false alarms thereby eroding credibility of the warning system. Murty has pointed out that for every real tsunami event, there are two or three false alarms which is a very serious problem. An Al-Nino storm in the Western Pacific and constant extreme winds carried huge swells upto 80 feet high onto the Hawaiian shores in 1998. The Hawaiian authorities declared the ocean Condition Black and no one was allowed miles near the stunning mountains of water. In the past half of the 20$^{th}$ century, Pacific-wide, destructive tsunamis occurred in 1946, 1952, 1957, 1960, 1964, 1975, 1983, 1985, 1992, 1993, 1995, 1998, 1999 and 2001. But none of these tsunamis matched the fury of the December 26, 2004 tsunami generated by Sumatra earthquake with intensity of 9.5 on the Richter Scale.

## Typhoon

Of the most frequent occuring natural calamities, though rarely reported, mention may be made of typhoon. As a result hundreds of persons are reported missing or dead every year from different parts of the world from the ships that get sunk or are reportedly missing in highwaters. According to Yoshitaka Murata, Japan's minister for disaster management (Times of India, 22.1.2005, p. 8): "After World War II, every major typhoon cost us thousands of lives".

Super Typhoon (Bilis) hit northeastern coast of Taiwan at a

speed of 240km per hour on 21st August, 2000. As a result 600,000 people were reported to have been rendered homeless due to the collapse of tens of thousands of houses. 11 persons were reported dead after having been burried due to mudslides at two places. The worst typhoon that hit Taiwan on 30th July, 2001 roared across the island, killing at least 35 persons in floods, mud and rock slides and leaving more than 100 missing, many believed to be burried alive. In addition, hundreds of homes and thousands of acres of farmland had also been destroyed in Toraji's rampage overnight. The eastern coastal county of Hualien took the brunt when typhoon "Toraji" swept ashore. Toraji, packing winds of 150km per hour, was downgraded to a tropical storm after the landfall at Hualien's Hsiuguluan river. The typhoon passed through Vietnam and southern China (175km south of Fu Chow). Nine persons (including two Indians who were drowned in Halong Bay when their boat sank off the coast of the northern Quang Ninh province) are reported to have been killed and four injured when typhoon Kaemi hit Vietnam's coastline on 21st August, 2000. In October, 2004 a deadliest typhoon killed at least 80 people.

According to a recent report, at least 160 people are dead or missing around the city of Fuzhou, a large port city, after Typhoon Chebi pounded the southeastern coast of China in the last week of June, 2001 (Business Times, 26.6.2001, p. 15). The intensity of this typhoon could very well be gauzed from the fact that a 17,000-tonne ship under construction for an European shipping consortium got blown from a nearby shipyard to quayside in Fuzhou, China's eastern Fujian province.

Development of sophisticated storm tracking modern communication system has helped to give timely warning and evacuation of people living in the affected areas. To cite an example mention may be made of the death of only 14 persons in 1985 when Hurricane Kate swept Cuba, Jamaica and the nearby American coast.

According to United Nations sources, a net-based atlas to track down ocean threats is reported to have been launched. This online atlas of the ocean which has been prepared with John

Everett as the Project Manager is considered as the most ambitious global scientific information collaboration over online and covers issues even beyond environment. The atlas contains an initial 14 global maps with links to hundreds of others covering different aspects pertaining to oceans. Among contributing scientific bodies to this atlas are the United States National Geographic Society and the Russian Head Department of Navigation and Oceanography, which has provided 100 charts showing global ice cover, earthquake and volcanic activity, temperature gradients, sea-bottom contours, salinity and other characteristics. Accoring to Mr Serge Garcia, Director of the fisheries division in the UN's Food and Agriculture Organisation in Rome: "The atlas is not just an information system, but it is also a communication system and it contains resources to resolve conflicts........The atlas will be updated continuously and is freely available as a public good source.......In particular, it will contain data about the climate changes which many meterologists believe could cause partial melting of the polar ice caps and rises in sea levels at low-lying swamp regions." The UN Environment Programme has estimated that a one-metre rise in sea levels would affect 70 million people in coastal China, 10 per cent of the population of Egypt and 60 per cent of the population of Bangladesh (The Straits Times, Singapore, 8th June, 2002, p. H 24).

## Droughts

Drought conditions prevail in some part or the other of the world at a given time. India, Pakistan, China, South Korea, several countries in Africa and innumerable other developing countries are worst affected by such droughts resulting in the death of thousands of persons and large number of animals every year. Scarcity of water available, especially drinking water, is the main cause for such deaths. Of the recent droughts in our country mention may be made of the state of Orissa which had continuously remained under drought from 1995 to 1998. Things improved in 1999, but the state was hit by another natural calamity, super cyclone. The drought again returned to the state in 2000. Similar drought conditions were also been reported during this period from some parts of Gujarat and Rajasthan. Nearly 16 per cent of India's total area is reported to be drought prone and approximately 50 million people are affected annually by droughts.

South Korea was hit by the worst drought in the century in the year 2001 as it suffered from the worst heat wave in the country since 1904. This drought had driven President Kim Dae Jung to forsake the luxury of soaking in a bath and to opt for a modest shower instead. Mr Kim also urged the people of his country to save water in the worsening drought conditions to reduce water consumption and to help minimise drought damage. Water rationing was also introduced in the country to overcome the worsening conditions. Farmers in different parts of the country were provided funds to help them buy pumps to fight drought damage.

The famine of 1958-60 in the rural areas of China killed more than 30 million people. Lack of rainfall coupled with extreme temperatures and frequent sandstorms produced droughts in northern China in 2001 – the worst during decades. The cities of Yantai and Weihai in eastern provinces of Shandong were among the worst hit areas. Water shortage emerged as the leading problem in China due to this drought, even more serious than flooding and deterioration of water quality. To combat a catastrophic shortage of water, authorities in northern China came up with a host of drastic measures such as cutting off water supply to bath houses, banning the use of tap water for washing cars and slashing water rations. Defaulters were heavily fined. To address the water crisis in Weihai, the authorities planned to divert water from sections of Yellow River. In Tianjin, 180 km east of Beijing, city authorities banned the use of tap water for car washes and stopped issuing licences to new bath houses. Similar restrictions were imposed in places in Beijing where water level at the Miyun Reservoir dropped drastically. The Guanting Reservoir in Beijing had not been providing drinking water to the city since 1997. Under a longer-term plan, Chienese authorities would undertake massive water diversion plan that would send water from the floodprone Yangtze River in the south to cities and farmlands in the north.

# APPENDICES

## APPENDIX - 1

# THE ENVIRONMENT ACT

---

## ENVIRONMENT (PROTECTION) ACT, 1986*

**An Act to provide for the protection and improvement of environment and for matters connected therewith.**

Whereas decisions were taken at the United Nations Conference on the Human Environment held at Stockholm in June, 1972, in which India participated, to take appropriate steps for the protection and improvement of human environment.

And whereas it is considered necessary further to implement the decisions aforesaid in so far as they relate to the protection and improvement of environment and the prevention of hazards to human beings, other living creatures, plants and property.

Be it enacted by Parliament in the Thirty-seventh Year of the republic of India as follows:

### CHAPTER 1

### PRELIMINARY

**1. Short title, extent and commencement—**

(1) This act may be called the Environment (Protection) Act, 1986).

(2) It extends to the whole of India.

---

* Received the assent of the President on 23 May 1986, published in the Gazette of India, Extraordinary pt. II, Sec 1 dated 26 May 1986. pp. 1-11.

(3) It shall come into force on such date as the Central Government may, by notification in the Official Gazette, appoint and different dates may be appointed for different provisions of this Act and for different areas.

2. **Definitions**—In this Act, unless the context otherwise requires—

(a) 'environment' includes water, air and land and the inter-relationship which exists among and between water, air and land, and human beings, other living creatures, plants, micro-organism and property;

(b) 'environmental pollutant' means any solid, liquid or gaseous substance present in such concentration as may be or tend to be, injurious to environment;

(c) 'environmental pollution' means the presence in the environment of any environmental pollutant;

(d) 'handling', in relation to any substance, means the manufacture, processing, treatment, package, storage, transportation, use, collection, destruction, conversion, offering for sale, transfer or the like of such substance;

(e) 'hazardous substance' means any substance or preparation which, by reason of its chemical or physico-chemical properties or handling, is liable to cause harm to human beings, other living creatures, plants, micro-organism, property or the environment;

(f) 'occupier', in relation to any factory or premises, means a person who has control over the affairs of the factory or the premises and includes in relation to any substance, the person in possession of the substances;

(g) 'prescribed' means prescribed by rules made under this Act.

## CHAPTER II

## GENERAL POWERS OF THE CENTRAL GOVERNMENT

3. **Power of Central Government to take measures to protect and improve environment—**

(1) Subject to the provisions of this Act, the Central Government

shall have the power to take all such measures as it deems necessary or expedient for the purpose of protecting and improving the quality of the environment and preventing, controlling and abating environmental pollution.

(2) In particular and without prejudice to the generality of the provisions of sub-section (1), such measures may include measures with respect to all or any of the following matters, namely:

(i) co-ordination of actions by the stage governments, officers and other authorities—

(a) under this Act, or the rules made there under; or

(b) under any other law for the time being in force which is relatable to the objects of this Act;

(ii) planning and execution of a nation-wide programme for the prevention, control and abatement of environmental pollution;

(iii) laying down standards for the quality of environment in its various aspects;

(iv) laying down standards for emission or discharge of environmental pollutants from various sources whatsoever:

Provided that different standards for emission or discharge may be laid down under this clause from different sources having regard to the quality or composition of the emission or discharge of environmental pollutants from such sources;

(v) restriction of areas in which any industries, operations or processes or class of industries, operations or processes shall not be carried out or shall be carried out subject to certain safeguards;

(vi) laying down procedures and safeguards for the prevention of accidents which may cause environmental pollution and remedial measures for such accidents;

(vii) laying down procedures and safeguards for the handling of hazardous substances;

(viii) examination of such manufacturing processes, materials and substances as are likely to cause environmental pollution;

(ix) carrying out and sponsoring investigations and research relating to problems of environmental pollution;

(x) inspection of any premises, plant, equipment, machinery, manufacturing or other processes, materials, or substances and giving, by order, of such directions to such authorities, officers or persons as it may consider necessary to take steps for the prevention, control and abatement of environmental pollution;

(xi) establishment or recognition of environmental laboratories and institutes to carry out the functions entrusted to such environmental laboratories and institutes under this Act;

(xii) collection and dissemination of information in respect of matters relating to environmental pollution;

(xiii) preparation of manuals, codes or guides relating to the prevention, control and abatement of environmental pollution;

(xiv) such other matters as the Central Government deems necessary or expedient for the purpose of securing the effective implementation of the provisions of this Act.

(3) The Central Government may, if it considers it necessary or expedient so to do for the purposes of this Act, by order, published in the Official Gazette, constitute an authority or authorities by such name or names as may be specified in the order for the purpose of exercising and performing such of the powers and functions (including the power to issue directions under section 5) of the Central Government under this Act and for taking measures with respect to such of the matters referred to in sub-section (2) as may be mentioned in the order and subject to the supervision and control of the Central Government and the provisions of such order, such order, such authority or authorities may exercise

the powers or perform the functions or take the measures so mentioned in the order as if such authority or authorities had been empowered by this Act to exercise those powers or perform those functions or take such measures.

**(4) Appointment of officers and their powers and functions**—

(1) Without prejudice to the provisions of sub-section (3) of section 3, the Central Government may appoint officers with such designations as it thinks fit for the purposes of this Act and may entrust to them such of the powers and functions under this Act as it may deem fit.

(2) The officers appointed under sub-section (1) shall be subject to the general control and direction of the Central Government or, if so directed by that Government, also of the authority or authorities, if any, constituted under sub-section (3) of section 3 or of any other authority or officer.

**(5) Power to give directions**—Notwithstanding anything contained in any other law but subject to the provisions of the this Act, the Central Government may, in the exercise of its powers and performance of its functions under this Act, issue directions in writing to any person, officer or any authority and such person, officer or authority shall be bound to comply with such directions.

*Explanations*—For the avoidance of doubts it is hereby declared that the power to issue direction under this section includes the power to direct—

(a) the closure, prohibition or regulation of any industry, operation or process; or

(b) stoppage or regulation of the supply of electricity or water or any other service.

**(6) Rules to regulate environmental pollution**—(1) The Central Government may, by notification in the Official Gazette, make rules in respect of all or any of the matters referred to in section 3.

(2) In particular, and without prejudice to the generality of

the foregoing power, such rules may provide for all or any of the following matters, namely:

(a) the standards of quality of air, water or soil for various areas and purposes;

(b) the maximum allowable limits of concentration of various environmental pollutants (including noise) for different areas;

(c) the procedures and safeguards for the handling of hazardous substances;

(d) the prohibition and restrictions on the handling of hazardous substances in different areas;

(e) the prohibition and restrictions on the location of industries and the carrying on of processes and operations in different areas;

(f) the procedures and safeguards for the prevention of accidents which may cause environmental pollution and for providing for remedial measures for such accidents.

## CHAPTER III

## PREVENTION, CONTROL AND ABATEMENT OF ENVIRONMENTAL POLLUTION

**7. Persons carrying on industry, operation, etc., not to allow emission or discharge of environmental pollutants in excess of the standards.**—No person carrying on any industry, operation or process shall discharge or emit or permit to be discharged or emitted any environmental pollutant in excess of such standards as may be prescribed.

**8. Persons handling hazardous substances to comply with procedural safeguards.**—No person shall handle or cause to be handled any hazardous substance except in accordance with such procedure and after complying with such safeguards as may be prescribed.

**9. Furnishing of information to authorities and agencies**

**in certain cases.**—(1) Where the discharge of any environmental pollutant in excess of the prescribed standards occurs or is apprehended to occur due to any accident or other unforeseen act or event, the person responsible for such discharge and the person in charge of the place at which such discharge occurs or is apprehended to occur shall be bound to prevent or mitigate the environmental pollution caused as a result of such discharge and shall also forthwith—

(a) intimate the fact of such occurrence or apprehension of such occurrence; and

(b) be bound, if called upon, to render all assistance to such authorities or agencies as may be prescribed.

(2) On receipt of information with respect to the fact or apprehension of any occurrence of the nature referred to in sub-section (1), whether through intimation under that sub-section or otherwise, the authorities or agencies referred to in sub-section (1) shall, as early as practicable, cause such remedial measures to be taken as are necessary to prevent or mitigate the environmental pollution.

(3) The expenses, if any, incurred by any authority or agency with respect to the remedial measures referred to in sub-section (2), together with interest (at such reasonable rate as the Government may, by order, fix) from the date when a demand for the expenses is made until it is paid, may be recovered by such authority or agency from the person concerned as arrears of land revenue or of public demand.

**10. Powers of entry and inspection.**—(1) Subject to the provisions of this section, any person empowered by the Central Government in this behalf shall have a right to enter, at all reasonable times with such assistance as he considers necessary any place—

(a) for the purpose of performing any of the functions of the Central Government entrusted to him;

(b) for the purpose of determining whether and if so in what manner, any such functions are to be performed or whether any provisions of this Act or the rules made thereunder or nay notice, order, direction or authorisation served, made, given or granted under this Act is being or has been complied with;

(c) for the purpose of examining and testing any equipment, industrial plant, record, register, document or any other material object or for conducting a search of any building in which he has reason to believe that an offence under this Act or the rules made thereunder has been or is being or is about to be committed and for seizing any such equipment, industrial plant, record, register, document or other material object if he has reasons to believe that it may furnish evidence of the commission of an offence punishable under this Act or the rules made thereunder or that such seizure is necessary to prevent or mitigate environmental pollution.

(2) Every person carrying on any industry, operation or process or handling any hazardous substance shall be bound to render all assistance to the person empowered by the Central Government under sub-section (1) for carrying out the functions under that sub-section and if he fails to do so without any reasonable cause or excuse, he shall be guilty of an offence under this Act.

(3) If any person wilfully delays or obstructs any person empowered by the Central Government under sub-section (1) in the performance of his functions, he shall be guilty of an offence under this Act.

(4) The provisions of the Code of Criminal Procedure, 1973 or, in relation to the State of Jammu and Kashmir, or any area in which that Code is not in force, the provisions of any corresponding law in force in that State or area shall, so far as may be, apply to any search or seizure under this section as they apply to any search or seizure made under the authority of a warrant issued under section 94 of the said Code or, as the case may be, under the corresponding provisions of the said law.

**11. Power to take sample and procedure to be followed in connection therewith**—(1) The Central Government or any officer empowered by it in this behalf, shall have power to take, for the purpose of analysis, samples of air, water, soil or other substance from any factory, premises or other place in such manner as may be prescribed.

(2) The result of any analysis of a sample taken under sub-section (1) shall not be admissible in evidence in any legal proceeding unless the provisions of sub-sections (3) and (4) are complied with.

(3) Subject to the provisions of sub-section (4) the person taking the sample under sub-section (1) shall—

(a) serve on the occupier or his agent or person incharge of the place, a notice, then and there, in such form as may be prescribed of his intention to have it so analysed;

(b) in the presence of the occupier or his agent or person, collect a sample for analysis;

(c) cause the sample to be placed in a container or containers which shall be marked and sealed and shall also be signed both by the person taking the sample and the occupier or his agent or person;

(d) send without delay, the container or the containers to the laboratory established or recognised by the Central Government under section 12.

(4) When a sample is taken for analysis under sub-section (1) and the person taking the sample serves on the occupier or his agent or person, a notice under clause (a) of sub-section (3), then—

(a) in a case where the occupier, his agent or person wilfully absents himself, the person taking the sample shall collect the sample for analysis to be placed in a container or containers which shall be marked and sealed and shall also be signed by the person taking the sample, and

(b) in a case where the occupier or his agent or person present at the time of taking the sample refuses to sign the marked and sealed container or containers of the sample as required under clause (c) of sub-section (3), the marked and sealed container or containers shall be signed by the person taking the samples.

and the container or containers shall be sent without delay by the person taking the sample for analysis to the laboratory established or recognised under section 12 and such person shall inform the Government Analyst appointed or recognised under section 13 in writing, about the willful absence of the occupier or his agent or person, or, as the case may be, his refusal to sign, the container or containers.

**12. Environmental laboratories**—(1) The Central Government may, by notification in the Official Gazette—

(a) establish one or more environmental laboratories;

(b) recognise one or more laboratories or institutes as environmental laboratories to carry out the functions entrusted to an environmental laboratory under this Act.

(2) The Central Government may, by notification in the Official Gazette, make rules specifying—

(a) the functions of the environmental laboratory;

(b) the procedure for the submission to the said laboratory of samples of air, water, soil or other substance for analysis or tests the form of the laboratory report thereon and the fees payable for such report;

(c) such other matters as may be necessary or expedient to enable that laboratory to carry out its functions.

**13. Government Analysts**— The Central Government may by notification in the Official Gazette, appoint or recognise such persons as it thinks fit and having the prescribed qualifications to be Government Analysts for the purpose of analysis of samples of air, water, soil or other substance sent for analysis to any environmental laboratory established or recognized under sub-section (1) of section 12.

**14. Reports of Government Analysts**—Any document purporting to be a report signed by a Government analyst may be used as evidence of the facts stated therein in any proceeding under this Act.

**15. Penalty for contravention of the provisions of the Act and the rules, orders and directions**—(1) Whoever fails to comply with or contravenes any of the provisions of this Act, or the rules made or orders or directions issued thereunder, shall in respect of each such failure or contravention, be punishable with imprisonment for a term which may extend to five years or with fine which may extend to one lac rupees, or with both, and in case the failure or contravention continues, with additional fine which may extend to five thousand rupees for every day during which such failure or contravention continues after the conviction for the first such failure or contravention.

(2) If the failure or contravention referred to in sub-section (1) continues beyond a period of one year after the date of conviction, the offender shall be punishable with imprisonment for a term which may extend to seven years.

**16. Offences by companies.**—(1) Where any offence under this Act has been committed by a company, every person who, at the time the offence was committed, was directly in charge of and was responsible to, the company for the conduct of the business of the company as well as the company, shall be deemed to be guilty of the offence and shall be liable to be proceeded against and punished accordingly:

Provided that nothing contained in this sub-section shall render any such person liable to any punishment provided in this Act, if he proves that the offence was committed without his knowledge or that he exercised all due diligence to prevent the commission of such offence.

(2) Notwithstanding anything contained in sub-section (1), where an offence under this Act has been committed by a company and it is proved that the offence has been committed with the consent or connivance of or is attributable to any neglect on the part of, any director, manager, secretary or other officer of the company, such director, manager, secretary or other officer shall also be deemed to be guilty of that offence and shall be liable to be proceeded against and punished accordingly.

*Explanation.*—For the purposes of this section—

(a) 'company' means any body corporate and includes a firm or other association of individuals;

(b) 'director', in relation to a firm, means a partner in the firm.

**17. Offences by Government Departments.**—(1) Where an offence under this Act has been committed by any Department of Government, the Head of the Department shall be deemed to be guilty of the offence and shall be liable to be proceeded against and punished accordingly:

Provided that nothing contained in this section shall render such Head of the Department liable to any punishment if he proves that the offence was committed without his knowledge or that he exercised all due diligence to prevent the commission of such offence.

(2) Notwithstanding anything contained in sub-section (1), where an offence under this Act has been committed by a Department of Government and it is proved that the offence has been committed with the consent or connivance of, or is attributable to any neglect on the part of, any officer, other than the Head of the Department, such officer shall also be deemed to be guilty of that offence and shall be liable to be proceeded against and punished accordingly.

## CHAPTER IV

## MISCELLANEOUS

**18. Protection of action taken in good faith**—No suit, prosecution or other legal proceeding shall lie against the Government or nay officer or other employee of the Government or any authority constituted under this Act or any member, officer or other employee of such authority in respect of anything which is done or intended to be done in good faith in pursuance of this Act or the rules made or orders or directions issued thereunder.

**19. Cognisance of Offences**—No court shall take cognizance of any offence under this Act except on a complaint made by—

(a) the Central Government or any authority or officer authorized in this behalf by that Government; or

(b) any person who has given notice of not less than sixty days, in the manner prescribed, of the alleged offence and of his intention to make a complaint, to the Central Government or the authority or officer authorized as aforesaid.

**20. Information, reports or returns**—The Central Government may, in relation to its functions under this Act, from time to time, require any person, officer, State Government or other authority to furnish to it or any prescribed authority or officer any reports, returns, statistics, accounts and other information and such person, officer, State Government or other authority shall be bound to do so.

**21. Members, officers and employees of the authority constituted under section 3 to be public servants**—All the members of the authority, constituted, if any, under section 3 and all officers and other employees of such authority when acting or purporting to act in pursuance of any provisions of this Act or the rules made or orders or directions issued thereunder shall be deemed to be public servants within than meaning of section 21 of the Indian Penal Code.

**22. Bar of Jurisdiction**—No civil court shall have jurisdiction to entertain any suit or proceeding in respect of anything done, action taken or order or direction issued by the Central Government or any authority or officer in pursuance of any power conferred by or in relation to its or his functions under this Act.

**23. Power to delegate**—Without prejudice to the provisions of sub-section (3) of section 3, the Central Government may, by notification in the Official Gazette, delegate, subject to such conditions and limitations as may be specified in the notification, such of its powers and functions under this Act (except the power to constitute an authority under sub-section (3) of section 3 and to make rules under section 25) as it may deem necessary or expedient, to any officer, State Government or other authority.

**24. Effect of other laws**—(1) Subject to the provisions of sub-section (2), the provisions of this Act and the rules or orders made therein shall have effect notwithstanding anything inconsistent therewith contained in any enactment other than this Act.

(2) Where any act or omission constitutes an offence punishable

under this Act and also under any other Act then the offender found guilty of such offence shall be liable to be punished under the other Act and not under this Act.

**25. Power to make rules**—(1) The Central Government may, by notification in the Official Gazette, make rules for carrying out the purposes of this Act.

(2) In particular, and without prejudice to the generality of the foregoing power, such rules may provide for all or any of the following matters, namely:

(a) the standards in excess of which environmental pollutants shall not be discharged or emitted under section 7;

(b) the procedure in accordance with and the safeguards in compliance with which hazardous substances shall be handled or cause to be handled under section 8;

(c) the authorities or agencies to which intimation of the fact of occurrence or apprehension of occurrence of the discharge of any environmental pollutant in excess of the prescribed standards shall be given and to whom all assistance shall be bound to be rendered under sub-section (1) of section 9;

(d) the manner in which in which samples of air, water, soil or other substance for the purpose of analysis shall be taken under sub-section (1) of section 11;

(e) the form in which notice of intention to have a sample analysed shall be served under clause (a) of sub-section (3) of section 11;

(f) the functions of the environmental laboratories, the procedure for the submission to such laboratories of samples of air, water, soil and other substances for analysis or test; the form of laboratory report; the fees payable for such report and other matters to enable such laboratories to carry out their functions under sub-section (2) of section 12;

(g) the qualifications of Government Analyst appointed or recognised for the purpose of analysis of samples of air, water, soil or other substances under section 13;

(h) the manner in which notice of the offence and of the intention to make a complaint to the Central Government shall be given under clause (b) of section 19;

(i) the authority or office to whom any reports, returns, statistics, accounts and other information shall be furnished under-section 20;

(j) any other matter which is required to be, or may be, prescribed.

**26. Rules made under this Act to be laid before Parliament.**—Every rule made under this Act shall be laid, as soon as may be after it is made, before each House of Parliament, while it is in session, for a total period of thirty days which may be comprised in one session or in two or more successive sessions, and if, before the expiry of the session immediately following the session or the successive sessions aforesaid, both Houses agree in making any modification in the rule or both Houses agree that the rule should not be made, the rule shall thereafter have effect only in such modified form or be of no effect, as the case may be; so, however, that any such modification or annulment shall be without prejudice to the validity of anything previously done under that rule.

APPENDIX -2

# THE ENVIRONMENT RULES

## ENVIRONMENT (PROTECTION) RULES, 1986

*Notification No. S.O. 844 (E), dated 19 November 1986*[1]

In exercise of powers conferred by sections 6 and 25 of the Environment (Protection) Act, 1986 (29 of 1986), the Central Government hereby makes the following rules, namely:

**1. Short title and commencement.**—(i) These rules may be called the Environment (Protection) Rules, 1986.

(ii) They shall come into force on the date of their publication in the Official Gazette.

**2. Definitions.**—In these rules, unless the context otherwise requires,--

(a) 'Act' means the Environment (Protection) Act, 1986 (29 of 1986);

[2][(aa) 'areas' means all areas where the hazardous substances are handled;]

(b) 'Central Board' means the Central Board for the Prevention and Control of Water Pollution constituted under section 3 of the Water (Prevention and Control of Pollution) Act, 1974 (6 of 1974);

(c) 'form' means a form set forth in Appendix A to these rules;

(d) 'Government Analyst' means a person appointed or recognized as such under section 13;

(e) 'person' in relation to any factory or premises means a person or occupier or his agent who has control over the affairs of the factory or premises and includes in relation to any substance, the person in possession of the substance;

[3][(ee) 'prohibited substance' means the substance prohibited for handling;]

(f) 'recipient system' means the part of the environment, such as, soil, water, air or other which receives the pollutants;

[4][(ff) 'restricted substance' means the substance restricted for handling;]

(g) 'section' means a section of the Act;

(h) 'schedule' means a schedule appended to these rules'

(i) 'standards' means standards prescribed under these rules;

(j) 'State Board' means a State Board for the Prevention and Control of Water Pollution constituted under section 4 of the Water (Prevention and Control of Pollution) Act, 1974 (6 of 1974), or a State Board for the Prevention and Control of Air Pollution constituted under section 5 of the Air (Prevention and Control of Pollution) Act, 1981 (14 of 1981).

**3. Standards for emission or discharge of environmental pollutants.**—(1) For the purposes of protecting and improving the quality of the environment and preventing and abating environmental pollution, the standards for emission of discharge of environmental pollutants from the industries, operations or processes shall be as specified in [5][Schedule I to IV].

[6][***]

(2) Notwithstanding anything contained in sub-rule (1), the Central Board or a State Board may specify more stringent standards from those provided in [7][Schedule I to IV] in respect of any specific industry, operation or process depending upon the quality of the recipient system and after recording reasons, therefor, in writing.

[8][(3) The standards for emission or discharge of environmental pollutants specified under sub-rule (1) or sub-rule (2) shall be

complied with by an industry operation or process within a period of one year of being specified.]

[9][(3A) (i) Notwithstanding anything contained in sub-rules (1) and (2), on and from the 1st day of January, 1994, emission or discharge of environmental pollutants from the [10][industries, operations or processes other than those industries, operations or processes for which standards have been specified in Schedule I shall] not exceed the relevant parameters and standards specified in Schedule VI:

Provided that the State Boards may specify more stringent standards for the relevant parameters with respect to specific industry or locations after recording reasons thereof in writing;

(ii) The State Board shall while enforcing the standards specified in Schedule VI follow the guidelines specified in Annexures I and II in the Schedule.]

[11][(3B) The combined effect of emission or discharge of environmental pollutants in an area from the industries, operations, processes, automobiles and domestic sources, shall not be permitted to exceed the relevant concentration in ambient air as indicated and set out against each pollutant in columns (3) to (5) of Schedule VII.]

(4) Notwithstanding anything contained in sub-rule (3),—

(a) the Central Board or a State Board, depending on the local conditions or nature of discharge of environmental pollutants, may, by order, specify a lesser period than a period specified under sub-rule (3) within which the compliance of standards shall be made by an industry, operation or process;

(b) the Central Government in respect of any specified industry, operation or process, by order, may specify any period other than a period specified under sub-rule (3) within which the compliance of standards shall be made by such industry, operation or process.

(5) Notwithstanding anything contained in sub-rule (3), the standards for emission or discharge of environmental pollutants

specified under sub-rule (1) or sub-rule (2) in respect of an industry, operation or process before the commencement of the Environment (Protection) Amendment Rules, 1991, shall be complied with by such industry, operation or process by the 31st day of December, 1991.]

[12][(6) Notwithstanding anything contained in sub-rule (3), an industry, operation or process which has commenced production on or before 16th May 1981, and has shown adequate proof of at least commencement of physical work for establishment of facilities to meet the specified standards within a time-bound programme, to the satisfaction of the concerned State Pollution Control Board, shall comply with such standards latest by the 31st day of December, 1993.

(7) Notwithstanding anything contained in sub-rule (3) or sub-rule (6), an industry, operation or process which has commenced production after the 16th day of May, 1981, but before the 31st day of December 1991, and has shown adequate proof of at least commencement of physical work for establishment of facilities to meet the specified standards within a time-bound programme, to the satisfaction of the concerned State Pollution Control Board, shall comply with such standards latest by the 31st day of December, 1992.]

[13][(8) On and from the 1st day of June 2001, the following coal based thermal power plants shall use [14][raw or blended or beneficiated coal with an ash content not exceeding thirty-four per cent on an annual average basis], namely:

(a) any thermal power plant located beyond one thousand kilometers from the pit-head; and

(b) any thermal power plant located in urban area or sensitive area or critically polluted area irrespective of their distance from pit-head except any pit-head power plant.

[15][Provided that any thermal power plant using Fluidised Bed Combustion or Circulating Fluidised Bed Combustion or Pressurised Fluidised Bed Combustion or Integrated Gasification Cycle technologies or any other clean technologies as may be notified by the Central Government in the Official Gazette shall

be exempted from clause (a) and (b).]

*Explanation:* For the purpose of this rule—

(a) 'beneficiated coal' means coal containing higher calorific value but lower ash than the original ash content in the raw coal obtained through physical separation or washing process;

(b) 'pit-head power plant' means power stations having captive transportation system for its exclusive use for transportation of coal from the loading point at the mining end up to the unloading point at the power station without using the normal public transportation system;

(c) 'sensitive area' means an area whose ecological balance is prone to be easily disturbed;

(d) 'critically polluted area' means the area where pollution level has reached or likely to reach the critical level and which has been identified as such by the Central Government or Central Pollution Control Board or State Pollution Control Board.]

[16][(e) 'Urban area' means an area limit of a city having a population of more than 1 million according to 1991 census.]

**4. Directions.**—(1) Any direction issued under section 5 shall be in writing.

(2) The direction shall specify the nature of action to be taken and the time within which it shall be complied with by the person, officer or the authority to whom such direction is given.

[17][(3-a)] The person, officer or authority to whom any direction is sought to be issued shall be served with a copy of the proposed direction and shall be given an opportunity of not less than fifteen days from the date of service of a notice to file with an officer designated in this behalf the objections, if any, to the issue of the proposed direction.

[18][(3-b) Where the proposed direction is for the stoppage or regulation of electricity or water or any other service affecting the carrying on of any industry, operation or process and is sought

to be issued to an officer or an authority, a copy of the proposed direction shall also be endorsed to the occupier of the industry, operation or process, as the case may be, and objections, if any, filed by the occupier with an officer designated in this behalf shall be dealt with in accordance with the procedures under sub-rules (3-a) and (4) of this rule:

Provided that no opportunity of being heard shall be given to the occupier if he had already been heard earlier and the proposed direction referred to in sub-rule (3-b) above for the stoppage or regulation of electricity or water or any other service was the resultant decision of the Central Government after such earlier hearing.]

(4) The Central Government shall within a period of 45 days from the date of receipt of the objections, if any, or from the date up to which an opportunity is given to the person, officer or authority to file objections whichever is earlier, after considering the objections, if any, received from the person, officer or authority sought to be directed and for reasons to be recorded in writing, confirm, modify or decide not to issue the proposed direction.

(5) In a case where the Central Government is of the opinion that in view of the likelihood of a grave injury to the environment it is not expedient to provide an opportunity to file objections against the proposed direction, it may, for reasons to be recorded in writing, issue direction without providing such an opportunity.

(6) Every notice or direction required to be issued under this rule shall be deemed to be duly served—

(a) where the person to be served is a company, if the document is addressed in the name of the company at its registered office or at its principal office or place of business and is either,--

(i) sent by registered post; or

(ii) delivered at its registered office or at the principal office or place of business;

(b) where the person to be served is an officer serving Government, if the document is addressed to the person and a copy thereof is endorsed to the Head of the Department and also to the Secretary to the Government, as the case may be, incharge of the Department in which for the time being the business relating to the Department in which the officer is employed is transacted and is either,--

(i) sent by registered post; or

(ii) is given or tendered to him;

(c) in any other case, if the document is addressed to the person to be served and—

(i) is given or tendered to him; or

(ii) if such person cannot be found, is affixed on some conspicuous part of his last known place of residence or business or is given or tendered to some adult member of his family or is affixed on some conspicuous part of the land or building, if any, to which it relates; or

(iv) is sent by registered post to that person.

*Explanation*.—for the purposes of this subrule,—

(a) 'company' means any body corporate and includes a firm or other association of individuals;

(b) 'a servant' is not a member of the family.

**5. Prohibition and restriction on the location of industries and the carrying on processes and operations in different areas.**—(1) The Central Government may take into consideration the following factors while prohibiting or restricting the location of industries and carrying on of processes and operations in different areas—

(i) Standards for quality of environment in its various aspects laid down for an area.

(ii) The maximum allowable limits of concentration of various environment pollutants (including noise) for an area.

(iii) The likely emission or discharge of environmental pollutants from an industry, process or operation proposed to be prohibited or restricted.

(iv) The topographic and climatic features of an area.

(v) The biological diversity of the area which, in the opinion of the Central Government, needs to be preserved.

(vi) Environmentally compatible land use.

(vii) Net adverse environmental impact likely to be caused by an industry, process or operation proposed to be prohibited or restricted.

(viii) Proximity to a protected area under the Ancient Monuments and Archaeological Sites and Remains Act, 1958 or a sanctuary, National Park, game reserve or closed area notified, as such under the Wild Life (Protection) Act, 1972, or places protected under any treaty, agreement or convention with any other country or countries or in pursuance of any decision made in any international conference, association or other body.

(ix) Proximity to human settlements.

(x) Any other factors as may be considered by the Central Government to be relevant to the protection of the environment in an area.

(2) While prohibiting or restricting the location of industries and carrying on of processes and operations in an area, the Central Government shall follow the procedure hereinafter laid down.

(3) (a) Whenever it appears to the Central Government that it is expedient to impose prohibition or restrictions on the location of an industry or the carrying on of processes and operations in an area, it may, by notification in the Official Gazette and in such other manner as the Central Government may deem necessary from time to time, give notice of its intention to do so.

(b) Every notification under clause (a) shall give a brief description of the area, the industries, operations, processes in that are about which such notification pertains and also specify the reasons for the imposition of prohibition or restrictions on the location of the industries and carrying on of processes or operations in that area.

(c) Any person interested in filing an objection against the imposition of prohibition or restriction on carrying on of processes or operations as notified under clause (a) may do so in writing to the Central Government within sixty days from the date of publication of the notification in the Official Gazette.

(d) The Central Government shall, within a period of one hundred and twenty days from the date of publication of the notification in the Official Gazette, consider all the objections received against such notification and may [19][within] [20][three hundred sixty five days] from such date of publication] impose prohibition or restrictions on location of such industries and the carrying on of any process or operation in an area.

[21][(4) Notwithstanding anything contained in sub-rule (3), whenever it appears to the Central Government that it is in public interest to do so, it may dispense with the requirement of notice under Clause (a) of sub-rule (3).]

[22][**6. Procedure for taking samples**—The Central Government or the officer empowered to take samples under section 11 shall collect the sample in sufficient quantity to be divided into two uniform parts and effectively seal and suitably mark the same and permit the person from whom the sample is taken to add his own seal or mark to all or any of the portions so sealed and marked. In case where the sample is made up in containers or small volumes and is likely to deteriorate or be otherwise damaged if exposed, the Central Government or the officer empowered shall take two of the said samples without opening the containers and suitably seal and mark the same. The Central Government or the officer empowered shall dispose of the samples so collected as follows:

(i) one portion shall be handed over to the person from whom the sample is taken under acknowledgement; and

(ii) the other portion shall be sent forthwith to the environmental laboratory for analysis.]

**7. Service of notice**—The Central Government or the officer empowered shall serve on the occupier or his agent or person in charge of the place a notice then and there in Form I of his intention to have the sample analysed.

**8. Procedure for submission of samples for analysis, and the form of laboratory report thereon**—(1) Sample taken for analysis shall be sent by the Central Government or the officer empowered to the environmental laboratory by registered post or through special messenger along with Form II.

(2) Another copy of Form II together with specimen impression of seals of the officer empowered to take samples along with the seals/marks, if any, of the person from whom the sample is taken shall be sent separately in a sealed cover by registered post or through a sealed messenger to the environmental laboratory.

(3) The findings shall be recorded in Form III in triplicate and signed by the Government Analyst and sent to the officer from whom the sample is received for analysis.

(4) On receipt of the report of the findings of the Government Analyst, the officer shall send one copy of the report to the person from whom the sample was taken for analysis, the second copy shall be retained by him for his records and the third copy shall be kept by him to be produced in the Court before which proceedings, if any, are instituted.

**9. Functions of environmental laboratories**—The following shall be the functions of environmental laboratories;

(i) to evolve standardized methods for sampling and analysis of various types of environmental pollutants;

(ii) to analyse samples sent by the Central Government or the officers empowered under sub-section (1) of section 11;

(iii) to carry out such investigations as may be directed by the Central Government to lay down standards for the quality of environment and discharge of environmental pollutants, to monitor and to enforce the standards laid down;

(iv) to send periodical reports regarding its activities to the Central Government;

(v) to carry out such other functions as may be entrusted to it by the Central Government from time to time.

**10. Qualification of Government Analyst**—A person shall not be qualified for appointment or recognised as a Government

Analyst unless he is a—

(a) graduate in science from a recognized university with five years experience in a laboratory engaged in environmental investigations, testing or analysis; or

(b) post-graduate in science or a graduate in engineering or a graduate in medicine or equivalent with two years' experience in a laboratory engaged in environmental investigations, testing or analysis; or

(c) post-graduate in environmental science from a recognized university with two yeas experience in a laboratory engaged in environmental investigations, testing or analysis.

**11. Manner of giving notice.**—The manner of giving notice under clause (b) of section 19 shall be as follows, namely:

(1) The notice shall be in writing in Form IV.

(2) The person giving notice may send notice to,—

(a) if the alleged offence has taken place in a union territory:

(A) the Central Board; and

(B) the Ministry of Environment and Forests (represented by the Secretary of the Government of India);

(b) if the alleged offence has taken place in a State:

(A) the State Board; and

(B) the Government of the State (represented by the Secretary to the State Government incharge of environment); and

(C) the Ministry of Environment and Forests (represented by the Secretary to the Government of India).

(3) The notice shall be sent by registered post acknowledgement due; and

(4) The period of sixty days mentioned in clause (b) of section 19 of the Environment (Protection) Act, 1986 shall be reckoned from the date it is first received by one of the authorities mentioned above.

[23][12. **Furnishing of information to authorities and agencies in certain cases.**—Where the discharge of environmental pollutant in excess of the prescribed standards occurs or is apprehended to occur due to any accident or other unforeseen act or event, the person in charge of the place at which such discharge occurs or is apprehended to occur shall forthwith intimate the fact of such occurrence or apprehension of such occurrence to all the following authorities or agencies, namely:

(i) The officer-in-charge of emergency or disaster relief operations in a district or other region of a State or Union Territory specified by whatever designation, by the Government of the said State or Union Territory, and in whose jurisdiction the industry, process or operation is located.

(ii) The Central Board or a State Board, as the case may be, and its regional officer having local jurisdiction who have been delegated powers under sections 20, 21, 23 of the Water (Prevention and Control of Pollution) Act, 1974 (6 of 1974), and section 24 of the Air (Prevention and Control of Pollution) Act, 1981 (14 of 1981).

(iii) The statutory authorities or agencies specified in column 3 in relation to places mentioned in column 2 against thereof of] [24][Schedule V.]

[25][13. **Prohibition and restriction on the handling of hazardous substances in different areas:**—(1) The Central Government may take into consideration the following factors while prohibiting or restricting the handling of hazardous substances in different areas:

(i) the hazardous nature of the substance (either in qualitative or quantitative terms) as far as may be in terms of its damage causing potential to the environment, human beings, other living creatures, plants and property;

(ii) the substances that may be or likely to be or readily available as substitutes for the substances proposed to be prohibited or restricted;

(iii) the indigenous availability of the substitute or the state of technology available in the country for developing a safe substitute;

(iv) the gestation period that may be necessary for gradual introduction of a new substitute with a view to bringing about a total prohibition of the hazardous substance in question; and

(v) any other factor as may be considered by the Central Government to be relevant to the protection of environment.

(2) While prohibiting or restricting the handling of hazardous substances in an area including their imports and exports the Central Government shall follow the procedure hereinafter laid down:

(i) Whenever it appears to the Central Government that it is expedient to impose prohibition or restriction on the handling of hazardous substances in an area, it may, by notification in the Official Gazette and in such other manner as the Central Government may deem necessary from time to time, give notice of its intention to do so.

(ii) Every notification under clause (i) shall give a brief description of the hazardous substances and the geographical region or the area to which such notification pertains and also specify the reasons for the imposition of prohibition or restriction on the handling of such hazardous substances in that region or area.

(iii) Any person interested in filing an objection against the imposition of prohibition or restrictions on the handling of hazardous substances as notified under clause (i) may do so in writing to the Central Government within thirty days from the date of publication of the notification in the Official Gazette.

(iv) The Central Government shall within a period of sixty days from the date of publication of the notification in the Official Gazette consider all the objections received against such notification and may impose prohibition or restrictions on the handling of hazardous substances in a region or an area.]

[26][**14. Submission of environmental** [27]**[statement]:** —Every person carrying on an industry, operation or process requiring consent under section 25 of the Water (Prevention and Control

of Pollution) Act, 1974 (6 of 1974), or under section 21 of the Air (Prevention and Control of Pollution) Act, 1981 (14 of 1981), or both or authorisation under the Hazardous Wastes (Management and Handling) Rules, 1989, issued under the Environment (Protection) Act, 1986 (29 of 1986), shall submit an environmental [28][statement] for the financial year ending the 31st March, in Form V to the concerned State Pollution Control Board on or before the [29][30th day of September] every year, beginning 1993.]

## SCHEDULE [30][I]

(*See* Rule 3)

| *Sl. No.* | *Industry* | *Parameter* | *Standards* |
|---|---|---|---|
| *1* | *2* | *3* | *4* |
| 1. | Caustic Soda Industry (except for PH | | Concentration not to Industry exceed, milligramme per litre and flow) |
| | | Total concentration of mercury in the final effluent* | 0.01 |
| | | Mercury bearing waste-water generation (flow) | 10 kilolitres/tonne of caustic soda produced. |
| | | pH | 5.5 to 9.0 |

*Final effluent is the combined effluent from (a) cell house, (b) brine plant, (c) chlorine handling, (d) hydrogen handling, (e) hydrochloric acid plant.

| | | | |
|---|---|---|---|
| 2. | Man-made fibres (synthetic) | | Concentration not to exceed, milligramme per litre (except for pH) |
| | | Suspended solids | 100 |
| | | [31][Bio-chemical oxygen demand, (3-days at 27°C) | 30 |
| | | pH | 5.5 to 9.0 |
| 3. | Oil-refinery | | Concentration, quantum, not to exceed, kg/1000 milligramme tones crude per litre (except processed |

| *Sl. No.* | *Industry* | *Parameter* | *Standards* | |
|---|---|---|---|---|
| *1* | *2* | *3* | *4* | |
| | | | for pH) | |
| | | Oil and Grease | 10 | 7 |
| | | Phenol | 1 | 0.7 |
| | | Sulphide | 0.5 | 0.35 |
| | | [31][Bio-chemical oxygen demand, (3-days at 27°C)] | 15 | 10.5 |
| | | Suspended solids | 20 | 14 |
| | | pH | 6 to 8.5 | |
| 4. | Sugar industry | | Concentration not to exceed, milligramme per litre | |
| | | [31][Bio-chemical oxygen demand, (3-days at 27°C)] | 100 for disposal on land<br>30 for disposal in surface waters | |
| | | Suspended solids | 100 for disposal on land<br>30 for disposal in surface waters | |
| 5. | Thermal power plants | | Maximum, limiting concentration, milligramme per litre (except for pH and temperature) | |
| | Condenser cooling waters (once through cooling system) | pH | 6.5—8.5 | |
| | | Temperature | Not more than 5°C higher than the intake water temperature | |
| | | Free available chlorine | 0.5 | |
| | Boiler Blowdowns | Suspended solids | 100 | |
| | | Oil and Grease | 20 | |
| | | Copper (total) | 1.0 | |
| | | Iron (total) | 1.0 | |
| | Cooling-tower blowdown | Free available chlorine | 0.5 | |
| | | Zinc | 1.0 | |
| | | Chromium (total) | 0.2 | |
| | | Phosphate | 5.0 | |
| | | Other corrosion | Limit to be established on | |

| *Sl. No.* | *Industry* | *Parameter* | *Standards* |
|---|---|---|---|
| *1* | *2* | *3* | *4* |
| | | inhibiting material | case by case basis by Central Board in case of Union territories and State Boards in case of states |
| | Ash-pond effluent | pH | 6.5—8.5 |
| | | Suspended solids | 100 |
| | | Oil and Grease | 20 |
| 6. | Cotton textile industries (composite and processing) | | Concentration not to exceed, milligramme per litre (except for pH and bio-assay) |
| | Common: | | |
| | | pH | 5.5 to 9 |
| | | Suspended solid | 100 |
| | | [32][Bio-chemical oxygen demand, (3-days at 27°C)] | 150 |
| | | Oil and Grease | 10 |
| | | Bio-assay test | 90% survival of fish after 96 hours |
| | Special: | | |
| | | Total chromium (as Cr) | 2 |
| | | Sulphide (as S) | 2 |
| | | Phenolic compounds (as $C_6H_5OH$) | 5 |

The special parameters are to be stipulated by the Central Board in case of Union Territories and State Boards in case of states depending upon the dye used in the industry. Where the industry uses chrome dyes, sulphur dyes and/or phenolic compounds in the dyeing/printing process, the limits on chromium of 2 mg/litre, sulphides of 2 mg/litre, and phenolic compounds of 5 mg/litre, respectively shall be imposed.

Where the quality requirement of the recipient system so warrants, the limit of BOD should be lowered up to 30 according to the requirement by the State Boards for the States and the Central Board for the Union Territories.

A limit on sodium absorption ratio of 26 should be imposed by the State Boards for the States and the Central Board for the Union Territories if the disposal of effluent is to be made on land.

| *Sl. No.* | *Industry* | *Parameter* | *Standards* |
|---|---|---|---|
| *1* | *2* | *3* | *4* |
| 7. | Composite woollen mills | | Concentration not to exceed, milligramme per litre (except for pH and bio-assay) |
| | Common: | | |
| | | Suspended solids | 100 |
| | | pH | 5.5 to 9.0 |
| | | [33][Bio-chemical oxygen demand, (3-days at 27°C)] | 10 |
| | | | 10 |
| | | Oil and Grease | 10 |
| | | Bio-assay test | 90% survival of fish after 96 hours |
| | Special: | Total chromium (as Cr) | 2 |
| | | Sulphide (as S) | 2 |
| | | Phenolic compounds (as $C_8H_5OH$) | 5 |

The special parameters to be stipulated by the Central Board in case of Union territories and State Boards in case of States depending upon the dye used in the industry. Where the industry uses chromes dyes, sulphur dyes and/or phenolic compounds in the dyeing/printing process, the limits on chromium of 2 mg/litre, sulphide of 2 mg/litre and phenolic compounds of 5 mg/litre, respectively shall be imposed.

Where the quality requirement of the recipient system so warrants, the limit of BOD should be lowered up to 30 according to the requirement by the State Boards for the state and the Central Board for the Union territories.

A limit on sodium absorption ratio of 26 should be imposed by the State Boards for the States and the Central Board for the Union territories if the disposal of effluent is to be made on land.

| | | | |
|---|---|---|---|
| [34][8. | Dye and Dye Intermediate Industries | | Concentration not to exceed, milligrammes per litre (except for pH, temperature and bio-assay) |
| | | Suspended Solids | 100 |
| | | pH | 6 to 8.5 |
| | | Temperature | Shall not exceed 5°C above the ambient temperature of the receiving body |
| | | Mercury (as Hg) | 0.01 |

| *Sl. No.* | *Industry* | *Parameter* | *Standards* |
|---|---|---|---|
| *1* | *2* | *3* | *4* |
| | | Hexavalent Chromium (as Cr) | 0.1 |
| | | Total Chromium (as Cr) | 2.0 |
| | | Copper (as Cu) | 3.0 |
| | | Zinc (as Zn) | 5.0 |
| | | Nickel (as Ni) | 3.0 |
| | | Cadmium (as Cd) | 2.0 |
| | | Chloride (as Cl) | 1000 |
| | | Sulphate (as $SO_4$) | 1000 |
| | | Phenolic Compounds (as $C_6H_5OH$) | 1.0 |
| | | Oil and Grease | 10 |
| | | Bio-assay Test (with 1:8 dilution of effluents) | 90% survival of test animals after 96 hours |

The standards of chlorides and sulphates are applicable for discharge into inland and surface watercourses. However, when discharged on land for irrigation, the limit for chloride shall not be more than 600 milligrammes per litre and the sodium absorption ratio shall not exceed 26.

| *Sl. No.* | *Industry* | *Parameter* | *Standards* |
|---|---|---|---|
| 9. | Electroplating | | Concentration not to exceed, milligrammes per litre (except for pH and temperature) |
| | | pH | 6.0 to 9.0 |
| | | Temperature | Shall not exceed 5°C above ambient temperature of the receiving body |
| | | Oil and Grease | 10 |
| | | Suspended Solids | 100 |
| | | Cyanides (as CN) | 0.2 |
| | | Ammonical Nitrogen (as N) | 50 |
| | | Total Residual Chloride (as Cl) | 1.0 |
| | | Cadmium (as Cd) | 2.0 |
| | | Nickel (as Ni) | 3.0 |
| | | Zinc (as Zn) | 5.0 |
| | | Hexavalent Chromium (as Cr) | 0.1 |
| | | Total Chromium (as Cr) | 2.0 |
| | | Copper (as Cu) | 3.0 |

| Sl. No. | Industry | Parameter | Standards |
|---|---|---|---|
| 1 | 2 | 3 | 4 |
| | | Lead (as Pb) | 0.1 |
| | | Iron (as Fe) | 3.0 |
| 10. | Cement Plants | | Not to exceed-milligrammes per normal cubic metre |
| | *Plant Capacity:* | | |
| | 200 tonnes per day | Total dust (All sections) | 400 |
| | Greater than 200 tonnes per day | Total dust (All sections) | 250 |

The Central and State Pollution Control Boards may fix stringent standards, not exceeding 250 milligrammes per normal cubic metre for smaller plants and 150 milligrammes per normal cubic matre for larger plants if the industry is located in an area which, in their opinion, requires more stringent standards.

Where continuous monitoring integrators are provided on dust emission lines, the integrated average values over a period, to be fixed by the Central and State Boards but not exceeding 72 hours shall be considered instead of momentary dust emission values for conformity to standards.

| Sl. No. | Industry | Parameter | Standards |
|---|---|---|---|
| [35][11. | Stone-crushing unit | Suspended particulate matter | The suspended particulate matter measured between 3 metres and 10 metres from any process equipment of a stone-crushing unit shall not exceed 600 microgrammes per cubic metre.] |
| [36][12. | Coke ovens | | Concentration in the effluents when discharged into inland surface waters not to exceed milligrammes per litre (except for pH). |
| | | pH | 5.5—90 |
| | | [37][Biochemical Oxygen Demand (3 days at 27°C)] | 30 |
| | | Suspended Solids | 100 |
| | | Phenolic Compounds (as $C_6H_5OH$) | 5 |
| | | Cyanides (as CN) | 0.2 |
| | | Oil & Grease | 10 |

| *Sl. No.* | *Industry* | *Parameter* | *Standards* |
|---|---|---|---|
| *1* | *2* | *3* | *4* |
| | | Ammonical Nitrogen (as N) | 50 |
| 13. | Synthetic Rubber | | Concentration in the effluent when discharged into inland surface waters not to exceed milligramme per litre (except for colour, and pH) |
| | | Colour | Absent |
| | | pH | 5.5—9.0 |
| | | [37][Biochemical Oxygen Demand (3 days at 27°C)] | 50 |
| | | Chemical Oxygen Demand | 250 |
| | | Oil & Grease | 10.0 |
| 14. | Small Pulp and Paper Industry * | | Concentration not to exceed milligramme per litre (except for pH and sodium absorption ratio) |
| | *Discharge into inland surface water | pH | 5.5—9.0 |
| | | Suspended solids | 100 |
| | | BOD | 30 |
| | Disposal on land | pH | 5.5—9.0 |
| | | Suspended Solids | 100 |
| | | BOD | 100 |
| | | Sodium Absorption Ratio | 26 |

*[38][*Note (1):*] Waste water generation shall not exceed 250 cubic metre per tonne of paper produced.

| *Sl. No.* | *Industry* | *Parameter* | *Standards* |
|---|---|---|---|
| 15. | Fermentation Industry (Distilleries, Maltries and Breweries) | | Concentration in the effluent not to exceed milligramme per litre (except for pH and colour & odour) |
| | | pH | 5.5—9.0 |
| | | Colour & odour | [39][All efforts should be made to remove colour and unpleasant odour as far as practicable] |

| *Sl. No.* | *Industry* | *Parameter* | *Standards* |
|---|---|---|---|
| *1* | *2* | *3* | *4* |
| | | Suspended solids | 100 |
| | | [40][BOD (3 days at 27°C)] | |
| | | —disposal into inland surface water/river/ stream | 30 mg/l |
| | | —** Disposal on land for irrigation | 100 mg/l.] |

[41][ * * *]

16. Leather Tanneries — Concentration in the effluents not to exceed milligramme per litre (except for pH and percent sodium)

| | Inland Surface Waters (a) | Public Sewers (b) | Land for Irrigation (c) | Marine Coastal areas (d) |
|---|---|---|---|---|
| Suspended Solids | 100 | 600 | 200 | 100 |
| [42][BOD (3 days at 27°C)] | 30 | 350 | 100 | 100 |
| pH | 6.0-9.0 | 6.0-9.0 | 6.0-9.0 | 6.0-9.0 |
| Chlorides (as Cl) | 1000 | 1000 | 600 | – |
| Hexavalent Chromium (Cr + 6) | 0.1 | 0.2 | 0.1 | 1.0 |
| Total Chromium (as Cr) | 2.0 | 2.0 | 2.0 | 2.0 |
| Sulphides (as S) | 2.0 | 5.0 | – | 5.0 |
| Sodium percent | – | 60 | – | – |
| Boron (as B) | 2.0 | 2.0 | 2.0 | – |
| Oil & Grease | 10 | 20 | 10 | 20 |

17. Fertilizer Industry — Concentration in the effluents not to exceed milligramme per litre (except for pH)

*Effluents*—
Straight
Nitrogenous
Fertilizers.

| *Sl. No.* | *Industry* | *Parameter* | *Standards* | |
|---|---|---|---|---|
| *1* | *2* | *3* | *4* | |
| | excluding the Calcium Ammonium Nitrate and Ammonium Nitrate Fertilizer | Plants Commissioned 1 January 1982 onwards | Plants Commissioned prior to 1 January 1982 | |
| | | | (a) | (b) |
| | | pH | 6.5—8.0 | 6.5—8.0 |
| | | Ammonical Nitrogen | 50 | 75 |
| | | Total Kjeldahl Nitrogen | 100 | 150 |
| | | Free Ammonical Nitrogen | 4 | 4 |
| | | Nitrate Nitroen | 10 | 10 |
| | | Cyanide as CN | 0.2 | 0.2 |
| | | Vanadium as V | 0.2 | 0.2 |
| | | Arsenic as As | 0.2 | 0.2 |
| | | Suspended Solids | 100 | 100 |
| | | Oil and Grease | 10 | 10 |
| | | *Hexavalent Chromium as Cr | 0.1 | 0.1 |
| | | *Total Chromium as Cr | 2.0 | 2.0 |

*To be complied with at the outlet of Chromate removal unit.

| Industry | Parameter | Standards | |
|---|---|---|---|
| Straight Nitrogenous Fertilisers, including Calcium Ammonium Nitrate and Ammonium nitrate Fertilisers | Plants Commissioned 1 January 1982 onwards | Plants Commissioned prior to 1 January 1982 | |
| | | (a) | (b) |
| | pH | 6.5—8.0 | 6.5—8.0 |
| | Ammonical Nitrogen | 50 | 75 |
| | Total Kjeldahl Nitrogen | 100 | 150 |
| | Free Ammonical Nitrogen | 4 | 4 |

| *Sl. No.* | *Industry* | *Parameter* | *Standards* | |
|---|---|---|---|---|
| *1* | *2* | *3* | *4* | |
| | | Nitrate Nitrogen | 20 | 20 |
| | | Cyanide as CN | 0.2 | 0.2 |
| | | Vanadium as V | 0.2 | 0.2 |
| | | Arsenic as As | 0.2 | 0.2 |
| | | Suspended Solids | 100 | 100 |
| | | Oil and Grease | 10 | 10 |
| | | * Hexavalent Chromium as Cr | 0.1 | 0.1 |
| | | * Total Chromium as Cr | 2.0 | 2.0 |

* To be complied with at the outlet of Chromate removal unit.

| | Industry | Parameter | Plants commissioned 1 January 1982 onwards | Plants commissioned prior to 1 January 1982 |
|---|---|---|---|---|
| | | | (a) | (b) |
| | Complex Fertilizers, excluding Calcium Ammonium Nitrate, Ammonium Nitrate & Ammonium Nitrophosphate Fertilizers | pH | 6.5—8.0 | 6.5—8.0 |
| | | Ammonical Nitrogen | 50 | 75 |
| | | Free Ammonical Nitrogen | 4 | 4 |
| | | Total Kjeldahl Nitrogen | 100 | 150 |
| | | Nitrate Nitrogen | 10 | 10 |
| | | Cyanide as CN | 0.2 | 0.2 |
| | | Vanadium as V | 0.2 | 0.2 |
| | | Arsenic as As | 0.2 | 0.2 |
| | | Phosphate as P | 5 | 5 |
| | | Oil and Grease | 10 | 10 |
| | | Suspended Solids | 100 | 100 |
| | | *Fluorideas F | 10 | 10 |
| | | **Hexavalent Chromium as Cr | 0.1 | 0.1 |
| | | **Total Chromium as Cr | 2.0 | 2.0 |

| *Sl. No.* | *Industry* | *Parameter* | *Standards* | |
|---|---|---|---|---|
| *1* | *2* | *3* | *4* | |
| | Complex Fertilizers, including Calcium Ammonium Nitrate, Ammonium Nitrate & Ammonium Nitrophosphate Fertilizers | | Plants commissioned 1 January 1982 onwards | Plants commissioned prior to 1 January 1982 |
| | | | (a) | (b) |
| | | pH | 6.5—8.0 | 6.5—8.0 |
| | | Ammonical Nitrogen | 50 | 75 |
| | | Free Ammonical Nitrogen | 100 | 100 |
| | | Nitrate Nitrogen | 20 | 20 |
| | | Cyanide as CN | 0.2 | 0.2 |
| | | Vanadium as V | 0.2 | 0.2 |
| | | Arsenic as As | 0.2 | 0.2 |
| | | Phosphate as P | 5 | 5 |
| | | Oil and Grease | 10 | 10 |
| | | Suspended Solids | 100 | 100 |
| | | *Fluoride as F | 10 | 10 |
| | | **Hexavalent Chromium as Cr | 0.1 | 0.1 |
| | | **Total Chromium as Cr | 2.0 | 2.0 |

* To be complied with at the outlet of Fluoride removal unit. If the recipient system so demands, Fluoride as F shall be limited to 1.5 mg/1.

** To be complied with at the outlet of Chromate removal unit.

| | | | |
|---|---|---|---|
| | Straight Phosphatic Fertilizers | | |
| | | pH | 7.0—9.0 |
| | | Phosphate as P | 5 |
| | | Oil and Grease | 10 |
| | | Suspended Solids | 100 |
| | | *Fluoride as F | 10 |
| | | **Hexavalent | 0.1 |

| *Sl. No.* | *Industry* | *Parameter* | *Standards* |
|---|---|---|---|
| *1* | *2* | *3* | *4* |
| | | Chromium as Cr | |
| | | **Total Chromium as Cr | 2.0 |
| *Emissions* | | | |
| | —Phosphatic Fertilizers (Fluoride and Particulate matter emission) | Phosphoric acid manufacturing unit | 25 milligrammes per normal cubic metre as total Fluoride |
| | | Granulation, mixing and grinding of rock Phosphate | 150 milligrammes per normal cubic metre of particulate matter |
| | —Urea (particulate matter emission) | Prilling Tower Commissioned prior to 1-1-1982 | 150 milligramme per normal cubic metre or 2 kilogramme per tonne of product |
| | | Commissioned after 1-1-1982 | 50 milligramme per normal cubic metre or 0.5 kilogramme per tonne of product |

* To be complied with at the outlet of Fluoride removal unit. If the recipient system so demands, Fluoride as F shall be limited to 1.5 mg./1.

** To be complied with at the outlet of Chromate removal unit.

| | | | |
|---|---|---|---|
| 18. | Aluminium | Particulate Matter Emissions: | |
| | | —Calcination | 250 milligramme per normal cubic metre of particulate matter |
| | | —Smelting | 150 milligramme per normal cubic metre of particulate matter |
| 19. | Calcium Carbide | Particulate Matter Emission: | |
| | | —Kiln | 250 milligramme per normal cubic metre |
| | | —Arc Furnace | 150 milligramme per normal cubic metre |
| 20. | CarbonBlack | Particulate Matter Emisison: | 150 milligramme per normal cubic metre |
| 21. | Copper, Lead and Zinc | Particulate Matter Emission in concent-rator | 150 milligramme per normal cubic metre |
| | Smelting | Emission of Oxides of | |
| | | | Off-gases must be utilised for |

| *Sl. No.* | *Industry* | *Parameter* | *Standards* |
|---|---|---|---|
| *1* | *2* | *3* | *4* |
| | | sulphur in smelter & Converter | sulphuric acid manufacture. The limits of sulphur dioxide emission from stock shall not exceed 4 kilogramme per tonne of concentrated (one hundred per cent) acid produced. |
| 22. | Nitric acid (emission of oxides of nitrogen) | Emission of Oxides of Nitrogen | 3 kilogramme of oxides of nitrogen per tonne of weak acid (before concentration) produced. |
| 23. | Sulphuric Acid (emission of Sulphur dioxide & acid mist) | sulphur dioxide emissions | 4 kilogramme per tonne of concentrated (One hundred per cent) acid produced |
| | | Acid Mist | 50 milligramme per normal cubic metre |
| 24. | Iron & Steel (Integrated) | Particulte Matter Emission | |
| | | —Sintering Plant | 150 milligrammes per normal cubic metre |
| | | —Steel making | |
| | | —during normal operations | 150 milligrammes per normal cubic metre |
| | | —during oxygen lancing | 400 milligrammes per normal cubic metre |
| | | —Rolling Mill | 150 milligrammes per normal cubic metre |
| | | Carbon monoxide from coke oven | 3 kilogrammes per tonne of code produced.] |
| [43][25. | Thermal Power Plants | *Particulate Matter Emissions: | |
| | | —generation capacity 210 MW or more | 150 milligramme per normal cubic metre |
| | | —generation capacity less than 210 MW | 350 milligramme per normal cubic metre |

*Depending upon the requirement of local situation, such as protected area, the State Pollution Control Boards and other implementing agencies under the Environment (Protection) Act, 1986, may prescribe a limit of 150 milligramme per normal cubic metre, irrespective of generation capacity of the plant.

| *Sl. No.* | *Industry* | *Parameter* | *Standards* |
|---|---|---|---|
| *1* | *2* | *3* | *4* |
| 26. | Natural Rubber industry | | Concentrations in the effluents not to exceed milligramme per litre (except for pH) |
| | —Discharge into inland surface waters | Colour & Odour | Absent |
| | | pH | 6.0—9.0 |
| | | BOD | 50 |
| | | COD | 250 |
| | | Oil & Grease | 10 |
| | | Sulphides | 2 |
| | | Total Kjeldhal Nitrogen | 100 |
| | | Dissolved phosphate (as P) | 5 |
| | | Suspended solids | 100 |
| | | Dissolved solids (inorganic) | 2100 |
| | | Ammonical nitrogen (as N) | 50 |
| | | Free ammonia (as $NH_3$) | 5 |
| | — Disposal on land for irrigation | Colour & Odour | Absent |
| | | pH | 6.0—8.0 |
| | | BOD | 100 |
| | | COD | 250 |
| | | Oil & Grease | 10 |
| | | Suspended solids | 200 |
| | | Dissolved solids | 2100] |
| [44][27. | All types of Asbestos manufacturing units: (including all processes involving the use of Asbestos) | Emissions | |
| | | -- Pure asbestos material | 4 Fibre*/cc |
| | | —Total dust | 2mg/$m^3$ (normal) |

*Fibre of length more than 5 micrometre and diametre less than 3 micrometre with an aspect ratio of 3 or more.

| Sl. No. | Industry | Parameter | Standards |
|---|---|---|---|
| 1 | 2 | 3 | 4 |
| 28. | Chlor Alkali (Caustic soda) | Emissions | Concentrations in mg/m² (normal) |
| | (a) Mercury Cell | Mercury (from hydrogen gasholder stack) | 0.2 |
| | (b) All processes | Chlorine (from hypo tower) | 15.0 |
| | (c) All processes | Hydrochloric acid vapour and mist (from (hydrochloric acid plant) | 35.0 |
| 29. | Large pulp and Paper | Emissions | Concentration in mg/m² (normal) |
| | | Particulate matter | 250** |
| | | $H_2S$ | 10 |

**'This standard of 250 mg/m³ (normal) shall apply only for a period of 3 years with effect from the date on which the Environment (Protection) Second Amendment Rules, 1989, came into force. After three years the standard to be applicable in 15 mg/m³ (normal).

| Sl. No. | Industry | Parameter | Standards |
|---|---|---|---|
| 30. | Integrated Iron and Steel Plants: | | |
| | | I. Emissions | |
| | (a) Coke oven | Particulate matter | 50 |
| | (b) Refractory material plant | Particulate matter | 150 |
| | | II. Effluents | Concentration in mg/litre (except for pH) |
| | (a) Coke oven | | |
| | By product plant: | pH | 6.0—8.5 |
| | | Suspended solids | 100 |
| | | Phenol | 1.0 |
| | | Cyanide | 0.2 |
| | | [45][BOD (3 days at 27°C)] | 30 |
| | | COD | 250 |
| | | Ammonical nitrogen | 50 |
| | | Oil and Grease | 10 |

| *Sl. No.* | *Industry* | *Parameter* | *Standards* |
|---|---|---|---|
| *1* | *2* | *3* | *4* |
| | (b) Other plants such as sintering plant, blast furnace, steel melting and rolling mill: | pH | 6.0-9.0 |
| | | Suspended solids | 100 |
| | | Oil and Grease | 10 |

| Sl. No. | Industry | Parameter | Standards ($mg/Nm^3$) |
|---|---|---|---|
| 1 | 2 | 3 | 4 |
| 31. | Reheating (Reverberatory) Furnaces: | Emissions | Concentration in $mg/m^3$ (normal) |
| | Capacity: 'All 'sizes | | |
| | Sensitive area | Particulate matter | 150 |
| | Other area | Particulate matter | 450] |
| [46][32. | Foundries: | Emissions | |
| | (a) Cupola Capacity (melting rate): | | |
| | Less than 3 MT/hr. | Particulate Matter | 450 |
| | 3 MT/hr. and above | Particulate matter | 150 |
| | (b) Arc furnaces | | |
| | Capacity: All sizes | Particulate Matter | 150 |
| | (c) Induction furnaces | | |
| | Capacity: All Sizes | Particulate Matter | 150 |

*Note:* In respect of arc furnaces and induction furnaces, provision has to be made for collecting the fumes before discharging the emissions through the stack.

| | | | |
|---|---|---|---|
| 33. | Thermal Power Plants | Stack height/limits | |
| | | *Power generation capacity*: | |
| | | —500 MW and above | 275 |
| | | —200 MW/210 MW and above to less than 500 MW | 220 |
| | | —Less than 200 MW/ | $H=14(Q)^{0.3}$ where Q is |

| Sl. No. | Industry | Parameter | Standards (mg/Nm³ |
|---|---|---|---|
| 1 | 2 | 3 | 4 |
| | | 210 MW | emission rate of $SO_2$ in kg/hr. and H is stack height in metres |
| | | *Steam generating capacity:* | |
| | | —Less than 2 ton/hr. | 2 ½ times the neighbouring building height or 9 metres (whichever is more) |
| | | —More than 2 ton/hr. to 5 ton/hr. | 12 |
| | | —More than 5 ton/hr. to 10 ton/hr. | 15 |
| | | —More than 10 ton/hr. | 18 |
| | | —More than 15 ton/hr. to 25 ton/hr. | 15 |
| | | —More than 20 ton/hr. to 25 ton/hr. | 24 |
| | | —More than 25 ton/hr. to 30 ton/hr. | 27 |
| | | —More than 30 ton/hr. | 30 or using formula $H=14(Q)^{0.3}$ (whichever is more) where Q is emission rate of $SO_2$, in kg/hr. and H is stack height in meters. |
| 34. | Small boilers | Emissions* Particulate Matter | |
| | *Capacity of boiler* | | |
| | —Less than 2 ton/hr | | 1600 |
| | —2 to 15 ton/hr. | | 1200 |
| | —More than 15 ton/hr. | | 150 |

*All emissions normalized to 12 per cent carbon dioxide

| | | | |
|---|---|---|---|
| 35. | Oil Refineries (Sulphur dioxide) | Emissions | |
| | | —Distillation (atmospheric plus vacuum) | 0.25 kg/MT of feed** |

| *Sl. No.* | *Industry* | *Parameter* | *Standards* |
|---|---|---|---|
| *1* | *2* | *3* | *4* |
| | | —Catalytic cracker | 2.5 kg/MT of feed |
| | | —Sulphur recovery unit | 120 kg/MT of sulphur in the feed |

**Feed indicates the feed for that part of the process under consideration only.

| | | | |
|---|---|---|---|
| 36. | Aluminium Plants | Emissions | |
| | (a) Alumina plant: | | |
| | (i) Raw material handling | Primary and secondary crusher Particulate Matter | 150 |
| | (ii) Precipitation area | Particulate Matter | 250 |
| | | Carbon monoxide | 1% max. |
| | –Calcination | Stack height | $H = 14(Q)^{0.3}$ where Q is emission rate of $SO_2$ in kg/hr and H is stack height in metres |
| | (b) Smelter point | | |
| | (i) Green anode shop | Particulate Matter | 150 |
| | (ii) Anode bake oven | Particulate Matter | 150 |
| | | Total flouride (F) | 0.3 kg/MT of Aluminium |
| | (iii) Potroom | Particulate Matter | 150 |
| | | Total fluoride (F) | |
| | | VSS | 4.7 kg/MT of Aluminium produced |
| | | HSS | 6.0 kg/MT of Aluminium produced |
| | | PBSW | 2.5 kg/MT of Aluminium produced |
| | | PBCW | 1.0 kg/MT. of Aluminuim produced. |
| | | Stack height | $H = 14(Q)^{0.3}$ where Q is emission rate of $SO_2$ in kg/hr. and H is stack height in metres |

| *Sl. No.* | *Industry* | *Parameter* | *Standards* |
|---|---|---|---|
| *1* | *2* | *3* | *4* |

Note: VSS = Vertical stud soderberg
HSS = Horizontal stud soderberg
PBSW = Prebacked side worked
PBCW = Prebacked centre worked

| | | | |
|---|---|---|---|
| 37. | Stone crushing unit | Suspended Particulate Matter (SPM) | The standards consist of two parts:<br>(i) *Implementation of the following pollution control measures:*<br>(a) Dust containment cum suppression system for the equipment.<br>(b) Construction of wind breaking walls.<br>(c) Construction of the metalled roads within the premises.<br>(d) Regular cleaning and wetting of the ground within the premises.<br>(e) Growing of a green belt along the periphery.<br>*(ii) Quantitative standard for the SPM:*<br>The Suspended Particulate Matter contribution value at a distance of 40 metres from a controlled isolated as well as from a unit located in a cluster should be less than 600 mg/$Nm^3$. The measurements are to be conducted at least twice a month for all the 12 months in a year. |

| Sl. No. | Industry | Parameter | Standards (concentrations in mg./l except for pH, temperature, specific pesticides and Bio-assay test) |
|---|---|---|---|
| 1 | 2 | 3 | 4 |
| 38. | Petrochemicals (Basic and intr mediates) | Effluents | |
| | | pH | 6.5-8.5 |
| | | *[47] [(BOD (3 days at 27°C)] | 50 |
| | | **Phenol | 5 |
| | | Sulphide (as S) | 2 |
| | | COD | 250 |
| | | Cyanide (as CN) | 0.2 |
| | | ***Fluoride (as F) | 15 |
| | | Total suspended solids | 1000 |
| | | Hexavalent Chromium (as CR) | 0.1 |
| | | ****Total Chromium (as CR) | 2.0 |

* State Boards may prescribe the BOD value of 30 mg/l if the recipient system so demands.

** The limit for phenol shall be conformed to at the outlet of effluent treatment of phenol plant. However, at the final disposal point, the limit shall be less than 1mg/1.

***The limit for fluoride shall be conformed to at the outlet of fluoride removal unit. However. at the disposal point, fluoride concentration shall be lower than 5 mg/1.

****The limits for total and hexavalent chromium shall be conformed to at the outlet of the chromate removal unit. This implies that in the final treated effluent, total and hexavalent chromium shall be lower than prescribed herein.

| Sl. No. | Industry | Parameter | Standards |
|---|---|---|---|
| 39. | Pharmaceutical manufacturing and formation industry | Effluents | |
| | | 1. pH | 5.5—9.0 |
| | | 2. Oil and Grease | 10 |
| | | 3. Total suspended solids | 100 |
| | | 4. [48][BOD (3 days at 27°C)] | 30 |
| | | 5. Bio-assay test | 90% survival of fish after 96 hrs. in 100% effluent |

| *Sl. No.* | *Industry* | *Parameter* | *Standards (concentrations in mg./l except for pH, temperature, specific pesticides and Bio-assay test)* |
|---|---|---|---|
| *1* | *2* | *3* | *4* |
| | | 6. Mercury | 0.01 |
| | | 7. Arsenic | 0.20 |
| | | 8. Chromium (Hexavalent) | 0.10 |
| | | 9. Lead | 0.10 |
| | | 10. Cyanide | 0.10 |
| | | 11. Phenolics (as $C_6H_5OH$) | 1.00 |
| | | 12. Sulphides (as S) | 2.00 |
| | | 13. Phosphates (as P) | 5.00 |

*Notes:*

1. Parameters listed as 1 to 13 are compulsory for formulators. However, the remaining parameters (6 to 13) will be optional for others.
2. State Board may prescribe limit for chemical oxygen demand (COD) correlated with BOD limit.
3. State Board may prescribe limit for total dissolved solids depending upon uses of recipient water body.
4. Limits should be complied with at the terminal of the treatment until before letting out of the factory boundary limits.
5. For the compliance of limits, analysis should be done in the composite sample collected every hour for a period of 8 hours.

| | | | |
|---|---|---|---|
| 40. | Pesticide Manufacturing and Formulation industry | Effluents | |
| | | 1. Temperature | Shall not exceed 5°C above the receiving water tempeature |
| | | 2. pH | 6.5—8.5 |
| | | 3. Oil and Grease | 10 |
| | | 4. [49][(BOD (3 days at 27°C)] | 30 |

| Sl. No. | Industry | Parameter | Standards (concentrations in mg./l except for pH, temperature, specific pesticides and Bio-assay test) |
|---|---|---|---|
| 1 | 2 | 3 | 4 |
| | | 5. Total suspended solids | 100 |
| | | 6. Bio-assay test | 90% survival of fish after 96 hours in 100 per cent effluent |
| | | 7. (a) Specific pesticides: | |
| | | Benzene | 10 |
| | | Hexachloride Carboryl | 10 |
| | | DDT | 10 |
| | | Endosulfan | 10 |
| | | Diamethoate | 450 |
| | | Fenitrothion | 10 |
| | | Malathion | 10 |
| | | Phorate | 10 |
| | | Methyl parathion | 10 |
| | | Phenthoate | 10 |
| | | Pyrethrums | 10 |
| | | Copper Oxychloride | 9600 |
| | | Copper sulphate | 50 |
| | | Ziram | 1000 |
| | | Sulphur | 30 |
| | | Paraquat | 2300 |
| | | Proponil | 7300 |
| | | Nitrogen | 780 |
| | | (b) Heavy metals: | |
| | | Copper | 1.00 |
| | | Manganese | 1.00 |
| | | Zinc | 1.00 |
| | | Mercury | 0.01 |
| | | Tin | 0.10 |
| | | Any other metal like Nickel, etc. | Shall not exceed 5 times the drinking water standards of BIS |
| | | (c) Organics: Phenol and phenolic compounds as $C_6H_5OH$ | 1.0 |

| *Sl. No.* | *Industry* | *Parameter* | *Standards (concentrations in mg./l except for pH, temperature, specific pesticides and Bio-assay test)* |
|---|---|---|---|
| 1 | 2 | 3 | 4 |

*Notes:*

1. Limits should be complied with at the end of the treatment plant before any dilution.
2. Bio-assay test should be carried out with available species of fish in receiving water.
3. State Board may prescribe limits of total dissolved solids (TDS) sulphates and chlorides depending on the uses of recipient water body.
4. State Board may prescribe COD limit correlated with BOD limit.
5. Pesticides are known to have metabolites and isomers. If they are founding significant concentration, standards may be prescribed for those in the list by Central or State Board.
6. Industries are required to analyze pesticides in waste by advanced analytical method such a GLC/HPLC.
7. All the parameters will be compulsory for formulators, for others, the 7th will be optional.

| | | | |
|---|---|---|---|
| 41. | Tannery (after primary treatment Disposal: Channel/Conduit Carrying waste waters to secondary treatment plants Type of tanneries | Effluents | |
| | –Chrome tanneries/ Combined chrome and vegetable tanneries | pH | 6.5—9.0 |
| | | SS | Not to exceed 600 |
| | | Chromium concentration after treatment in the chrome waste water stream | 45 |
| | —Vegetable tanneries | pH | 6.5—9.0 |
| | | SS | Not to exceed 600 |

*Note:*

The above standards will apply to those tannery units which have made full contribution to a Common Effluent Treatment Plant (CETP) comprising secondary treatment. Those who have not contributed will be governed by earlier Notification No. S.O. 64(E), dated January 18th, 1988.

| Sl. No. | Industry | Parameter | Standards (concentrations in mg./l except for pH, temperature, specific pesticides and Bio-assay test) |
|---|---|---|---|
| 1 | 2 | 3 | 4 |
| 42. | Paint industry (Waste-water discharge) | Effluents | |
| | | pH | 6.0-8.5 |
| | | Suspended Solids | 100 |
| | | [50][BOD (3 days at 27°C)] | 50 |
| | | Phenolics as $C_6H_5OH$ | 1.0 |
| | | Oil and Grease | 10.0 |
| | | Bio-assay test | 90 per cent survival in 96 hours |
| | | Lead as Pb | 0.1 |
| | | Chromium as Cr | 0.1 |
| | | Hexavalent | |
| | | Total | 2.0 |
| | | Copper as Cu | 2.0 |
| | | Nickel as Ni | 2.0 |
| | | Zinc as Zn | 5.0 |
| | | Total heavy metals | 7.0 |
| 43. | Inorganic chemical industry (Waste-water discharge) Part 1 (metal compounds of Chromium, Manganese, Nickel, Copper, Zinc, Cadmium, Lead and Mercury) | Effluents | |
| | | pH | 6.0—8.5 |
| | | Chromium as Cr | 0.1 |
| | | Hexavalent | |
| | | Total | 2.0 |
| | | Manganese as Mn | 2.0 |
| | | Nickel as Ni | 2.0 |
| | | Copper as Cu | 2.0 |
| | | Zinc as Zn | 5.0 |
| | | Cadmium as Cd | 0.2 |
| | | Lead as Pb | 0.1 |
| | | Mercury as Hg | 0.01 |
| | | Cyanide as CN | 0.2 |
| | | Oil and Grease | 10.0 |
| | | Suspended solids | 30.0 |

In addition to the above, total heavy metals are to be limited to 7 mg/1.

| *Sl. No.* | *Industry* | *Parameter* | *Standards (concentrations in mg./l except for pH, temperature, specific pesticides and Bio-assay test)* |
|---|---|---|---|
| 1 | 2 | 3 | 4 |
| 44. | Bullion Refining (Waste-water discharge) | Effluents | |
| | | pH | 6.5—8.5 |
| | | Cyanide as CN | 0.2 |
| | | Sulphide as S | 0.2 |
| | | Nitrate as N | 10.0 |
| | | Free $Cl_2$ and Cl | 1.0 |
| | | Zinc as Zn | 5.0 |
| | | Copper as Cu | 2.0 |
| | | Nickel as Ni | 2.0 |
| | | Arsenic as As | 0.1 |
| | | Cadmium as Cd | 0.2 |
| | | Oil and Grease | 10.0 |
| | | Suspended solids | 100 |
| 45. | Dye and Dye Intermediate Industry (Waste-water discharge) | Effluents | |
| | | pH | 6.0—8.5 |
| | | Colour, Hazen Unit | 400.0 |
| | | Suspended solids | 100.0 |
| | | [51][BOD (3 days at 27°C)] | 100.0 |
| | | Oil and Grease | 10.0 |
| | | Phenolic as $C_6H_5OH$ | 1.0 |
| | | Cadmium as Cd | 0.2 |
| | | Copper as Cu | 2.0 |
| | | Manganese as Mn | 2.0 |
| | | Lead as Pb | 0.1 |
| | | Mercury as Hg | 0.01 |
| | | Nickel as Ni | 2.0 |
| | | Zinc as Zn | 5.0 |
| | | Chromium as Cr | 0.1 |
| | | Hexavalent | |
| | | Total | 2.0 |
| | | Bio-assay test | 90% survival in 96 hours |

| *Sl. No.* | *Company* | *Standards, d B (A)* |
|---|---|---|
| *1* | *2* | *3* |
| 46. | Noise limits for automobiles (free field at one metre in dB(A) at the manufacturing stage) to be achieved by the year 1992 | |
| | (a) Motorcycles, scooters and three wheelers | 80 |
| | (b) Passenger cars | 82 |
| | (c) Passenger or commercial vehicles up to 4 MT | 85 |
| | (d) Passenger or commercial vehicles above 4 MT and up to 12 MT | 89 |
| | (e) Passenger or commercial vehicles exceeding 12 MT | 91 |
| 47. | Domestic appliances and construction equipments at the manufacturing state to be achieved by the year 1993 | |
| | (a) Window air-conditioners of 1 ton to 1.5 ton | 68 |
| | (b) Air-coolers | 60 |
| | (c) Refrigerators | 46 |
| | (d) Diesel generators for domestic purposes | 85-90 |
| | (e) Compactors (rollers) front loaders, concrete mixers, cranes (movable) vibrators and saws | 75] |

| *Sl. No.* | *Industry* | *Parameter* | *Standards* |
|---|---|---|---|
| *1* | *2* | *3* | *4* |
| [52][48. | Glass Industry | Emissions | |
| | A. Sodalime and Borosilicate and other special glass (other than Lead) | | |
| | (a) Furnace: Capacity | | |
| | (i) Up to a product draw capacity of 60 Mt/Day | Particulate matter | 20 kg/hr. |
| | (ii) Product draw capacity more than 60 Mt/Day | Particulate matter | 0.8 kg/Mt. Of product drawn |

| *Sl. No.* | *Industry* | *Parameter* | *Standards* |
|---|---|---|---|
| *1* | *2* | *3* | *4* |
| (iii) | For all capacities | Stack height | $H=14(Q)^{0.3}$ where Q is the emission rate of $SO_2$ in Kg/hr. and H is stack height in metres |
| | (b) Implementation of the following measures for fugitive emission control from other sections: | Total fluorides | 5.0 mg/NM³ |
| | | NOx | Use of low NOx burners in new plants |
| | (i) Raw material should be transported in leak proof containers. | | |
| | (ii) Cullet preparation should be dust-free using water spraying. | | |
| | (iii) Batch preparation section should be covered. | | |
| | B. Lead glass | | |
| | (a) Furnace: | | |
| | All capacities | Particulate matter | 50 mg/NM³ |
| | | Lead | 20 mg/NM³ |
| | (b) Implementation of the following measures for fugitive emission control from other sections. | | |
| | (i) Batch mixing, proportioning sections and transfer points should be covered and it should be connected to control equipments to meet following standards: | | |
| | | Particulate matter | 50 mg/NM³ |
| | | Lead | 20 mg/NM³ |
| | (ii) Minimum stack height should be 30 metre in lead glass units. | | |
| | (c) Pot Furnace at Firozabad | | |
| | Furnace: | Particulate matter | 1200 mg/NM³ |

*Note:*
Depending upon local environmental conditions, State/Central Pollution Control Board can prescribe more stringent standards than those prescribed above.

| | Industry | Parameter | Standards |
|---|---|---|---|
| | Glass Industry (For all categories) | Effluents: | |
| | | pH | 6.5-8.5 |
| | | Total suspended solids | 100 mg/1 |
| | | Oil and Grease | 10 mg/1 |
| | Lime Kiln | Stack height | |
| 49. | Capacity:- | | |
| | Up to 5T/Day | Stack Height | A hood should be provided with a stack of 30 metre height from ground level (including kiln height). |

| Sl. No. | Industry | Parameter | Standards |
|---|---|---|---|
| 1 | 2 | 3 | 4 |
| | Above 5T/Day | Stack Height | H = 14 $(Q)^{0.3}$ where Q is emission rate of $SO_2$ in Kg/hr and H = Stack height in metres. |
| | More than 5T/ Day and upto 40T/Day | Particulate Matter | 500 mg/$NM^3$ |
| | Above 40T/Day | Particulate matter | 150 mg/$NM^3$ |
| 50. | *Slaughter House, Meat and Sea Food Industry: | Effluents | |
| A. | Slaughter house | | |
| | (a) Above 70 TLWK | [53][BOD (3 days at 27°C | 100 |
| | | Suspended solids | 100 |
| | | Oil and Grease | 10 |
| | (b) 70 TLWK and below | [53][BOD (3 days at 27°C)] | 500 |
| B. | Meat processing | | |
| | (a) Frozen Meat | [53] [BOD (3 days at 27°C)] | 30 |
| | | Suspended solids | 30 |
| | | Oil and Grease | 10 |
| | (b) Raw Meat from own slaughter house | [53][BOD (3 days at 27°C)] | 50 |
| | | Suspended solids | 50 |
| | | Oil and Grease | 10 |
| | (c) Raw meat from other sources | | Disposal *via* screen and septic tank |
| C. | Sea Food Industry | [53] [BOD (3 days at 27°C)] | 30 |
| | | Suspended solids | 50 |
| | | Oil and Grease | 10 |

*Notes:*

(i) TLWK—Total Live Weight Killed. (ii) In case of disposal into municipal sewer where sewage is treated the industries shall in stall screen and oil and grease separation units. (iii) The industries having slaughter house along with meat processing units will be considered in meat processing category as far as standards are concerned.

* The emission standards from Boiler House shall conform to the standards already prescribed under E(P) Act. 1986, *vide* notification No. GSR 742 (E), dated 30-08-1990.

| *Sl. No.* | *Industry* | *Parameter* | *Standards* | |
|---|---|---|---|---|
| *1* | *2* | *3* | *4* | |
| 51. | Food and Fruit Processing Industry Category: | Effluents | Concentration not to exceed mg/l except pH | Quantum gm/MT of product |
| A. | Soft Drinks | | | |
| | (a) Fruit based synthetic (More than 0.4 MT/Day) Bottles and tetrapack | pH | 6.5—8.5 | – |
| | | Suspended solids | 100 | |
| | | Oil and Grease | 10 | |
| | | [54][BOD (3 days at 27°C)] | 30 | |
| | (b) Synthetic (Less than 0.4 MT/Day) | | Disposal via Septic tank | – |
| B. | Fruit and vegetables (a) Above 0.4 MT/Day | pH | 6.5—8.5 | |
| | | Suspended solids | 50 | |
| | | Oil and Grease | 10 | |
| | | [54][BOD (3 days at 27°C)] | 30 | |
| | (b) 0.1-0.4 MT/ Day (10 MT/Yr) | | Disposal *via* Septic tank | -- |
| C. | Bakery | | | |
| | (a) Bread & bread and biscuit | | | |
| | (i) Continuous process (more than 20T/Day) | pH | 6.5-8.5 | |
| | | [54][BOD (3 days at 27°C)] | 200 | 25 |
| | (ii) Non-continuous process (less than 20 MT/Day) | | Disposal via Septic tank | |
| | (b) Biscuit Production | | | |
| | (i) 10T/Day and above | pH | 6.5—8.5 | |
| | | [54][OD (3 days at 27°C)] | 300 | 35 |

| *Sl. No.* | *Industry* | *Parameter* | *Standards* |
|---|---|---|---|
| *1* | *2* | *3* | *4* |
| | (ii) Below 10 T/ Day | | Disposal via Septic tank |
| | D. Confectioneries | Effluents | |
| | (a) 4 T/Day and above | pH | 6.5-8.5 |
| | | Suspended solids | 50 |
| | | Oil and Grease | 10 |
| | | [54][BOD (3 days at 27°C)] | 30 |
| | (b) Below 4 T/Day | | Disposal *via* Septic tank |

*Notes:*

To ascertain the category of 'unit fails' the average of daily production and waste water discharge for the preceding 30 operating days from the date of sampling shall be considered. The emission from the boiler house shall conform to the standards already prescribed under the Environment (Protection) Act, 1986, vide Notification No. GSR 742 (E), dated 30-08-1990.

| | | | |
|---|---|---|---|
| 52. | *Jute Processing Industry: | Effluents | Concentration in mg/l except pH and water consumption |
| | | pH | 5.5-9.0 |
| | | [55][BOD (3 days at 27°C)] | 30 |
| | | Suspended solids | 100 |
| | | Oil and Grease | 10 |
| | | Water consumption | 1.60 Cum/Ton of product produced. |

*Notes:* 1. Water consumption for the jute processing industry will be 1.5 Cum/ton of product from January, 1992.

2. At present no limit for colour is given for liquid effluent. However, as far as possible, colour should be removed.

* Stack emissions from boiler house shall conform to the standards already prescribed under Environment (Protection) Act, 1986, vide Notification No. GSR 742 (E), dated 30-8-90.

| | | | |
|---|---|---|---|
| 53. | Large Pulp and Paper/News Print/ Rayon Grade Plants of Capacity above 24,000 mt/annum | | |

| *Sl. No.* | *Industry* | *Parameter* | *Standards* |
|---|---|---|---|
| *1* | *2* | *3* | *4* |
| | | pH | 7.0—85 |
| | | [56][BOD (3 days at 27°C)] | 30 |
| | | COD | 350 |
| | | Suspended solids | 50 |
| | | TOCL | 2.0 kg.Ton of product |
| | | Flow (total waste Water discharge | |
| | | **(i) Large pulp and paper | 200 Cum/ton of paper produced |
| | | (ii) Large rayon grade/ News print | 150 Cum/Ton of paper produced |

*Notes:*

* The Standards for Total Organic Chloride (TOCL) will be applicable from January 1992.

** The Standards with respect to total waste water discharge for the large pulp and paper mills to be established from 1992, will meet standards of 100 Cum/ Ton of paper produced.

| | | | |
|---|---|---|---|
| 54. | Small Pulp and Paper, Plant of Capacity Upto 24,000 MT/Annum: | Effluent | |
| | *Category:* | | |
| | A. *Agro-based | Total waste-water Discharge | 2000 cum/Ton of paper produced |
| | B. **Waste-paper based | -do- | 75 Cu/Tom of paper produced |

*Notes:*

* The agro-based mills to be established from January, 1992 will meet the standards of 150 Cum/Ton of paper produced.

** The waste-paper mills to be established from January, 1992 will meet the standards of 50 Cum/Ton of paper produced.

| | | | |
|---|---|---|---|
| 55. | Common Effluent Treatment Plants: | Effluents (inlet effluent quality for CETP) | (Concentration in mg/1) |
| | A. Primary Treatment | pH | 5.5-9.0 |
| | | Temperature °C | 45 |

| *Sl. No.* | *Industry* | *Parameter* | *Standards* |
|---|---|---|---|
| *1* | *2* | *3* | *4* |
| | | Oil and Grease | 20 |
| | | Phenolic compounds (as $C_6H_5OH$) | 5.0 |
| | | Ammonical Nitrogen (as N) | 50 |
| | | Cyanide (as CN) | 2.0 |
| | | Chromium (hexavalent) (as Cr+6) | 2.0 |
| | | Chromium (total) (as Cr) | 2.0 |
| | | Copper (as Cu) | 3.0 |
| | | Lead (as Pb) | 1.0 |
| | | Nickel (as Ni) | 3.0 |
| | | Zinc (as An) | 15 |
| | | Arsenic (as As) | 0.2 |
| | | Mercury (as Hg) | 0.01 |
| | | Cadmium (as Cd) | 0.1 |
| | | Selenium (Se) | 0.05 |
| | | Fluoride (as F) | 15 |
| | | Boron (as B) | 2.0 |
| | | Radioactive Materials | |
| | | Alpha emitters, HC/mL | 10.7 |
| | | Beta emitters, Hc/mL | 10.8 |

*Notes:*

1. These standards apply to the small scale industries. *i.e.*, total discharge upto 25 KL/Day.
2. For each CETP and its constituent units, the State Board will prescribe standards as per the local needs and conditions, these can be more stringent than those prescribed above.

| | | Into inland surface waters | On land for Irrigation | Into Marine Coastal areas |
|---|---|---|---|---|
| | | (a) | (b) | (c) |
| B. Treated Effluent | Quality of common effluent treatment plant | | Concentration in mg/l except pH and Temperature | |
| | pH | 5.5—9.0 | 5.5-9.0 | 5.5-9.0 |
| | [57] [BOD (3 days at 27°C)] | 30 | 100 | 100 |

| *Sl. No.* | *Industry* | *Parameter* | *Standards* | | |
|---|---|---|---|---|---|
| *1* | *2* | *3* | *4* | | |
| | | Oil and Grease | 10 | 10 | 20 |
| | | Temperature | | — | |
| | | | Shall not exceed 40°C in any section of the stream within 15 metres downstream from the effluent outlet | | 45°C at the point of discharge |
| | | Suspended solids | 100 | 200 | (a) For process waste waters 100 (b)For cooling water effluents 10 percent above total suspended matter of influent cooling water |
| | | Dissolved solids (Inorganic) | 2100 | 2100 | – |
| | | Total residual chlorine | 1.0 | – | 1.0 |
| | | Ammonical Nitrogen (as N) | 50 | – | 50 |
| | | Total Kjeldahl Nitrogen (as N) | 100 | – | 100 |
| | | Chemical Oxygen Demand | 250 | – | 250 |
| | | Arsenic (as As) | 0.2 | 0.2 | 0.01 |
| | | Mercury (as Hg) | 0.01 | – | 001 |
| | | Lead (as Pb) | 0.1 | – | 0.1 |
| | | Cadmium (as Cd) | 1.0 | – | 2.0 |
| | | Total Chromium (as Cr) | 2.0 | – | 2.0 |
| | | Copper (as Cu) | 3.0 | – | 3.0 |
| | | Zinc (as Zn) | 5.0 | – | 15 |
| | | Selenium (as Se) | 0.05 | – | 0.05 |
| | | Nickel (as Ni) | 3.0 | – | 5.0 |
| | | Boron (as B) | 2.0 | 2.0 | – |
| | | Percent Sodium | – | 60 | – |
| | | Cyanide (as CN) | 0.2 | 0.2 | 0.2 |
| | | Chloride (as Cl) | 1000 | 600 | – |
| | | Fluoride (as F) | 2.0 | – | 15 |
| | | Sulphate (as $SO_4$) | 1000 | 1000 | – |
| | | Sulphide (as S) | 2.8 | – | 5.0 |

| Sl. No. | Industry | Parameter | Standards | | |
|---|---|---|---|---|---|
| 1 | 2 | 3 | 4 | | |
| | | Pesticides | Absent | Absent | Absent |
| | | Phenolic Compounds (as $C_6H_5OH$) | 1.0 | – | 5.0 |

*Note:*
All efforts should be made to remove colour and unpleasant odour as far as possible.]

| [58][56. Diary | Effluents | Concentration in mg./l, except pH | Quantum per product processed |
|---|---|---|---|
| | pH | 6.5-8.5 | |
| | *[59][BOD (3 days at 27°C)] | 100 | -- |
| | **Suspended solids | 150 | – |
| | Oil and Grease | 10 | – |
| | Waste water generation | – | $3m^3$/Kl of milk |

*Notes:*
* BOD may be made stringent up to 30 mg/l if the recipient fresh water body is a source for drinking water supply. BOD shall be up to 350 mg/l for the chilling plant effluent for applying on land provided the land is designed and operated as a secondary treatment system with suitable monitoring facilities. The drainage water from the land after secondary treatment has to satisfy a limit of 30 mg/l of BOD and 10 mg/l of nitrate expressed as 'N'. The net addition to the groundwater quality should not be more than 3 mg/l of BOD and 3 mg/l of nitrate expressed as 'N'. This limit for applying on land is allowed subject to the availability of adequate land for discharge under the control of the industry. BOD value is relaxable up to 350 mg/l, provided the waste water is discharged into a town sewer leading to secondary treatment of the sewage.
** Suspended solids limit is relaxable upto 450 mg/l, provided waste water is discharged into a town sewer leading to secondary treatment of the sewage.

| 57. Tanneries | Effluents | Concentration in mg/l, except pH | Quantum Per raw hide processed |
|---|---|---|---|
| | pH | 6.5-9.0 | |
| | *[60][BOD (3 days at 27°C)] | 100 | |
| | Suspended solids | 100 | |

| *Sl. No.* | *Industry* | *Parameter* | *Standards* | |
|---|---|---|---|---|
| *1* | *2* | *3* | *4* | |
| | | Sulphides (as S) | 1 | -- |
| | | Total Chromium (as Cr) | 2 | -- |
| | | Oil and Grease | 10 | -- |
| | | Waste water generation | -- | 28m³/T |

*Note:* * for effluent discharge into inland surface waters BOD limit shall be made stricter to 30 mg/l by the concerned State Pollution Control Board

| ****58. Natural Rubber Rubber Processing Industry | Centrifuging and creaming units | | Crap and crumb units | |
|---|---|---|---|---|
| | For disposal into inland surface water | For disposal on land for irrigation | For disposal into inland surface water | For disposal on and for irrigation |
| | (a) | (b) | (a) | (b) |
| | (concentration in mg. l, except pH and quantum of waste generation) | | (Concentration mg/l, except pH and quantum of waste water generation) | |
| pH | 6-8 | 6-8 | 6-8 | 6-8 |
| Total Kjeldahl Nitrogen (as N) | 200 (100*) | *** | 50 | *** |
| Amonical Nitrogen (as N) | 100 (50*) | *** | 25 | *** |
| [61] [BOD (3 days at 27°C)] | 50 | 100 | 30 | 100 |
| COD | 250 | *** | 250 | *** |
| Oil and Grease | 10 | 20 | 10 | 20 |
| Sulphide (as S) | 2 | *** | 2 | *** |
| TDS | 2100 | NP** | 2100 | NP** |
| SS | 100 | 200 | 100 | 200 |
| Quantum of waste water generation | 5 lit/kg of product processed | 8 lit/kg of product processed | 40 lit/kg product processed | 40 lit/kg of product processed |

* To be achieved in three years.

** Not prescribed in case effluent is used for rubber plantation of their own, in other cases suitable limit, as necessary may be prescribed by the State Board.

*** Not specified.

**** These standards supersede the standards notified at serial No. 26 vide Notification No. S.O.8(E), dated 3 January 1989

| *Sl. No.* | *Industry* | *Parameter* | *Standards* |
|---|---|---|---|
| *1* | *2* | *3* | *4* |
| 59. | Bagasse-fired fired Boilers | Emissions | (Concentration in mg./l) |
| | (a) Step grate | Particulate matter | 250 |
| | (b) Horse shoe/ pulsating grate | Particulate matter | 500 (12% $CO_2$) |
| | (c) Spreader stroker | Particulate matter | 800 (12% $CO_2$) |

*Note:* In the case of the horse shoe and spreader stroker boilers, if more than one boiler is attached to a single stack, the standard shall be fixed based on added capacity of all the boilers connected with the stack.

| *Sl. No.* | *Industry* | *Parameter* | *Standards* |
|---|---|---|---|
| 60. | Man-made fibre industry (semi-synthetic) | Effluents | (Concentrate in mg/l except for pH) |
| | | pH | 5.5-9.0 |
| | | Suspended solids | 100 |
| | | [62][BOD (3 days at 27°C)] | 30 |
| | | Zinc (as Zn) | 1 |
| 61 | Ceramic industry | Emissions | (Concentration in mg/NM³) |
| | A. Kilns | | |
| | (a) Tunnel, Top Hat, Chamber | Particulate matter | 150 |
| | | Fluoride | 10 |
| | | Chloride | 100 |
| | | Sulphur dioxide | ** |
| | (b) Down-draft | Particulate matter | 1200 |
| | | Fluoride | 10 |
| | | Chloride | 100 |
| | | Sulphur dioxide | ** |
| | (c) Shuttle | Particulate matter | 150 |
| | | Fluoride | 10 |
| | | Chloride | 100 |
| | | Sulphur dioxide | ** |
| | (d) Vertical shaft kiln | Particulate matter | 250 |
| | | Fluoride | 10 |
| | | Sulphur dioxide | ** |
| | (e) Tank furnace | Particulate matter | 150 |
| | | Fluoride | 10 |
| | | Sulphur dioxide | ** |
| | B. Raw material handling, processing and operations | | |

| *Sl. No.* | *Industry* | *Parameter* | *Standards* |
|---|---|---|---|
| *1* | *2* | *3* | *4* |
| | (a) Dry raw materials handling and processing operations | Particulate matter | 150 |
| | (b) Basic raw materials handling and processing operations | Particulate matter | * |
| | (c) Other sources of air pollution generation | Particulate matter | * |
| C. | Automatic spray unit | | |
| | (a) Dryers | | |
| | (i) Fuel fired dryers | Particulate matter | 150 |
| | (ii) For heat recovery dryers | Particulate matter | * |
| | (b) Mechanical finishing operation | Particulate matter | * |
| | (c) Lime/plaster of paris manufacture Capacity | | |
| | Up to 5T/day | Stack height<br>-do- | A Hood should be provided with a stack of 30 metre height from ground level (including kiln height) |
| | Above 5T/day | -do- | $H = 14 (Q)^{0.3}$<br>Where Q is emission rate of $SO_2$ in kg/hr and H is Stack height in metres |
| | More than 5T/ day and upto 40T/day | Particulate matter<br>-do | 500 mg/NM³<br>150 mg/NM³ |

*Note:* Oxygen reference level for particulate matter concentration for kilns mentioned at A(c) is 18% and for those at A(b), A(d) and A(e) is 8%.

* All possible preventive measures should be taken to control pollution as far as practicable.

** The standard for sulphur dioxide in terms of stack height limits for kilns with various capacities of coal consumption shall be as indicated below:

| *Sl. No.* | *Industry* | *Parameter* | *Standards* |
|---|---|---|---|
| *1* | *2* | *3* | *4* |

| *Coal consumed per day* | *Stack height* |
|---|---|
| Less than 8.5 MT | 9 m |
| More than 8.5 to 21 MT | 2 m |
| More than 21 to 42 MT | 15 m |
| More than 42 to 64 MT | 18 m |
| More than 64 to 104 MT | 21 m |
| More than 104 to 105 MT | 24 m |
| More than 105 to 126 MT | 27 m |
| More than 126 MT | 30 m or using formula $H=14\ (Qg)^{0.3}$ (whichever is more) |

*Note:* Inthis notification, H-Physical height of the stack, Qg-Emission of sulphur dioxide in kg/hr., MT-Metric tones and m-metres.]

| | | | |
|---|---|---|---|
| [63][62. Viscose-filament Yarn (sub-sector of man-made fibre semi-synthetic industry | Effluents | | (Concentration in mg/l except for pH) |
| | pH | | 5.5-9.0 |
| | Suspended Solids | | 100 |
| | [64][BOD (3 days at 27°C)] | | 30 |
| | Zinc (as Zn) | | 5] |
| [65][63. Starch Industry (Maize products) | Effluents | | Concentration not to exceed mg./l (except PH and waste water discharge) |
| | pH | | 6.5—8.5 |
| | BOD (3 days at 27°C) | | 100 |
| | Suspended solids | | 150 |
| | Waste water discharge | | 8 $m^3$/tonne of maize processed |

*Notes:* The prescribed limits for BOD and suspended solids shall be made more stringent or less stringent depending upon the conditions and local requirements as mentioned below:

| *Sl. No.* | *Industry* | *Parameter* | *Standards* |
|---|---|---|---|
| *1* | *2* | *3* | *4* |

(i) BOD shall be made stringent upto 30mg/l if the recipient fresh water body is a source for drinking water supply.

(ii) BOD shall be allowed upto 350 mg/l for applying on land, provided the land is designed and operated as a secondary treatment system with the requisite monitoring facilities. The drainage water from the land after secondary treatment has to satisfy a limit of 30 mg/l of BOD and 10 mg/l of nitrate expressed as 'N'. The net addition to ground water quality should not be more than 3 mg/l of BOD and 10 mg/l of nitrate expressed as 'N'.

(iii) BOD shall be allowed upto 350 mg/l for discharge into a town sewer, if such sewer leads to a secondary biological treatment system.

(iv) Suspended solids shall be allowed upto 450 mg/l for discharge into a town sewer, if such sewer leads to a secondary biological system.

(v) In the event of bulking of sludge, the industry shall immediately apprise the respective State Pollution Control Board.

| *Sl. No.* | *Industry* | *Parameter* | *Standards* |
|---|---|---|---|
| 64. | Beehive hard coke oven | Emissions: | |
| | (i) New unit | Particulate Matter (corrected to 6% $CO_2$) | 150 mg/Nm$^3$ |
| | (ii) Existing units | Hydrocarbons | 25 ppm |
| | | Particulate matter (corrected to 6% $CO_2$) | 350 mg/Nm$^3$ |

*Note:* For control of emissfons and proper dispensation of pollutants the following guidelines shall be followed:

(i) Units set up after the publication of this notification shall be treated as new units.

(ii) A minimum stack height of 20 metres shall be provided by each unit.

(iii) Emissions for coke ovens shall be channelised through a tunnel and finally emitted through a stack. Damper adjustment techniques shall be used to have optimum heat utilisation and also to control the emission of unburnt carbon particles and combustible flue gases.

(iv) Wet scrubbing system or waste heat utilization for power generation or byproduct recovery systems should be installed preferably to achieve the prescribed standards.

(v) After four years from the date of this notification, all the existing units shall comply with the standards prescribed for the new units.

| *Sl. No.* | *Industry* | *Parameter* | *Standards* |
|---|---|---|---|
| *1* | *2* | *3* | *4* |
| 65. | Briquette Industry (Coal) | Emissions: | |
| | (a) Units having capacity less | Particulate matter (corrected to 6% $CO_2$) | 350 mg/Nm$^3$ |
| | (b) Units having capacity 10 tones or more | Particulate matter (corrected to 6% $CO_2$) | 150 mg/Nm$^3$ |

*Notes:* For control of emissions/proper disposal of pollutants, the following guidelines shall be followed by the industry;

(i) A minimum stack height of 20 metres shall be provided.

(ii) All ovens shall be modified to single chimney multi-oven systems.

(iii) Emissions from ovens shall be channelised through inbuilt draft stack. Optimum heat utilisation technique shall be used.

(iv) In case of units having capacity 10 tonnes and above, wet scrubbing system shall be provided to control air pollution.

| | | | |
|---|---|---|---|
| 66. | Soft Coke Industry | Particulate matter (corrected to 6% $CO_2$) | 350 mg/Nm$^3$ |

*Notes:* Wet scrubbing systems alongwith by product recovery system shall be provided.
Guidelines for Emission Control to Improve Work Zone Environment (applicable for industries at serial numbers 64, 65 and 66):

(a) Water used for quenching and wet scrubbing shall be recirculated and reused through catch-pits.

(b) Leakages in the oven shall be sealed by bentonite or by any suitable paste and by proper maintenance to avoid fugitive emission.

Guidelines for Coal Handling and Crushing Plant (applicable to industries at serial numbers 64, 65 and 66):

(i) Unloading of coal trucks shall be carried out with proper care avoiding dropping of the materials from height. It is advisable to moist the material by sprinkling water while unloading.

(ii) Pulversiation of coal shall be carried out in an enclose placed and water sprinkling arrangement shall be provided at coal heaps, crushing area and on land around he crushing unit.

(iii) Work area surrounding the plant shall be asphalted or concreted.

(iv) Green belt shall be developed along the boundary of the industry.

(v) Open burning of coal to manufacture soft coke shall be stopped.

| *Sl. No.* | *Industry* | *Parameter* | *Standards* |
|---|---|---|---|
| *1* | *2* | *3* | *4* |
| 67. | Edible oil & Vanaspati | Effluents: | |
| | | Temperature | Not more than 5°C above ambient temperature of the recipient waterbody. |
| | | PH | 6.5-8.5 |
| | | Suspended solids | 150 mg/l |
| | | Oil & Grease | 20 mg/l |
| | | BOD (3 days at 27°C) | 100 mg/l |
| | | COD | 200 mg/l |
| | | Waste water discharge | |
| | | (i) Solvent extraction | 2.0 cum/tonne of product (oil) |
| | | (ii) Refinery/Vanaspati | 2.0 cum/tonne of product (refined oil/vanaspati) |
| | | (iii) Integrated unit of solvent extraction & refinery/vanaspati | 4.0 cum/tonne of refined oil/ vanaspati produced |
| | | (iv) Barometric cooling water/deodorizer water | 15.0 cum/tonne of refined oil/ vanaspati |

*Notes:*

(i) The above standards shall be applicable to wastewater from processes and cooling.

(ii) BOD shall be made stringent upto 30 mg/l if the recipient fresh water body is source of drinking water supply.

(iii) The standards-for boiler emissions shall be applicable as prescribed under Schedule I of these rules

| | | | |
|---|---|---|---|
| 68. | Organic Chemicals manufacturing industry | Effluents: | |
| (a) | Compulsory Parameters | pH | 6.5-8.5 |
| | | BOD (3 days at 27°C) | 100 mg/l |
| | | Oil & Grease | 10 mg/l |
| | | Bioassay test | Minimum 90% survival after 96 hours with fish at 100% effluent |
| (b) | Additional parameters | | (mg/l) |
| | | Nitrate (as N) | 10 |
| | | Arsenic | 0.2 |
| | | Hexavalent Chromium | 0.1 |

| Sl. No. | Industry | Parameter | Standards |
|---|---|---|---|
| 1 | 2 | 3 | 4 |
| | | Total Chromium | 1.0 |
| | | Lead | 0.1 |
| | | Cyanide as CN | 0.2 |
| | | Zinc | 0.5 |
| | | Mercury | 0.01 |
| | | Copper | 2.0 |
| | | Nickel | 2.0 |
| | | Phenolics as $C_6H_5OH$ | 5.0 |
| | | Sulphide | 2.0 |

*Notes:*

(i) No limit for COD is prescribed but it shall be monitored. If the COD in a treated effluent is persistently greater than 250 mg/l, such industrial units are required to identify chemicals causing the same. In case these are found to be toxic as defined in Hazardous Chemicals Rules, 1989 in Part I of Schedule-I, the State Boards in such cases may direct the industries to install tertiary treatment system stipulating time limit. This may be done on case-to-case basis.

(ii) These standards are not applicable to small-scale detergent (formulating units).

(iii) The standards for boiler emissions shall be applicable as per the existing emission regulations.

(iv) Industry covered under this group are haloaliphatics, plasticizers, aromatics (calcohols, phenols, esters, acids and salts, aldehydes and ketones), substituted aromatics, aliphatic (alcohols, esters, acids, aldehydes, ketones, amines and amides) and detergents.

| Sl. No. | Industry | Parameter | Standards |
|---|---|---|---|
| 69. | Flour Mills | Effluents | |
| | | pH | 6.5-8.5 |
| | | BOD (3 days at 27°C) | 100 mg/l |
| | | Total Suspended solids | 100 mg/l |
| | | Oil & Grease | 10mg/l |
| | | Waste water discharge | 2 cubic metre per tonne of wheat processed. |

*Notes:*

(i) BOD shall be made stringent upto 30 mg/l if the recipient fresh water body is a source for drinking water supply.

(ii) BOD shall be allowed upto 350 mg/l for applying on land, provided the land is designed and operated as a secondary treatment system with the requisite

| *Sl. No.* | *Industry* | *Parameter* | *Standards* |
|---|---|---|---|
| *1* | *2* | *3* | *4* |

monitoring facilities. The drainage water from the land after secondary treatment has to satisfy a limit of 30 mg/l of BOD and 10 mg/l of nitrate expressed as 'N'. The net addition to ground water quality should not be more than 3 mg/l of BOD and 10 mg/l of nitrate expressed as 'N'.

(iii) BOD shall be allowed upto 350 mg/l for discharge into a town sewer, if such sewer leads to a secondary biological treatment system.

(iv) Suspended solids shall be allowed upto 450 mg/l for discharge into a town sewer, if such sewer leads to a secondary biological treatment system.

| | | |
|---|---|---|
| 70. Boilers (Small) | Steam generation Capacity (ton/hour) | Particulate emission matter (mg/Nm³) |
| | Less than 2 | 1200* |
| | 2 to less than 10 | 800* |
| | 10 to less than 15 | 600* |
| | 15 and above | 150** |

* to meet the respective standards, cyclone/multicyclone is recommended as control equipment with the boiler.

** to meet the standard, bag filter/ESP is recommended as control equipment with the boiler.

*Notes:* (i) 12% of $CO_2$, correction shall be the reference value for particulate matter emission standards for all categories of boilers.

(ii) These limits shall supersede the earlier limits notified under Schedule I at serial number 34 of Environment (Protection) Act, 1986 *vide* notification GSR 742 (E), dated 30th August, 1990

(iii) Stack height for small boilers.

For the small boilers using coal or liquid fuels, the required stack height with the boiler shall be calculated by using the formula

$H = 14\ Q^{0.3}$

Where H—Total stack height in metres from the ground level.

Q = $SO_2$ emission rate in kg/hr.

In no case the stack height shall be less than 11 metres. Where providing all stacks are not feasible using above formula the limit of 400 mg/NM³ for $SO_2$ emission shall be met by providing necessary control equipment with a minimum stack height of 11 metres.

| | | | |
|---|---|---|---|
| 71. | Pesticide Industry | (i) Compulsory Parameters | mg/l except pH |
| | | pH | 6.5—8.5 |
| | | BOD (3 days at 27°C) | 100 |

| *Sl. No.* | *Industry* | *Parameter* | *Standards* |
|---|---|---|---|
| *1* | *2* | *3* | *4* |
| | | Oil & Grease | 10 |
| | | Suspended solids | 100 |
| | | Bioassay test: | Minimum 90% survival of fish after 96 hours with 90% effluent and 10% dilution water. Test shall be carried out as per IS:6502-1971. |
| | | (ii) Additional Parameters | mg/l |
| | | (a) Heavy metal | |
| | | Copper | 1.0 |
| | | Manganese | 1.0 |
| | | Zinc | 1.0 |
| | | Mercury | 0.01 |
| | | Tin | 0.1 |
| | | Any other like Nickel | shall not exceed 5 times the drinking water standards (BIS) individually. |
| | | (b) Organics Phenol & Phenolic Compounds as $C_6H_2OH$ | 1.0 |
| | | (c) Inorganics | |
| | | Arsenic as AS | 0.2 |
| | | Cyanide as CN | 0.2 |
| | | Nitrate as $NO_3$ | 50 |
| | | Phosphate as P | 5.0 |
| | | (d) Specific pesticide | (microgram/litre) |
| | | Benzene Hexachloride | 10 |
| | | DDT | 10 |
| | | Dimethoate | 450 |
| | | Copper oxychloride | 9600 |
| | | Ziram | 1000 |
| | | 2, 4D | 400 |
| | | Paraquat | 23000 |
| | | Propanil | 7300 |
| | | Nitrogen | 780 |
| | | Other/below mentioned pesticides individually) | 100 |

Other Pesticides:

Insecticides:

Aluminium | Lindane | Pyrethrum extract

| *Sl. No.* | *Industry* | *Parameter* | *Standards* |
|---|---|---|---|
| *1* | *2* | *3* | *4* |
| | Phosphide | | |
| | Dichlorovos | Malathion | Quinalphos |
| | EDTC Mixer | Methyl Bromide | Monocrotophos |
| | Ethylene Dibromide | Nicotine Sulphate | Carbaryl |
| | Ethion | Oxydemeton Methyl | Endosulfan |
| | Fenitrothion | Methhyl Parathion | Fenvalerate |
| | Lime-sulphur | Phosphamidon | Phorate |
| | Temephos | | |
| (ii) | Fungicides: | | |
| | Aurefungin | Organomercurials (MEMC & PMA) | |
| | Barium Polysulphide | Sulphur (Colloidal, Wettable & Dust) | |
| | Cuprous Oxide | Streptocycline | |
| | Ferbam | Thiram | |
| | Mancozeb | Zineb | |
| | Manab | Carbendazim | |
| | Nickel Chloride | Tridemorph | |
| (iii) | Rodenticides; | | |
| | Comafuryl | | |
| | Warfarin | | |
| | Zinc Phosphide | | |
| (iv) | Nematicides: | | |
| | Metham N-Sodium | | |
| (v) | Weedicides: | | |
| | Fluchloralin | | |
| | Isoproturon | | |
| | Butachlor | | |
| | Anilphos | | |
| (vi) | Plant Growth Regulants: | | |
| | Chloromequat Chloride | | |
| | Nemphalene | | |
| | Acetic Acid | | |
| (vii) | Any other pesticide not specified above | | |

*Notes:*

(1) Limits shall be compiled with at the end of the treatment plant before any dilution.

(2) From the 'Additional Parameters' specified in 71 (ii), only the relevant parameters

| *Sl. No.* | *Industry* | *Parameter* | *Standards* |
|---|---|---|---|
| *1* | *2* | *3* | *4* |

(based on the raw-materials used and products manufactured) may be prescribed by the concerned State Board on a case-to-case basis.

(3) No limit for COD is prescribed. If the COD in a treated effluent is persistently more than 250 mg/l, such industrial units are required to identify the chemicals causing the same. In case, these are found to be toxic as defined in Schedule I of the Hazardous Chemicals Rules, 1989, the State Boards in such cases may direct the industries to install tertiary treatment, stipulating time limit. This may be done on a case-to-case basis.

(4) Solar evaporation followed by incineration is a recognized practice, provided the Guidelines on solar evaporation as given below are followed.

(i) Solar evaporation pans shall be constructed in such a way that the bottom is atleast one metre above the ground level.

(ii) Solar evaporation pans shall be leak proof and of impervious construction and designed as per IS:7290.

(iii) The solar evaporation pans shall be designed on the basis of evaporation rate matching to the output of wastewater.

(iv) Wastewater must be pre-treated as below before subjecting to solar evaporation:

(a) Oil and grease and floating organics shall be removed so that the rate of evaporation is not effected.

(b) Acidic/Alkaline waste must be neutralized before solar evaporation to maintain pH in the range of 6.5 to 8.5.

(c) Toxic volatile matter shall be removed so as not to cause air pollution.

(v) During the rainy season, storm water shall not be allowed to mix with process waste and enter the pans. The waste-water shall in no case outflow from the evaporation pans. Alternative arrangements shall be made to hold the wastewater in proper impervious tanks and if necessary, force evaporated.

(vi) In no circumstances, the liquid effluent shall be discharged without conforming to the minimum national standards or stored in a holding arrangement which is likely to cause pollution.

(vii) The sludge from the solar evaporation pans shall be incinerated or disposed as per the guidelines for management and handling of hazardous waste, published by the Ministry of Environment and Forests, Government of India, after obtaining authorization from the State Pollution Control Board under the Hazardous Wastes (Handling and Management) Rules, 1989.

(viii) The facility shall be protected from flood and storm to prevent embankments from erosion or any other damage which may render any portion inoperable.

(ix) Facilities shall have protective enclosures to keep wildlife, domestic animals unauthorised persons, etc. away.

| *Sl. No.* | *Industry* | *Parameter* | *Standards* |
|---|---|---|---|
| *1* | *2* | *3* | *4* |
| 72. | Oil Drilling and Gas Extraction Industry | | |
| A. | Standards for Liquid Effluent 1.0 On-Shore facilities (For Marine Disposal) | | |
| | | pH | 5.5-9.0 |
| | | Oil & Grease | 10 mg/l |
| | | Suspended solids | 100 mg/l |
| | | BOD (3 days at 27°C) | 30 mg/l |

*Note:*

(i) For on-shore discharge of effluents. In addition to the standards prescribed above, proper marine outfall has to be provided to achieve the individual pollutant concentration level in sea water below their toxicity limits as given below, within a distance of 50 metre from the discharge point, in order to protect the marine aquatic life:

| Parameter | Toxicity limit, mg/l |
|---|---|
| Chromium as Cr | 0.1 |
| Copper, as Cu | 0.05 |
| Cyanide, as CN | 0005 |
| Fluoride, as F | 1.5 |
| Lead, as Pb | 0.05 |
| Mercury, as Hg | 0.01 |
| Nickel, as Ni | 0.1 |
| Zinc, as Zn | 0.1 |

(ii) Oil and gas drilling and processing facilities, situated on land and away from saline water sink, may opt either for disposal of treated water by on-shore disposal or by re-injection in abandoned well, which is allowed only below a depth of 1000 metres from the ground level. In case of a depth of 1000 metres from the ground level. In case of re-injection in abandoned well the effluent have to comply only with respect to suspended solids and oil and grease at 100 mg/l and 10 mg/l, respectively. For on-shore disposal, the permissible limits are given below:

| *S.No.* | *Parameter* | *On-shore discharge standards (Not to exceed)* |
|---|---|---|
| *1* | *2* | *3* |
| 1. | pH | -5.5—9.0 |
| 2. | Temperature | 40°C |
| 3. | Suspended Solids | 100 mg/l |
| 4. | Zinc | 2 mg/l |
| 5. | BOD | 30 mg/l |
| 6. | COD | 100 mg/l |
| 7. | Chlorides | 600 mg/l |
| 8. | Sulphates | 1000 mg/l |
| 9. | TDS | 2100 mg/l |
| 10. | % Sodium | 60 mg/l |
| 11. | Oil and Grease | 10 mg/l |
| 12. | Phenolics | 1.2 mg/l |
| 13. | Cyanides | 0.2 mg/l |
| 14. | Fluorides | 1.5 mg/l |
| 15. | Sulphides | 2.0 g/l |
| 16. | Chromium (Cr+6) | 0.1 mg/l |
| 17. | Chromium (Total) | 1.0 mg/l |
| 18. | Copper | 0.2 mg/l |
| 19. | Lead | 0.1 mg/l |
| 20. | Mercury | 0.01 mg/l |
| 21. | Nickel | 3.0 mg/l |

2.0 Off-shore facilities:

For off-shore discharge of effluents; the oil content of the treated effluent without dilution shall not exceed 40 mg/l for 95% of the observation and shall never exceed 10 mg/l. Three 8-hourly grab samples are required to be collected daily and the average value of oil and grease content of the three samples shall comply with these standards.

B. Guidelines for Discharge of Gaseous Emission;

1.0 DG Sets

1.1 DG sets at drill site as well as production station shall conform with the norm notified under the environment (Protection) Act, 1986.

2.0 Elevated/ground flares

2.1 Cold venting of gases shall never be resorted to and all the gaseous emissions are to be flared.

2.2 All flaring shall be done by elevated flares except where there is any effect on crop production in adjoining areas due to the flaring. In such cases, one may adopt ground flaring.

2.3 In case of ground flare, to minimise the effects of flaring the flare pit at Group Gathering Station (GGS), Oil Collecting Station (OCS) and Group Collection Station (GCS) shall be made of RCC surrounded by a permanent

| S.No. | Parameter | On-shore discharge standards (Not to exceed) |
|---|---|---|
| 1 | 2 | 3 |

wall (made of refractory brick) of minimum 5m height to reduce the radiation and glaring effect in the adjoining areas.

2.4 A green belt of 100m width may be developed around the flare after the refractory wall in case of ground glaring.

2.5 If the ground flaring with provision of green belt is not feasible, enclosed ground flare system shall be adopted, and be designed with proper enclosures height, to meet the ground level concentration (GLC) requirement.

2.6 In case of elevated flaring, the minimum stack height shall be 30 m. Height of the stack shall be such that the maximum GLC never exceeds the prescribed ambient air quality limit.

3.0 Burning of effluent in the pits shall not be carried out at any stage.

C. Guidelines for Disposal of Solid Waste:

1 Disposal of drill cuttings.

1.1 The drill cuttings shall be conveyed through a conveyor system to the disposal pit after proper washing.

1.2 No drill cuttings (of any composition) shall be disposed off-shore. For off-shore installation, drill cuttings separated from mud, shall be transported on-shore through supply vessels secured land-fill disposal as per Ministry of Environment and Forests' guidelines. The site shall be approved by the concerned authority (State Government/State Pollution Control Board).

1.3 The disposal of drill cuttings (on-shore/off-shore) shall conform to the guidelines provided by the Ministry of Environment and Forests.

1.4 The secured land-fill pit shall be covered with a thick layer of local top soil provided with proper top slope, after drilling operation is over

2.0 Disposal of drilling mud.

2.1 The unusuable portion of the drillingmud (of any composition), after reclamation shall be disposed of only at a secured land-fill site secured by the concerned authority (State Government/State Pollution Control Boards). The disposal of mud shall conform to the guidelines provided by the Ministry of Environment and Forests under the Hazardous Wastes (Management and Handling) Rules, 1989.

2.2 No mud (of any composition) shall be disposed off-shore. For off-shore installation, the unusable portion of the mud shall be brought back to the shore for disposal in a secured land-fill.

2.3 Only water-based mud system shall be used. Where oil-based muds are used, themuds, after they become unusual, shall be properly treated/incinerated, in a centralized treatment facility. In case of off-shore installation, these may be brought to the shore and treated.

| S.No. | Parameter | | On-shore discharge standards (Not to exceed) |
|---|---|---|---|
| *1* | *2* | | *3* |
| 3.0 | Production stage solid waste disposal. | | |
| 3.1 | The dried sludge from waste-water treatment plant and other solid wastest at production stage shall be disposed in a secured land-fill. | | |
| 3.2 | In case all content in the sludge is high, it shall be properly treated/ incinerated and ash shall be disposed of in a secured land-fill. | | |
| 73. | Pharmaceuticals Industry (Bulk Drugs) | | |
| | (i) | Compulsory Parameters | (mg/l except pH) |
| | | pH | 6.5-8.5 |
| | | Oil & Grease | 10 |
| | | BOD (3 days at 27°C) | 100 |
| | | Total Suspended solids | 100 |
| | | Bioassay test | 90% survival after 96 hours in 100% effluent test shall be carried out as per IS:6582—1971. |
| | (ii) | Additional parameters | mg/l |
| | | Mercury | 0.01 |
| | | Arsenic | 0.2 |
| | | Chromium (Hexavalent) | 0.1 |
| | | Lead | 0.1 |
| | | Cyanide | 0.1 |
| | | Phenolics ($C_6H_5OH$) | 1.0 |
| | | Sulphides (as s) | 2.0 |
| | | Phosphate (as P) | 5.0 |

*Notes:* (i) The limit of BOD (3 days at 27°C) shall be 30 mg/l if effluent is discharged directly to fresh water body.

(ii) The additional parameters are applicable to bulk drug manufacturing units depending upon the process and product.

(iii) No limit for COD is prescribed, but it shall be monitored. If the COD of the treated effluent is greater than 250 mg/1, such industrial units are required to identify chemicals causing the same. In case, there are found to be toxic, as defined in the Hazardous Chemicals Rules, 1989 (Schedule I), the State Boards in such cases shall direct the industries to install tertiary treatment system within the stipulated time limit. This may be done on a case-to-case basis.

74. Emission standards for brick kilns:

I. Minimal National Emission Standards for Brick Kilns:

| Size | Kiln Capacity | Maximum limit for the concentration of particulate matter (mg/N cu.m) |
|---|---|---|
| 1 | 2 | 3 |
| Small | Less than 15,000 bricks per day (less than 15 ft. trench width) | 1000 |
| Medium | 15,000-30,000 bricks per day (15-22 ft. trench width) | 750 |
| Large | More than 30,000 bricks per day (more than 22 ft. trench width) | 750 |

*Note:* The above particulate matter emission limits are achievable installing fixed chimney high draught kilns and/ or settling chamber.

II. Stack Height Regulation:

The following stack heights are recommended for optional dispersion of particulate matter.

| Kiln Capacity | Stack Height |
|---|---|
| 1 | 2 |
| Less than 15,000 bricks per day (less than 15 ft trench width) | Minimum stack height of 22 m or, Induced draught fan operating with minimum draught of 50 mm. Water Gauge with 12m stack height. |
| 15,000-30,000 bricks per day (15-22 ft. trench width) | Minimum stack height of 27m with gravitational settling chamber or, Induced draught fan operating with minimum draught of 50mm. Water Gauge with 15m tack height. |
| More than 30,000 bricks per day (more than 22 ft. trench width) | Minimum stack height of 30m with gravitational settling chamber or, Induced draught fan operating with minimum draught of 50mm. Water Gauge with 17 m stack height. |

[66][III. Existing moving chimney Bull's trench kilns shall be dispensed with by 30 June 2000 and no new moving chimney kilns shall be allowed to come up.]

IV. Considering the immediate need to protect the top soil and to find ways for safe disposal/utilization of fly ash, it is provided that from 1 January 1997, all brick manufacturing units within a radius of 50 kms from any thermal power plant, shall utilize fly ash in optimal proportion for making bricks.

75. Soda Ash Industry (Solvay Process)

| *Parameter Minas* | *(Recipient body specified)* | | |
|---|---|---|---|
| | *Marine* | *Brackish* | *Inland surface water* |
| pH | 6.5-9 | 6.5-9 | 6.5-9 |
| Temperature | 45°C or less | 45°C or less | 45°C or less |
| Oil & Grease | 2 mg/l | 20 mg/l | 10 mg/l |
| Suspended solids (SS) | 500 mg/l | 200 mg/l | 100 mg/l |
| Ammonical nitrogen | 5 mg/l | 50 mg/l | 50 mg/l |
| Bio-assay | 96 hours 90% survival | 96 hours 90% survival | 96 hours 90% survival |

*Note:* MINAS for disposal in brackish and inland surface water are without any dilution.
Standards for Dual Process Soda Ash Plants:

| *Parameter* | *Minas (Inland Surface Water)* |
|---|---|
| pH | 6.5-8.0 |
| Ammonical nitrogen as N (mg/l) | 50 |
| Nitrate nitrogen, as N (mg/l | 10 |
| Cyanide, as CN (mg/l) | 0.2 |
| Hexavalent chromium (mg/l) | 0.1 |
| Total chromium (mg/l) | 2.0 |
| Suspended solids (mg/l) | 100 |
| Oil and Grease (mg/l) | 10 |

*Note:* [67][The standards shall to be implemented by the industry in a time target schedule by December, 1999.] The progress on the time targetted implementation schedule shall be periodically submitted by the industry to the State Pollution Control Board and Central Pollution Control Board.

76. Emission Standard for $SO_2$ from Cupola furnace:

Standard for Sulphur Dioxide emission from Cupola Furnace:

| Characteristics | Emission limit |
|---|---|
| Sulphur dioxide ($SO_2$) emission | 300 mg/Nm3 at 12% $CO_2$ correction |

To achieve the standard, foundries may install scrubber; followed by a stack of height six times the diameter of the Cupola beyond the charging door.

*Note:* In case due to some technical reasons, installation of scrubber is not possible, then value of $SO_2$ to the ambient air has to be effected through the stack height.

77. Specification of Motor Gasoline for Emission Related Parametres:

| *Sl. No.* | *Characteristics* | *Requirement* | *Method of Test ref. To P:of IS:1448* |
|---|---|---|---|
| (i) | Reid Vapour Pressure at 38°C, KPa | 35 to 70 | P:39 |
| (ii) | Benzene, Percent by volume, Max | 5.0[1] | P:104 |
| (iii) | Lead Content as (Pb) g/l, Max | 0.15 (low leaded)[2]<br>0.013 (unleaded) | P:38 |
| (iv) | Sulphur, per cent by mass; Max | 0.10 (unleaded)<br>0.20 (leaded) | P:34 |
| (v) | Potential Gum, g/m³, Max | 50 | ASTM 873:8 |
| (vi) | Gum (Solvent Washed) g/m³ Max | 40 | P:29 |
| (vii) | Oxygenates Content Ether (MTBE, ETBE) Alcohol, per cent by volume, Max | 15 | |
| (viii) | Phosphorus | See Footnote[3] | ASTMD 3231 |

(1) 3.0 per cent by volume maximum in metro cities by 2000 A.D.

(2) 0.15 g/l by 31 December 1996 (for entire country);
0.13 g/l by 1 April 1995 (in four metro cities); by 1 December 1998 (for all State capitals/Uts and major metro cities) and by 1 April 2000 for the entire country.

(3) Phosphorous containing additives shall be absent.

*Note:*

(a) Above specifications applies to leaded as well as unleaded petrol except lead content.

(b) For new refineries coming up during or after 1997 the specification applicable by 2000 for existing refineries shall be applicable by 1997.

78. Specifications of Diesel Fuel for Emission Related Parameters:

| Sl. No. | Characteristics | Requirement | Method of Test ref. To P:of IS: 1448 |
|---|---|---|---|
| (i) | Density at 15°C, kg/$m^3$ | 820 to 880[1] | P:32 |
| (ii) | Cetane Number, Min | 45.0[2] | P:9 |
| (iii) | Distillation 85 per cent by volume recovery at °C Max 95 | 350 | |
| | percent by volume recovery at C Max | 370 | P:18 |
| (iv) | Sulphur, per cent by mass | 0.50[3] | P:33 |

(1) 820 to 860 by 2000 AD.

(2) 48 by 31 December 1998 (except in the refineries—Digboi, Gauhati and Bongaigaon refineries & Petrochemicals (Ltd.)

(3) (i) 0.50 per cent by mass by 1 April, 1996 in four metros and Taj Trapezium.
(ii) 0.25 per cent by mass by 1 October 1996 in Taj Trapezium.
(iii) 0.25 per cent by mass by 1 April 1999 throughout the country.

*Note:*

(a) Above specifications apply to HSD only.

(b) For new refineries coming during or after 1997 specification applicable by 2000 for existing refineries shall be applicable by 1997.

(c) 'P' refers to parts of IS:1448.]

| Sl.No. Industry | Parameter | Standards New Batteries | Standards Existing Batteries |
|---|---|---|---|
| [68][79. Coke oven plants (by product recovery type) | Fugitive Visible Emissions | | |
| | (a) Leakage from door | 5 (PLD)* | 10 (PLD)* |
| | (b) Leakage from charging lids | 1 (PLL)* | 1 (PLL)* |
| | (c) Leakage from AP Covers | 4 (PLO)* | 4 (PLO)* |
| | (d) Charging emission (second/charge) | 16 (with HPLA)* | 50 (with HPLA)* |
| Stack Emission of Coke Oven | | | |
| (a) $SO_2$ (mg/$Nm^3$) | | 800 | 800 |
| (b) NOx (mg/$Nm^3$) | | 500 | 500 |
| (c) SPM, (mg/$Nm^3$) | | 50 | 50 |
| (a) SPM emission | | 25 | 25 |

| | | |
|---|---|---|
| during charging (stack emission) mg/Nm³ | | |
| (b) SPM emission during coke pushing (stack emission) gm/ton of coke | 5 | 5 |
| Sulphurin Coke Oven gas used for heating (mg/Nm³) | 800 | 800 |
| Emission for quenching operation Particulate matter gm/MT of coke produced | 50 | 50 |
| Benzo-Pyerine (BOP) concentration in work zone air (ug/m³) | | |
| -Battery area (top of the battery) | 5 | 5 |
| -Other units in coke oven plant | 2 | 2 |
| -Ambient standards (ng/m³) | 10 | 10 |

For control of emissions and to maintain environmental quality in work zone area, the following guidelines shall be followed, namely:

(i) New coke oven units shall follow any of the low-emission procedures, such as, coke dry cooling, non-recovery coke-ovens, Indirect Quenching Process, Jumbo coke oven reactor. Modified Wet Quenching System with appropriate environmental controls (e.g. baffles, filtering media, collection and treatment of residual water from quench tower and recycling; Use of process water as quenching water shall not be permissible).

(ii) Effective pollution control measures (for e.g., Extensive maintenance and cleaning of oven doors and frame seals, ascension pipes, charging holes and lids and other equipment: On-main charging system (HPLA); Luting charging holes with clay-suspension; Modified guide/transfer car with emission control system, etc.) shall be taken to reduce coal charging and coke pushing emissions. The bleeder of the coke oven shall be flared.

(iii) In the case of existing coke ovens with wet quenching, the new procedure as in (i) and (ii) shall be adopted and emission standards achieved within four years (by 2001).

*Note:* Units set up after the publication of this notification shall be treated as new units.

* HPLA—Aspiration through high pressure liquor injection in goose neck.

* PLD—Percent leaking doors.

* PLL—Percent leaking lids.

*PLO—Percent leaking off takes.]

[69][80. Specification of two-stroke engine oil:

| *Specifications* | *Standard* | *Test procedure* |
|---|---|---|
| Two-stroke engine oil grade JASO-FC as per JASO M-345-93 specification and API TC is per specification No. ASTM D 4859 | Minimum Smoke Index of 85 | JASO-M342-92 for JASO-FC and ASTM D-4857 for API TC |

The above specification shall be effective from the 1 day of April 1999].

[70][81. Battery manufacturing industry—(i) Lead Acid Battery Manufacturing Industries.

Emission Standards

| *Source* | *Pollutant* | *Standards Conc. Based (mg/Nm³)* |
|---|---|---|
| Grid casting | Lead | 10 |
| | Particulate matter | 25 |
| Oxide manufacturing | Lead | 10 |
| | Particulate matter | 25 |
| Paste Mixing | Lead | 10 |
| | Particulate matter | 25 |
| Assembling | Lead | 10 |
| | Particulate matter | 25 |
| PVC section | Particulate matter | 150 |

— To comply with the respective standards, all the emissions from above mentioned sources shall be routed through stack connected with hood and fan. In addition to above, installation of control equipment, viz., bag filter/ventury scrubber, is also recommended —the minimum stack height shall be 30 m.

Liquid Effluent Discharge Standards

| *Pollutant* | *Concentration based standards* |
|---|---|
| pH | 6.5—8.5 |
| Suspended solids | 50 mg/l |
| Lead | 0.1 mg/l |

(ii) Dry Cell Manufacturing Industry

Emission Standards

| *Pollutant* | *Concentration based standards (mg/Nm³)* |
|---|---|
| Particulate matter | 50 |
| Manganese as Mn | 5 |

—To comply with the respective standards, all the emissions from above mentioned sources shall be routed through stack connected with hood and fan. In addition to above, installation of control equipment, *viz*:, bag filter/ventury scrubber, is also recommended.

—The minimum stack height shall be 30 m.

Effluent Standards

| *Pollutant* | *Concentration based standards* |
|---|---|
| pH | 6.5—8.5 |
| Total suspended solids | 100 mg/l |
| Manganese as Mn | 2 mg/l |
| Mercury as Hg | 0.02mg/l |
| Zinc as Zn | 5 mg/l |
| Lead as Pb | 10 mg/Nm³ |
| Particulate matter | 50 mg/Nm³ |
| Minimum stack height | 30m |

82. Environmental Standards for Gas/Naphtha-based Thermal Power Plants (i) Limit for emission of NOx (a) For existing units—150 ppm (v/v) at 15% excess oxygen. (b) For new units effect from 1-6-1999.

| | *Total generation of gas turbine* | | *Limit for Stack NOx emission [v/v. at 15% excess oxygen]* |
|---|---|---|---|
| (a) | 400 MW and above | (i) | 50 ppm for the units burning natural gas |
| | | (ii) | 100 ppm for the units burning naphtha |
| (b) | Less than 400 MW but upto 100MW | (i) | 75 ppm for the units burning natural gas |
| | | (ii) | 100 ppm for the units burning naphtha |
| (c) | Less than 100 MW | | 100 ppm for units burning natural gas or naphtha as fuel |
| (d) | For the plants burning gas in a conventional boiler | | 100ppm |

(ii) Stack height H in m should be calculated using the formula $H = 14Q^{0.3}$, where Q is the emission rate of $SO_2$ in kg/hr, subject to a minimum of 30 mts. (iii) Liquid waste discharge limit.

| *Parameter* | *Maximum limit of concentration (mg/l except for pH and temperature)* |
|---|---|
| pH | 6.5–8.5 |
| Temperature | As applicable for other thermal power plants |
| Free available chlorine | 0.5 |
| Suspended solids | 100.0 |
| Oil and Grease | 20.0 |
| Copper (total) | 1.0 |
| Iron (total) | 1.0 |
| Zinc | 1.0 |
| Chromium (total) | 0.2 |
| Phosphate | 5.0 |

83. Standards/Guidelines for Control of Noise Pollution from Stationary Diesel Generator (DG) Sets—(A) Noise Standards of DG sets (15-500 KVA).

The total sound power level, Lw, of a DG set should be less than 94 + 10 $\log_{10}$ (KVA), dB(A), at the manufacturing stage, where, KVA is the nominal power rating of a DG set.

This level should fall by 5 dB (A) every five years, till 2007, i.e., in 2002 and then in 2007.

(B) Mandatory acoustic enclosure/acoustic treatment of room for stationary DG sets (5 KVA and above).

Noise from the DG set should be controlled by providing at acoustic enclosure or by treating the room accoustically.

Theacoustic enclosures/acoustic treatment of the room should be designed for minimum 25 dB(A). Insertion Loss or for meeting the ambient noise standards, whichever is on the higher side (if the actual ambient noise is on the higher side, it may not be possible to check the performance of the acoustic enclosure/acoustic treatment. Under such circumstances the performance may be checked for noise reduction up to actual ambient noise level, preferably, in the night time). The measurement for Insertion Loss may be done at different points at 0.5 m from the acoustic enclosure/room, and then averaged.

The DG set should also be provided with proper exhaust muffler with Insertion Loss of minimum 25 dB(A).

(C) Guidelines for the manufacturers/users of DG sets (5 KVA and above)—

01 The manufacturer should offer to the user a standard acoustic enclosure of 25 dB (A) Insertion Loss and also a suitable exhaust muffler with Insertion Loss of 25 dB(A)

02 The user should make efforts to bring down the noise levels due to the DG set, outside his premises, within the ambient noise requirements by proper setting and control measures.

03 The manufacturer should furnish noise power levels of the unsilenced DG sets as per standards prescribed under (A).

04 The total sound power level of a DG set, at the user's end, shall be within 2 dB (A) of the total sound power level of the DG set, at the manufacturing stage, as prescribed under (A).

05 Installation of a DG set must be strictly incompliance with the recommendations of the DG set manufacturer.

06 A proper routine and preventive maintenance procedure for the DG set should be set and followed in consultation with the Dg set manufacturer which would help prevent noise levels of the DG set from deteriorating with use.

84. Temperature Limit for Discharge of Condenser Cooling Water from Thermal Power Plant—

A. New Thermal Power plants commissioned after 1 June 1999—

New Thermal power plants, which will be using water from rivers/lakes/ reservoirs. shall install cooling towers irrespective of location and capacity. For thermal power plants which will use sea water for cooling purposes, the condition below will apply.

B. New projects in coastal areas using sea water—

The thermal power plants using sea water should adopt suitable system to reduce water temperature at the final discharge point so that the resultant rise in the temperature of receiving water does not exceed 7°C over and above the ambient temperature of the receiving water bodies.

C. Existing thermal power plants—

Rise in temperature of condenser cooling water from inlet to the outlet of condenser shall not be more than 10°C.

D. Guidelines for discharge point—

1. The discharge point shall preferably be located at the bottom of the water body at midstream for proper dispersion of thermal discharge.
2. In case of discharge of cooling water into sea, proper marine outfall shall be designed to achieve the prescribed standards. The point of discharge may be selected in consultation with concerned State Authorities/NIO.
3. No cooling water discharge shall be permitted in estuaries or near ecologically sensitive areas such as mangroves, coral reefs/spawning and breeding grounds of acquatic flora and fauna.

85. Environmental Standards for Coal Washeries—

1. Fugitive emission standards:

— The difference in the value of suspended particulate matter, delta (Δ) measured between 25 and 30 metre from the enclosure of coal—crushing plant in the downward and leeward wind direction shall not exceed 150 microgram per cubic meter. Method of measurement shall be High Volume Sampling and Average Flow Rate, not less than 1.1 m³ per minute, using Upwind Downwind Method of measurement.

2. Effluent discharge standards:

— The coal washeries shall maintain the close-circuit operation with zero effluent discharge.

— If in case due to some genuine problems like periodic cleaning of the system, heavy rainfall etc. it becomes necessary to discharge the effluent into sewer/land/stream then the effluent shall conform to the following standards at the final outlet of the coal washery.

| *Sl. No.* | *Parameter* | *Limits* |
|---|---|---|
| 1. | pH | 5.5-9.0 |
| 2. | Total suspended solids | 100 mg/l |
| 3. | Oil & Grease | 10 mg/l |
| 4. | BOD (3 days 27°C) | 30mg/l |
| 5. | COD | 250 mg/l |
| 6. | Phenolics | 1.0 mg/l |

3. Noise level standards:

— Operational/Working zone—not to exceed 85 dB(A) Leq for 8 hours exposure.

— The ambient air quality standards, in respect of noise as notified under environmental (Protection) Rules, 1986 shall be followed at the boundary line of the coal washery.

4. Code of practice for Coal Washery:

— Water or Water mixed chemical shall be sprayed at all strategic coal transfer points such as conveyors, loading/unloading points etc. As far as practically possible conveyors, transfer points etc. shall be provided with enclosures.

— The crushers/pulverisers of the coal washeries shall be provided with enclosures, fitted with suitable air pollution control measures and finally emitted through a stack of minimum height of 30 m, conforming to particulate matter emission standard of 150 mg/Nm$^3$ or provided with adequate water sprinkling arrangement.

— Water-sprinkling by using fine atomizer nozzle arrangement shall be provided on the coal heaps and on and around the crushers/pulverisers.

— Area, in and around the coal washery shall be pucca either asphalted or concreted.

— Water consumption in the coal washery shall not exceed 1.5 cubic metre per tonne of coal.

— The efficiency of the settling ponds of the waste water treatment system of the coal washery shall not be less than 90%.

— Green belt shall be developed along the roadside, coal-handling plants, residential complex, office building and all around the boundary line of the coal washery.

— Storage bunkers, hoppers, rubber decks in chutes and centrifugal chutes shall be provided with proper rubber linings.

— Vehicles movement in the coal washery area shall be regulated effectively to avoid traffic congestion. High-pressure horn shall be prohibited. Smoke emission from heavy duty vehicles operating in the coal washeries should conform to the standards prescribed under Motor Vehicle Rules, 1989.

86. Water quality standards for coastal water marine outfall—In a coastal segment marine water is subjected to several types of uses. Depending on the types of uses and activities, water quality criteria have been specified to determine its suitability for a particular purpose. Among the various types of uses there is one use that demands highest level of water quality /purity and that is termed as 'designated best use' in that stretch of the coastal segment. Based on this primary water quality criteria have been specified for following five designated best uses—

| *Class* | *Designated best use* |
|---|---|
| SW-I (See Table 1.1) | Salt pans, Shell fishing, Mariculture and Ecologically Sensitive Zone. |
| SW-II (See Table 1.2) | Bathing, Contact Water Sports and Commercial fishing. |
| SW-III (See Table 1.3) | Industrial cooling, Recreation (non-contact) and Aesthetics. |
| SW-IV (See Table 1.4) | Harbour. |
| SW-V (See Table 1.5) | Navigation and Controlled Waste Disposal. |

The standards along with rationale/remarks for various parameters, for different designated best uses, are given in Tables A-II.1 to A-II.5

## TABLE A.II.1

### Primary Water Quality Criteria for Class SW-I Waters

(For Salt-pans, Shell Fishing, Mariculture and Ecolc gically Sensitive Zone)

| *Sl. No.* | *Parameter* | *Standards* | *Rationale/Remarks* |
|---|---|---|---|
| 1 | 2 | 3 | 4 |
| 1. | pH range | 6.5-8.5 | General broad range, conducive for propagation of aquatic lives, is given. Value largely dependent upon soil-water interaction. |
| 2. | Dissolved Oxygen | 5.0mg/l or 60 per cent saturation value, whichever is higher | Not less than 3.5 mg/l at any time of the year for protection of acquatic lives. |
| 3. | Colour and Odour | No noticeable colour or offensive odour | Specially caused by chemical compound like creosols, phenols, naphtha, pyridine, benzene, toluene etc. causing visible colouration of salt crystal and tainting of fish flesh. |

| 1 | 2 | 3 | 4 |
|---|---|---|---|
| 4. | Floating Matters | Nothing obnoxious or detrimental for use purpose | Surfactants should not exceed an upper limit of 1.0mg/l and the concentration not to cause any visible foam. |
| 5. | Suspended Solids | None from sewage or Industrial waste origin. | Settleable inert matters not in such concentration that would impair any usages specially assigned to this class. |
| 6. | Oil and Grease (including Petroleum Products) | 0.1 mg/l | Concentration should not exceed 0.1 mg/l because it has effect on fish eggs and larvae. |
| [71][7. | Heavy Metals: | | (i) Concentration in salt, fish and shell fish. |
| | Mercury (as Hg) | 0.001 mg/l | (ii) Average per capital consumption per day. |
| | Lead (as Pb) | 0.01 mg.l | |
| | Cadmium (as Cd) | 0.01 mg/l] | (iii) Minimum ingestion rate that induces symptoms of resulting diseases. |

*Note:* SW-I is desirable to safe and relatively free from hazardous chemicals like pesticides, heavy metals and radio nuclide concentrations. Their combined (synergestic or anatagonistic) effects on health and aquatic lives are not yet clearly known. These chemicals undergo bio-accumulation, magnification and transfer to human and other animals. Thorough test should be performed following appropriate methods for the purpose of setting case specific limits.

## TABLE A.II.2

## Primary Water Quality Criteria for Class SW-II Waters

(For Bathing, Contact Water Sports and Commercial Fishing)

| *Sl. No.* | *Parameter* | *Standards* | *Rationale/Remarks* |
|---|---|---|---|
| *1* | *2* | *3* | *4* |
| 1. | pH range | 6.5-8.5 | Range does not cause skin or eye irritation and is also conducive for propagation of aquatic lives. |
| 2. | Dissolved Oxygen | 4.0mg/l or 50 per cent saturation value, whichever is higher | Not less than 3.5 mg/l at anytime for protection of aquatic lives. |
| 3. | Colour and Odour | No noticeable colour or offensive odour | Specifically caused by chemical compound like creosols, phenols, naptha, benzene, pyridine, toluene etc., causing visible colouration |

| 1 | 2 | 3 | 4 |
|---|---|---|---|
| | | | of water and tainting of and odour in fish flesh. |
| 4. | Floating Matters assigned | Nothing obnoxious or detrimental for use purpose | None in concentration that would impair usages specifically to this class. |
| 5. | Turbidity | 30 NTU (Nephelo Turbidity Unit) | Measured at 0.9 depth. |
| 6. | Fecal Coliform | 100/100 ml (MPN) | The average value not exceeding 200/100 ml. In 20 per cent of samples in the year and in 3 consecutive samples in monsoon months. |
| 7. | Biochemical oxygen Demand (BOI) (3 days at 27°C) | 3mg/l | Restricted for bathing (aesthetic quality of water). Also prescribed by IS:2296-1974. |

## TABLE A.I1.3

### Primary Water Quality Criteria for Class SW-II Waters

[For Industrial Cooling, recreation (non-contact) and Aesthetics]

| *Sl. No.* | *Parameter* | *Standards* | *Rationale/Remarks* |
|---|---|---|---|
| *1* | *2* | *3* | *4* |
| 1. | pH range and | 6.5-8.5 | The range is conducive for propagation of aquatic species restoring natural system. |
| 2. | Dissolved Oxygen | 3.0 mg/l or 40 percent saturation value, whichever is higher | To protect aquatic lives. |
| 3. | Colour and Odour | No noticeable colour or offensive odour. | None is such concentration that would impair usage specifically assigned to this class. |
| 4. | Floating Matters | No visible, obnoxious floating debris, oil slick, scum | As in (3) above |
| 5. | Fecal 20 Coliform and monsoon | 500/100 ml (MPN) | Not exceeding 1000/100 ml in percent of samples in the year in 3 consecutive samples in months. |

| 1 | 2 | 3 | 4 |
|---|---|---|---|
| 6. | Turbidity | 30 NTU | Reasonable clear water for recreation, aesthetic appreciation and industrial cooling purposes. |
| *7. | Dissolved iron (as Fe) | 0.5 mg/l or less | It is desirable to have the collective concentration of dissolved Fe and Mn less or equal to 0.5 mg/l to avoid scaling effect. |
| *8 | Dissolved manganese (as Mn) | 0.5 mg/l or less | |

* Standards included exclusively for Industrial Cooling purpose. Other parameters same.

## TABLE A.II.4
## Primary Water Quality Criteria for Class Sw-IV Waters
(For Harbour Waters)

| *Sl.No.* | *Parameter* | *Standards* | *Rationale/Remarks* |
|---|---|---|---|
| *1* | *2* | *3* | *4* |
| 1. | pHrange | 6.5-9.0 | To minimize corrosive and scaling effect. |
| 2. | Dissolved oxygen | 3.0 mg/l or 40 per cent saturation value whichever is higher. | Considering bio-degradation of oil and inhibition to oxygen production through photosynthesis. |
| 3. | Colour and odour | No visible colour or offensive odour. | None from reactive chemicals Which may corrode paints/ metallic surfaces. |
| 4. | Floating from materials; oil grease and scum (including Petroleum products) | 10 mg/l | Floating matter should be free excessive living organism which may clog or coat operative parts of marine vessels/equipment. |

| 1 | 2 | 3 | 4 |
|---|---|---|---|
| 5. | Fecal coliform | 500/100 ml (MPN) | Not exceeding 1000/100ml in 20 percent of samples in the year and in 3 consecutive samples in monsoon months. |
| 6. | Biochemical oxygen demand (3 days at 27°C) | 5 mg/l | To maintain water relatively free from pollution caused by sewageand other decomposable wastes. |

## Table A.II.5
## Primary Water Quality Criteria for Class Sw-V Waters

(For Navigation and controlled Waste Disposal)

| *Sl. No.* | *Parameter* | *Standards* | *Rationale/Remarks* |
|---|---|---|---|
| *1* | *2* | *3* | *4* |
| 1. | pH range | 6.5-9.0 | As specified by the New England Interstate Water Pollution Control Commission. |
| 2. | Dissolved Oxygen | 3.0 mg/l or 40 per cent saturation value whichever is higher. | To protect aquatic lives. |
| 3. | Colour and Odour | None in such concentrations that would impair any usages specifically assigned to this class. | As in (1) above. |
| 4. | Sludge deposits, solid refuse, floating solids, oil, grease and scum | None except for such small amount that may result from discharge of appropriately treated sewage; and/or industrial waste effluents. | |
| 5. | Fecal coliform | 500/100 ml (MPN) | Not exceeding 1000/100 ml in 20 percent of samples in the year and in 3 consecutive samples in monsoon months. |

87. Emission regulations for Rayon Industry:

(a) Existing plants

Estimation of uncontrolled emission quality (EQ) of $CS_2$

For VSF,

EQ = 125 kg of $CS_2$/t of fibre

For VFY,

EQ = 225 kg of $CS_2$/t of fibre.

| *Stack Height (H) requirement, m* | *Remarks* |
|---|---|
| 11 $Q^{0.41}$–3 VsD/u | A minimum of 80 percent of total emission shall pass through stack. If the calculated stack height is less than 30 m, a minimum height of 30 m shall be provided. |

Where Q-$CS_2$ emission rate, kg./hr

Vs—stack exit velocity, m/sec.

D—diameter of stack, m

U—annual average wind speed at top of stack, m/sec.

Multiple stacks:

1. If there are more than one stack existing in the plant, the required height of all stacks shall be based on the maximum emission rate in any of the stacks. In other words, all the stacks carrying $CS_2$ emission shall be of same heights (based on the maximum emissions rate).
2. Number of stacks shall not be increased from the existing number. However the number of stacks may be reduced. The existing stacks may be rebuilt and if stacks are to be relocated, condition 3 below applies.
3. Spacing among the stacks (x) at the minimum shall be 3.0 H (in m). If distance, x, between two stacks is less than 3.0 H (in m), emission shall be considered as single point source and height of both the stacks shall be calculated considering all emission is going through one stack.

(b) Ambient air quality monitoring.

The industry shall install three air quality monitoring stations from $CS_2$ and $H_2S$ measurements in consultation with State Pollution Control Board (SPCB) to ensure attainment of WHO recommended ambient air quality norms ($CS_2$) = 100 ug/m$^3$ and $H_2S$ = 150 ug/m$^3$, 24 = hr, average).

(c) For new plants/expansion projects being commissioned on or after 1 June 1999.

Permissible emission limits are:

$CS_2$ = 21 kg/t of fibre

$H_2S$ = 6.3 kg/t of fibre

(*Note*: a. and b. above also apply to new plants/expansion projects)]

[72][88. Emission Standards for new generator sets (upto 19 kilowatt) run on petrol and kerosene with implementation schedule.

The emission standards for portable generator sets run on petrol and kerosene shall be as follows:

A. From June 1st, 2000

| *Class* | *Displacement (CC)* | *CO (g/kw-hr)* | | *HC+NOx (g/kw-hr)* | |
|---|---|---|---|---|---|
| | | *2-stroke engine* | *4-stroke engine* | *2-stroke engine* | *4-stroke engine* |
| 1. | ≤ 65 | 603 | 623 | 166 | 65 |
| 2. | > 65 ≤ 99 | — | 623 | — | 36 |
| 3. | > 99 ≤ 225 | — | 623 | — | 19.3 |
| 4. | > 225 | — | 623 | — | 16.1 |

B. From June 1, 2001

| *Class* | *Displacement (CC)* | *CO (g/kw-hr)* | *HC+NOx (g/kw-hr)* |
|---|---|---|---|
| 1. | < 65 | 519 | 54 |
| 2. | > 65 ≤ 99 | 519 | 30 |
| 3. | >99 ≤ 225 | 519 | 16.1 |
| 4. | > 225 | 519 | 13.4 |

C. Test method shall be as specified in SAEJ 1088. Measurement mode shall be DI cycle specified under ISO 8178 (Weighting Factor of 0.3 for 100% load, 0.5 for 75% load and 0.2 for 50% load).

D. Following organisations shall test and certify the generator sets:

(i) Automotive Research Association of India, Pune.

(ii) Indian Institute of Petroleum Dehradun.

(iii) Indian Oil Corporation , R&D Centre, Faridabad.

(iv) Vehicle Research Development Establishment, Ahmednagar.

These organisations shall submit the testing and certification details to the Central Pollution Control Board, annually. The Central Pollution Control Board may send the experts in the field to oversee the testing.

89. Noise standards for fire-crackers-

A. (i) The manufacture, sale or use of fire-crackers generating noise level exceeding 125 dB(AI) or 145 $dB(C)_{pk}$ at 4 meters distance from the point of bursting shall be prohibited.

(iii) For individual fire-cracker constituting the series (joined fire-crackers), the above mentioned limit be reduced by 5 $\log_{10}$ (N) dB, where N = number of crackers joined together.

B. The broad requirements for measurement of noise from fire-crackers shall be—

(i) The measurements shall be made on a hard concrete surface of minimum 5 meter diameter or equivalent.

(ii) The measurements shall be made in free field conditions i.e., there shall not be any reflecting surface up to 15 meter distance from the point of bursting.

(iii) The measurement shall be made with an approved sound level meter.

C. The Department of Explosives shall ensure implementation of these standards.

*Note:* dB (AI): A—weighted impulse Sound pressure Level in decibel.
DB $(C)_{pk}$: C—weighted Peak Sound Pressure Level in decibel.

## [73][SCHEDULE II]
(*See* Rule 3)

## SCHEDULE [74][III]
## Ambient Air Quality Standards in respect of Noise

| *Area Code* | *Category of Area* | *Limit in dB(A)* *day time* | *Leq.* *night time* |
|---|---|---|---|
| (A) | Industrial area | 75 | 70 |
| (B) | Commercial area | 65 | 55 |
| (C) | Residential area | 55 | 45 |
| (D) | Silence zone | 50 | 40 |

Notes-1 Day time is reckoned in between 6 a.m. and 9 p.m.

2 Night time is reckoned in between 9 p.m. and 6 a.m.

3 Silence zone is defined as areas upto 100 metres around such premises as hospitals, educational institutions and courts. The silence zones are to be declared by the Competent Authority.
Use of vehicular horns, loudspeakers and bursting of crackers shall be banned in these zones.

4 Mixed categories of areas should be declared as one of the four above mentioned categories by the Competent Authority and the corresponding standards shall apply.]

## [75][SCHEDULE IV
### (See Rule 3)
### Standard for Emission of Smoke, Vapour, etc. from Motor Vehicles

(1) Every motor vehicle shall be manufactured and maintained in such condition and shall be so driven that smoke, visible vapour, grit, sparks, ashes, cinders or oily substance do not emit therefrom.

(2) (2) On and from the 1st day of March 1990, every motor vehicle in use shall comply with the following standards—

(a) Idling CO (Carbon monoxide) emission limit for all four wheeled petrol driven vehicles shall not exceed 3 per cent by volume;

(b) Idling CO emission limit for all two and three wheeled petrol driven vehicles shall not exceed 4.5 per cent by volume;

(c) Smoke density for all diesel driven vehicles shall be as follows—

| | *Method of Test* | *Maximum smoke density* | | |
|---|---|---|---|---|
| | | *Light Absorption Coefficient m-1* | *Bosch Units* | *Harridge Units* |
| (a) | Full load at a speed of 605 to 70% of maximum engine rated speed declared | 3.1 | 5.2 | 75 |
| (b) | Free acceleration | 2.3 | - | 65 |

(3) On and from the 1st day of April 1991, all petrol driven vehicles shall be so manufactured that they comply with the mass emission standards as specified at Annexure 'I'. The breakdown of the operating cycle used for the test shall be as specified at Annexure 'II' and the reference fuel for all such tests shall be as specified in Annexure 'III' to this Schedule.

(4) On and from the 1st day of April 1991, all diesel vehicles shall be so manufactured that they comply with the mass emission standards based on exhaust gas capacity as specified at Annexure 'IV' to this Schedule.

(5) On and from the 1st day of April 1992, all diesel driven vehicles shall be so manufactured that they comply with the following levels of emissions under the Indian driving cycle—

| Mass of Carbon Monoxide (CO) Max. Grams per KWH | Mass of Hydro Carbons (HC) Max. Grams per KWH | Mass of Nitrogen Oxides (NO) Maxm. Grams per KWH |
|---|---|---|
| 14 | 3.5 | 18 |

(6) Each motor vehicle manufactured on and after the dates specified in paragraphs (2), (3), (4) and (5) shall be certified by the manufacturers to be conforming to the standards specified in the said paragraphs and the manufactures shall further certify that the component liable to effect the emission of gaseous pollutants are so designed, constructed and assembled as to enable the vehicle, in normal use, despite the vibration to which it may be subjected, to comply with the provisions of the said paragraphs.

(7) Tests for smoke emission level and carbon monoxide level for motor vehicles—

(a) Any officer not below the rank of a sub-inspector of police or an inspector of motor vehicles, who has reason to believe that a motor vehicle is by virtue of smoke emitted from it or other pollutants like carbon monoxide emitted from it, is likely to cause environmental pollution, endangering the health or safety of any other user of the road or the public, may direct the driver or any person incharge of the vehicle to submit the vehicle for undergoing a test to measure the standard of black smoke or the standard of any other pollutants.

(b) The driver or any person incharge of the vehicle shall upon demand by any officer referred to in sub-paragraph (a), submit the vehicle for testing for the purpose of measuring the standard of smoke or the levels of other pollutants or both.

(c) The measurement of standard smoke shall be done with a smoke meter of a type approved by the State Government and the measurement of other pollutants like carbon monoxide shall be done with instruments of a type approved by the State Government.

## REFERENCES

1. Published in *Gazette of India, Extraordinary*, Pt. II, See. 3(i), dated 19 November 1986.
2. *Ins.* by G.S.R. 931 (E) dated 27 October 1989.
3. *Ins.* by *Ibid.*
4. *Ins.* by *Ibid.*
5. *Subs.* by G.S.R. 422 (E), dated 19 May 1993.
6. *Omitted* by S.O. 23 (5), dated 16 January 1991.
7. *Subs.* by G.S.R. 422 (E), dated 19 May 1993.
8. *Ins.* by S.O. 23 (E), dated 16 January 1991.
9. *Ins.* by G.S.R. 422 (E), dated 19 May 1993.
10. *Ins.* G.S.R. 801 (E), dated 31 December 1993.
11. *Subs.* by G.S.R. 7, dated 22 December 1998.

12. *Ins.* by G.S.R. 95 (E), dated 12 February 1992.
13. *Ins.* by G.S.R. 560 (E) dated 19 September 1997.
14. *Subs. by* G.S.R. 378 (E). dated 30 1998.
15. *Ins.* by G.S.R. 378 (E), dated 30 June 1998.
16. *Ibid.*
17. *Renumbered* by S.O. 64 (E). dated 18 January 1988.
18. *Ins.* by ibid.
19. *Ins.* by G.S.R. 562 (E), dated 27 May 1992.
20. *Subs.* by G.S.R 884 (E), 20 November 1992.
21. *Ins.* by G.S.R. 320 (E), 16 March 1994.
22. *Subs.* by S.O. 64 (E), dated 18 January 1988.
23. *Ins.* by S.O. 82 (E), dated 16 February 1987.
24. *Ins.* by G.S.R. 422 (E), dated 19 May 1993.
25. *Ins.* by G.S.R. 431 (E), dated 27 October 1989.
26. *Ins.* by G.S. R. 329 (E), dated '3 March 1992.
27. *Subs.* by G.S.R. 386 (E), dated 22 April 1993.
28. *Ibid.*
29. *Ibid.*
30. *Renumbered* as Sch. 1 by S.O. 82 (E). dated 16 February, 1987.
31. *Subs.* by G.S.R. 176 (E), dated 2 April, 1996.
32. *Ibid.*
33. *Ibid.*
34. *Ins.* by S.O. 393 (E), dated 16 April 1987.Entries 8 to 10 were inserted by this notification.
35. *Ins.* by S.O. 443 (E). dated 28 April 1987. Entry 11 was inserted by this notification.
36. *Ins.* by S.O. 64 (E), dated 18 January 1988. Entries 12 to 24 were inserted by this notification.
37. *Subs.* by G.S.R. 176 (E), dated 2 April 1996.
38. *Renumbered* by S.O. 12 (E), dated 8 January 1990.
39. *Subs.* by S.O. 12 (E), dated 8 January 1990.
40. *Subs.* by G.S.R. 176 (E), dated 2 April 1996.
41. Notes *omitted* by G.S.R 176 (E), dated 2 April 1996.
42. *Subs.* by G.S.R. 176 (E), dated 2 April 1996.
43. *Ins.* by S. O. 8 (E). dated 3 January 1989. Entries 25 and 26 were inserted by this notification.
44. *Ins.* by G.S.R. 913 (E). October 1989. Entries 27 to 31 were inserted by this notification.

45. *Subs.* by G.S.R. 176 (E), dated 2 April 1996.
46. *Ins.* by G.S.R. 742 (E), dated 30 August 1990. Entries 32 to 47 were inserted by this notification.
47. *Subs.* by G.S.R. 176 (E). dated 2 April 1996.
48. *Ibid.*
49. *Ibid.*
50. *Subs. by G*.S.R. 176 (E), dated 2 April 1996.
51. *Ibid.*
52. *Ins.* by G.S.R. 93 (E), dated 21 Feb. 1991. Entries 48 to 55 were inserted by this notification.
53. *Subs.* by G.S.R. 176 (E) dated 2 April 1996.
54. *Ibid.*
55. *Ibid.*
56. *Subs.* by G.S.R. 176 (E), dated 2 April 1996.
57. *Ibid.*
58. *Ins.* by G.S.R. 475 (E), dated 5 May 1992. Entries 56 to 61 were inserted by this notification.
59. *Ibid.*
60. *Ibid.*
61. *Ibid.*
62. *Ibid.*
63. *Ins.* by G.S.R. 80 (E), dated 31 December 1993. Entry 62 was inserted by this notification
64. *Subs.* by G.S.R. 176 (E), dated 2 April 1996.
65. *Ins.* G.S.R. 176 (E), dated 2 April 1996. Entries 63 to 78 were inserted by this notification.
66. *Subs.* by G.S.R. 682 (E), dated 5 October 1999.
67. *Subs.* by *ibid.*
68. *Ins.* by G.S.R. 631 (E), dated 31 October 1997. Entry 79 was inserted by this notification.
69. *Ins.* by G.S.R. 504 (E), dated 20 August 1998. Entry 80 inserted by this notification.
70. *Ins.* by. G.S.R., dated 22 December 1998. Entries 81 to 87 were inserted by this notification.
71. *Subs.* by G.S.R. 682 (E), dated 5 October 1999.
72. *Ins.* by G.S.R. 682 (E), dated 5 October 1999. Entries 88 and 89 were

inserted this notification.

73. *Omitted* by G.S.R. 80 (E), dated 31 December 1993.
74. *Ins.* by G.S.R. 1063 (E), dated 26 December 1989.
75. *Ins.* by G.S.R. 54 (E), dated 5 February 1990.

# BIBLIOGRAPHY


Adlkins, W.G., and D. Burke. Jr. (1974), 'Social, Economic and Environmental Factors in Highway Decision Making." Research report 148-4. College Station: Texas Transportation Institute. Texas A & M University.

Aronsson, L. 2000, *The Development of Sustainable Tourism,* London: Continuum.

Bramwell, B. (1994), 'Rural Tourism and Sustainable Tourism', *Journal of Sustainable Tourism*, 2 (1 & 2): 1-6.

Barton, M.A. (1969), "Water pollution in remote remote recreational areas," *Journal of Soil and Water Conservation*, 24:132-134.

Bateille, R. (1968). "Tourism et milieu rural montagnard: l' example de Pitztal (Tirol autichein)", *Revue de Geographic Alphine*, 56: 367-376.

Busby, G. and Rendle, S. (2000), 'The Transition from Tourism on Farms to Farm Tourism', *Tourism Management,* 21 (6): 635—42.

Butler, R. and Clark, G. (1992), 'Tourism in Rural Areas: Canada and the UK', in I. Bowler, C. Bryant and M. Nellis, (eds.), *Contemporary Rural Systems in Transition*. Volume 2: Economy and Society, Wallingford: CAB International.

Butler, R., Hall, C.M. and Jenkins, J. (eds) (1998), *Tourism and Recreation in Rural Areas*, Chichester: John Wiley and Sons.

Canter, L. (1977). *Environmental Impact Assessment*. New York: